Warman's®
Sporting Collectibles

Identification and Price Guide

Russell E. Lewis

Published by

An Imprint of F+W Publications

700 East State Street • Iola, WI 54990-0001
715-445-2214 • 888-457-2873
www.krausebooks.com

Library of Congress Control Number: 2007924544

ISBN-13: 978-0-89689-563-8
ISBN-10: 0-89689-563-7

Designed by Kay Sanders
Edited by Kristine Manty

Printed in China

Contents

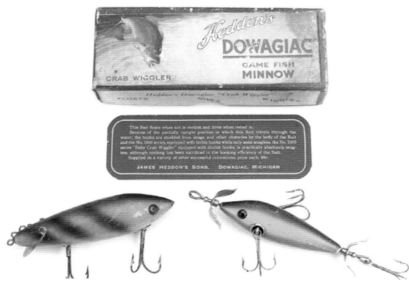

Introduction

This Crowell Preening Pintail set the world record price for wildfowl decoys, selling for **$801,500** at a 2003 auction held by Guyette & Schmidt and Christie's. The pintail was carved in 1915 by A. Elmer Crowell of Cape Cod, Mass. The same decoy brought a record price at the time of $319,000 in 1986, when it was purchased by Russ Aitken. The pintail decoy sold in 2003 broke the record price set for another Crowell decoy in 2000 of $684,000.

As the world's most prolific author on antique and collectible fishing tackle and duck decoys, I now bring you a "one-stop" source for the broader topic of sporting collectibles. I have written the book with general antiques dealers, beginning collectors, Americana aficionados and others interested in this field in mind. Numerous advanced references exist, many written by me, but there has not been a decent introductory book produced for some time and never in full color covering so many fields of sporting collectibles.

This book is intended to serve as a general introduction to the subject of sporting collectibles where the generalist can find references to all fields of sporting collectibles in one quick source. In discussing this recently with a number of antiques dealers visited, I found that many do not want the detail provided in many of the specialized works but do need to have a general idea as to value for the different types of sporting collectibles, such as fishing lures, old sporting equipment, shot shell boxes, fish and duck decoys, sporting prints, advertising items, licenses and pinbacks and more. There is always the need for specialized books, but those are generally better suited for the more advanced collector.

Also, a caveat about guns: I have purposely excluded coverage of guns in this book as the area is so specialized and has numerous current books available for both the beginning and more advanced collectors. Anyone interested in the value of collectible guns can easily find current values in any one of a number of books and can also follow values of older guns at auction sites such as www.juliaauctions.com, where many specialized auctions on sporting collectibles featuring rare and collectible guns are held at least once annually.

Sporting collectibles are often in the news and very hot right now. Recent auctions of fishing lures have reached $125,000 for one lure and duck decoys are about to break the million-dollar mark in the near future for one decoy with a recent high of $801,500 for the Crowell Preening Pintail sold at a joint auction held by Guyette & Schmidt and Christies which is shown on the previous page. Of course, these are the rare examples of

high values but the point is that these high prices have become newsworthy and even a recent article in *USA Today* (Aug. 17, 2006) and articles in many financial magazines are noting the possible investment potential of sporting collectibles.

This all leads to one fact: a quality resource is needed in this field. Most books available are either very old by collector standards or suffer from the problem of many collector books of having black and white photos. We need a good color book with accurate and realistic prices given for each item shown. Further, the prices need to be from the past one to three years to be meaningful. This has been my hallmark as an author—crisp and clear photographs and recent pricing based upon actual sales of items.

I hope you find this book about various sporting collectibles, broken into categories already recognized by collectors, to fill the gap. Each category has an introductory section explaining the most important attributes of that particular collectible, possible fakes, how to find them, etc. Have fun looking!

Other decoys that have high values include a rare Widgeon drake, at bottom, and a Mason Decoy Mallard pair, below. The Widgeon drake is Premier Grade and was produced by the Mason factory early in the 20th century. It has original paint, several tiny dents, with original newspaper wrapping visible, **$55,000**. The Mallard pair, also Premier Grade, is circa first quarter of the 20th century. They have original paint, minor roughness to tail tips and the hen has two small cracks in the underside of the bill, **$13,000**.
Guyette & Schmidt, Inc.

Chapter 1

Duck Decoys

It was difficult to decide where to begin but I have selected duck decoys, and other bird decoys, for the reason that they are America's first and foremost sporting collectible. Native Americans used decoys to lure birds close enough to capture or shoot and early American settlers soon thereafter followed in the tradition. Many scholars have argued that decoy carving is one of America's oldest folk art forms and I would certainly agree. It reached its hallmark from the late 1800s until about 1935 due to changes in both market and sport hunting and decoys made in this "vintage period" are truly in great demand. However, even factory decoys made from the early 1900s until about 1965 have a following of collectors and beginners need to be aware that some decoys are valuable whether made of wood, metal, cloth, paper, papier-mâché, or even plastic in some cases.

In addition to the decoys themselves, decoy weights, live bird holding devices, tags, boxes and related items are also gaining collector interest. Sometimes a decoy weight made by a particular company is harder to find than the decoy itself. Also, weights are often helpful in identifying the region from which a decoy came, such as the Illinois River lead strips often marked with the decoy maker's name or the manufacturer of the lead strip at least.

I have written two major books on decoy collecting, one the only full-color general introduction to decoys and with pricing current through 2006 titled *Warman's Duck Decoys*, 2006, Krause Publications. This full-color book is a great place to begin as it is broken into regional variations in America and Canada and has more than 1,000 color photos and prices, including prices from two major 2006 auctions by Guyette & Schmidt and Decoys Unlimited, Inc. My first book on decoys is also still available and has additional photos not found in *Warman's* and more details on owl, crow, swan and other decoys in addition to ducks. It is *Collecting Antique Bird Decoys and Duck Calls*, 3rd edition, by Carl F. Luckey and Russell E. Lewis, Krause Publications, 2005. I would recommend anyone interested in more history and details on individual carvers and/or factory decoys to purchase both of these books.

Assessing value

It is easy to hope to become rich and famous from a rare decoy find, but much harder to actually make such a rare find. Most decoys found are relatively common. Some are more difficult to find than others for sure, but the chances of finding a Preening Pintail by Elmer Crowell in an antiques store or a flea market are about zero; $801,500 duck decoys do not grow on trees. Also, the only reason a collectible ever reaches this value is because, as in this case, two very wealthy individuals decided to go after the same bird at auction. The Pintail is beautiful, no doubt, and it is rare and valuable, but is any one decoy worth so much? Yes, if someone is willing to pay for it. However, most duck decoys are within the $100 to $300 range and many are far less. A few bring $1,000 to $3,000, a few less bring $3,000 to $10,000 and even

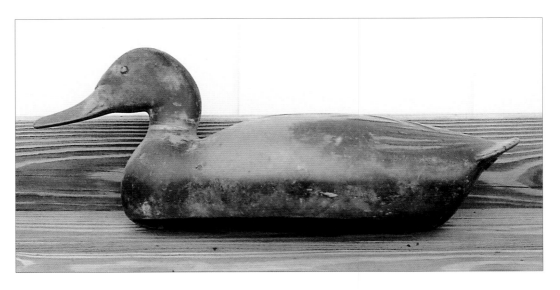

A Victor D-9 was sold by the author online in September 2002 for **$60.**

fewer bring more than $10,000 each. But it is without doubt that decoys have gone up in general the past 10 years at a rate far greater than most collectibles and seem to still be on the upward spiral. Be aware, though, that the bubble will not continue forever and we may be reaching a plateau in value for the rare ducks that will be hard to exceed in the near future.

Another issue about value is of course condition, condition, condition. A beat up old decoy with a reglued head missing 30 percent of its paint is just not worth much, period. Collectors and investors want decoys in original paint in very good to excellent condition. Repainted and repaired decoys drop in value rapidly, even from the better carvers. Provenance is also important for documentation as fakes are becoming an increasingly serious problem with rising values.

The best gauge of value is to follow results from auction houses such as Decoys Unlimited, Inc. or Guyette & Schmidt. Also, go online to such wonderful sites as http://www.old-decoys.com run by my friend and great decoy person, Gary Campbell. You can also subscribe to *Decoy Magazine* and other collector newsletters which feature articles on decoy history and valuation; see http://decoymag.com for more information. Also, go to the regional shows of decoys and handle and examine them in person, as it is the best way to learn the variations in makers and carvers. But the true value of any decoy is simply what one person is willing to pay for it on any given day. I do know that with the recent sale of the Crowell Preening Pintail, ducks have "come out of the woodwork" as they say because people are hoping they, too, have such a decoy stuck in their attic or garage. I am sure this will lead to some wonderful new finds, but it will also result in the flooding of the market of more common birds which may in turn drive pricing down for a bit. This certainly happened in the fishing lure market on various occasions.

But, and most importantly, you should not collect duck decoys merely as an investment but hopefully as pieces of art and artifact. Decoys have a life to them not found in many other sporting collectibles and there is nothing like a beautiful old Mason or a Charles Perdew on your mantel to give warmth and glow to a den or living room. Decoys are for display and enjoyment, not merely a diversion from buying stocks and bonds. Hopefully the decoys and information in this chapter will assist you in identifying some of your own collection or will lead to a desire for you to start finding some to begin a collection.

Current trends in decoy collecting

The reasons for the growing interest in these types of collectibles are many, but they boil down to three things:

1. A large population of "baby boomers" who grew up with these items.

2. The availability of items manufactured since 1940.

3. The affordability of items manufactured since 1940.

Collectors once laughed at papier-mâché duck decoys and Faulk game calls. Now, those same people are ready and willing to buy any and all high quality (e.g. good condition) papier-mâché duck decoys and company game calls they can find and are paying about three to five times the prices of 1995. When I offered a mint-condition Carry-Lite papier-mâché drake Mallard for $25 in 1995, it was too much. Now it is worth three to five times that amount. If it is one of those made for Sears or Montgomery Ward, it could be worth six times as much as it was in 1995. The $10 calls are now at least $30-$40 calls.

As the high-end Mason decoys can no longer be found, or not afforded if found, the beginning and intermediate collectors have searched elsewhere to satisfy a collecting desire and niche. Some collectors argue that there is no place in a duck decoy

A Mason tack eyed Bluebill is in the author's collection, **$125+.**

collection for plastics and I would have to vehemently disagree. I would love to add a mint D-11 Victor Pintail to my collection. Or how about the plastic Victor D-9 Mallard I sold for $60 on an online auction? Not bad for a plastic decoy.

There is indeed a place for plastic duck decoys, fiber decoys, rubber decoys, cardboard decoys and mass-produced calls. Many of our finest antiques were mass-produced and are now rare 100-plus years later. The same may become true of certain items made in the 1940s and '50s, and even later, if most collectors have bypassed them for something else. Would we all like a pair of pristine, never rigged, Charles Perdew Mallards? Of course. But not many of us will ever even handle a pair, let alone find some for sale at a price we can afford. Yet many of us will still find a string of Herter's Model 50s still in a gunnysack from their last use in 1959. They are not pricey or particularly rare, but they are getting harder and harder to find. I would be tickled to run into any of the Victors, Herter's, Carry-Lites, Ariduks or related decoys at a price that is affordable.

The main thing is that only you can decide what to collect. Do not let others tell you what to collect. Do not be taken in by the snobbery of those more fortunate than you financially to detract from the fun of the find, regardless of whether it is a Herter's or a Mason. We all want to find the best birds possible, but enjoy the fun of the hunt, whether for rare and pricey decoys or ones that fit into our collection.

One of the toughest decisions in any collecting venture is to decide what to concentrate on. I personally love Canvasbacks and Bluebills. I hardly ever see a Canvasback in the wild and Bluebills are very common in my Great Lakes region, but what I really like is the shape and symmetry of the decoys. Plain as they are, Bluebills are beautiful to me. Canvasbacks are beautiful to most, with their distinctive heads and frontal features.

I also concentrate on Michigan, Wisconsin and Great Lakes bird decoys, with a small influence from the Illinois River region. I live in Michigan, and have lived in Wisconsin, Illinois and Indiana, and I can find those decoys in my back yard. Sure, in this mobile society, you can find a Perdew in Arizona and an Eastern Seaboard decoy in Wisconsin, but a Michigan decoy is more likely to be found in Michigan than in Maine.

You must decide on the best way to build your collection. I would start with well-known, easily identified, factory decoys or those of prominent carvers that you can spot. I would add to a factory decoy collection decoys from your own region or flyway. These should be most familiar to you and hopefully will be available at antiques shops and shows. All of our collecting interests are still ultimately controlled by economics. Unless, like Bill Gates, you have earned a fortune by inventing a better mousetrap, you should consider your financial limitations.

Finally, you should always only buy what you want and can afford to keep. I have had three instances where I bought beautiful strings of decoys and then found that I was taken by the greed monster and sold most of them for a profit. Well, here I am years later wishing I had the opportunity to find the same strings. They were once in a lifetime deals. Hopefully you will learn from my three mistakes:

1. A string of one dozen (all drakes) Mason Standard grade tack eye Bluebills, all in moderate to very good plus condition: this was a hunting rig I broke up and only kept the poorest of the bunch.

2. A string of one dozen (nine drakes, three hens) Mason Standard grade painted eye Bluebills, all in above average to very good plus condition; a second hunting rig I broke up with none left.

3. A string of one dozen working decoys by an individual carver from Wisconsin. These were glass-eyed hollow decoys that were exceptional in quality but of a non-descriptive brown

A Wisconsin hollow decoy is from a string of a dozen, **$300+.**

wood color, not painted, just natural wood with painted wing details. Gorgeous and profitable, but now I wish I would have left them intact as a group.

Obviously, sometimes we sell items to make a profit, sometimes to upgrade a collection, and sometimes because our collecting interests change and grow. But do not sell decoys without first knowing the fact that they are difficult to replace, if not impossible. I collect and deal in both fishing and hunting collectibles, primarily lures and decoys, and I can assure you that there are far more Heddon Punkinseeds out there than there are strings of one dozen Masons. So learn from one collector's experience. Keep the really great items or you will likely miss them in the future. As the great collector Harvey Pitt, who collected for nearly 44 years, told me, "Every bird that lands in this nest stays here for life." That is good advice if you can afford to do it.

Decoy value trends

Values in antiques and collectibles are driven primarily by age, rarity, condition and desirability of a particular brand or maker. Usually, the older the item, the greater the rarity, but not always. Also, the older the item, the less important is condition compared to a newer item. With decoys, some collectors will only desire wooden ones, others cork, others anything. Overall, the field supports the values of wooden decoys the most, with fairly light interest in even the better quality carved cork decoys.

In the past 30 years, we have seen a revolution in decoy pricing. The breakout year when decoys started hitting five-figure amounts was 1971. Now we have unique, desirable, rare decoys selling for more than $800,000. This is double what the record-setting decoy brought just a few years back. Does that mean that all decoys are worth thousands of dollars? No. Most decoys are worth $50 to $500, with the range being toward the lower end. However, many decoys are now worth $1,000 to $5,000, a few are worth $5,000 to $50,000, and even fewer are worth more than $50,000. Most collectors could build a decent collection with $300 birds five years ago. Now, beginning prices are close to the $300 mark and an average of $1,200 would not be hard to believe for the better birds. Wildfowlers were fairly inexpensive five years ago, bringing less than $100 each, and now they have taken the place of the Masons in both pricing and collecting circles. Most collectors scoffed at papier-mâché and plastic ducks five years ago, but now they bring $25 to $150 each in pristine condition.

For specific values, see the sections on different decoys. In general, decoys have been going up on a 10 percent to 15 percent per year basis the last few years. Of course, this cannot be guaranteed to continue, but will likely keep rising slowly. They simply do not make any more of the rare and collectible birds, so the market will likely continue to grow in the future for these beautiful pieces of "floating sculpture."

Regarding advice on valuation, I would suggest keeping up with the sales data from auction houses, reviewing the Year in Review issue of *Decoys Magazine*, going to local auction houses and farm auctions, visiting antiques stores, and reading as much as you can find on decoys. Also, prudent following of online auctions is an excellent test of what people are actually willing to pay for a particular item. As to deciding the best place for an investment, again, only you can decide. However, I think it important to note that better birds retain and increase value more rapidly than mediocre birds. This is true in all antiques and collectibles areas. In other words, if you can afford to buy a Premier Grade Mason instead of a Standard Grade, you will more likely see a quicker increase in value on your investment; or if you buy wooden factory birds, you are going to see more value increase than if you buy a lot of plastic, rubber or cork decoys.

A collection of Mason Bluebills once lined the shelves at Harvey Pitt's home prior to his passing. Although Bluebills are fairly common, these included rare low head and oversize versions, Challenge and Premier grades and varied in value, starting at around **$300** for a common Bluebill to more than **$6,000** for the better birds. *Pitt Collection*

Some Major Factors That Determine the Value of Old Decoys

By Hal Sorenson (reprinted by permission)

Unlike the rather precise determinants of value assigned to individual stamps, coins, and other collectible items, one must contend with many variables when assessing old decoys. Five collectors could easily look at one decoy and come up with five different appraisals. In judging the general value of one decoy over another, the following major factors must be taken into consideration.

Rarity: The number of examples in existence of a particular species by a particular maker. How many or few examples constitute "rare" is difficult to discern. Usually the price assigned to a decoy by a knowledgeable seller is a good indicator of how unique the example is.

Maker: The relative importance of a carver's name, whether an individual or a factory, will have considerable bearing on the value of a decoy. For instance, with two different but equally handsome old Redhead drakes in similar condition, one by a "named" maker and the other by "maker unknown," the "named maker" decoy will undoubtedly command the higher price. The work of a "named maker" will also be worth more to a collector who specializes in that maker's decoys or who specializes in decoys from that region. However, many "known" carvers are not "named" carvers regardless of how many birds they may have produced. Collectors and publicity determine who is and who is not recognized as a "named" carver.

Condition: In the case of an old decoy, the word condition applies both to the physical appearance of the decoy and the painting. A Shourd's Merganser in fine original paint, but with the bill broken off and a large gouge in one side, would be comparable in condition to the same style decoy in near perfect physical state but with 90 percent of the original paint worn off, or the same decoy having been repainted.

Collectors vary in their interpretation of words such as excellent, very good, fair, etc. The breakdown between categories should be considered a general guideline.

Mint: 100 percent perfect, original condition. A decoy in mint condition would generally be unused.

Excellent: Near mint, with minor wear.

Very Good: At least 90 percent of the original paint is still intact; probably has a few nicks and bruises. A repaired bill is acceptable if not noticeable.

Good: Shows quite a bit of wear but still has 60 percent to 90 percent of the original paint left. Minor restoration such as bill repair and breast retouched are acceptable.

Fair: In pretty rough shape and probably needs restoration to make it worthy of a spot on the collector's shelf.

Poor: Both body and paint in bad condition; perhaps major body cracks. A decoy in this condition is hardly worth picking up unless it is exceedingly rare.

Repainted: Whether an old or new paint job, it was probably done by someone other than the carver. Certain of today's decoy artists specialize in restoring old named decoys with a sincere effort to capture the appearance of the originals. Others will take any old block, good or bad, and repaint it in whatever pattern or colors they happen to feel like at the moment.

Phonies, fakes, copies, etc.: A newly made decoy which appears to be an old original by a known maker; or a recently made decoy which looks old, but is unsigned or undated by the maker. Some fakes are so good they fool the experts. Study your proposed purchase carefully. Any honest dealer or collector will be glad to let you do so and most will give you a money-back guarantee. When in doubt, however, try to consult a third, knowledgeable party.

Species and sex: These two factors affect price because certain species are much rarer than others and some species are more highly prized than others. In addition, both the old hand carvers and the factories produced far more drakes than hens. Drake Wood duck decoys are very rare compared to most species; hen Wood duck decoys are almost non-existent. Species such as Merganser and Teal have wide appeal. While both were produced in pretty fair quantity, collectors tend to snap them up and hang onto them, resulting in a relative shortage in the marketplace.

Grade: Most factories and some individual carvers produced their decoys in two or more grades. The fancier the painting and the most detailed the carving, the higher the original selling price. In most cases, the same holds true when a collector goes to make a purchase today.

Style: Carving and painting patterns constitute "style." The Ward Brothers and the factory decoys made by Mason are two examples of those who produced a number of different styles—especially in carving pattern—over their many decoy-producing years. A collector who studies enough examples by a particular maker will be able to determine which of the styles he likes best.

Aesthetic and artistic preferences: Both of these factors are personal in nature except for certain classics agreed upon by the majority of decoy enthusiasts. Strip away a name, disregard rarity, species, etc., and one gets down to aesthetic consideration: do you like the decoy or not? Disagreements in preference will most likely arise over the primitives—those decoys with no pedigree, which border on crude workmanship and yet have appeal from aesthetic and artistic viewpoints.

Historical associations: Some people put considerable value on who-shot-over-what-decoy. Unless the association is a personal one, I consider it immaterial whose hands previously held one of my pride-and-joys.

Regional preferences: Because decoy styles vary from region to region, many collectors prefer to specialize in decoys from a specific area, i.e., Delaware River, Cape Cod, Barnegat Bay, Chesapeake Bay, Illinois River, etc. As mentioned above, a person who specializes in a certain area is likely to place a higher value on decoys that originate from there.

Age: All other factors considered, the actual age of a particular decoy is not very important. Take two similar decoys by the same maker: it matters not whether one is 10 or even 20 years older than the other. From a collector's standpoint, it also makes little difference if a clunker was made in 1970 or 1900…it is still a clunker.

Decoys in unusual poses: Sleeper, swimmers, feeders, preeners, callers, and the like are rare in the overall decoy picture. As a result, this factor probably belongs under the rarity category. Such poses add interest to the decoy shelves and dollars to the value.

A beautiful Charles/Edna Perdew sleeping Mallard was repainted by Carla Steele, **$250-$300.**

A Pratt Mallard, left, well worn, from a Henry, Illinois hunt club. Its poor condition limits its collector value. It is worth about **$150** in this condition.

A Mallard drake "minnow chaser," below, in a very rare pose, made by an unknown carver from the southern Gulf coast, likely Alabama or Louisiana. This was hunted over on Mobile Bay in the 1920s. It is made of one piece of cypress, hollowed from below with an inset bottom board, **$5,000.**
Hank and Judy Norman Collection

Using the Internet in collecting

The Internet became a viable tool for selling and buying collectibles and antiques beginning in 1995 with the birth of many online auction houses. Only a few remain today and most of the market is consumed and controlled by eBay. An entire decoy collection can be purchased without leaving the seat of my chair at my computer desk.

I make a substantial number of sales per year on eBay and frequently use it as a tool. However, for many, this is a bewildering area still not trusted or understood. Even if you do not buy even one decoy over the Internet, it is still a great tool to learn about decoys and related items. More and more dealers, auction houses and publishers are making online sites available for all of us to visit and expand our knowledge about decoys. Many collectors are sharing their collections and knowledge online by adding technically accurate listings of items for online sales with references given to major research works.

You can buy and sell on the Internet with confidence if only a few simple rules are followed. The first and most important rule is to do business only with those dealers with a positive reputation. This is the same for online dealers or those with storefronts. With online dealers, there is usually a mechanism known as "feedback" that can easily be checked to determine how others have fared in their business with the dealer. If all others are happy with the service, the timeliness of delivery, the quality of the items, the proper description of the items sold, etc., then it is likely you are dealing with a reputable individual or company. If the individual or company still lacks feedback, positive or negative, I would not spend a large amount of money in my purchases from them.

Make sure you know and can live with the seller's return policies. Also, for a $3,000 item, will the seller accept funds being escrowed to a third party until the transaction is completed? If not, that is not a guarantee of problems, but escrow does give one more option for very valuable items. Also, most auction services and electronic payment services (such as PayPal) are now offering guarantees that may be purchased at the time of electronic payment.

Finally, the best guarantee is in past dealings with the seller personally by the buyer. That way, you know first hand if you are satisfied with the past performance of a seller and with the product(s) supplied.

My advice to all with access to a computer and the Internet is to get on the "Net" and learn to use it as a tool. It is a great way to find items that trips to the local antiques store would take years to accomplish. Any item on the Internet is available to anyone for the looking and buying. It allows us to fill in our collections far more easily and more rapidly than any other technique, albeit at a more costly price in many cases. Sometimes there can be bargains had when a seller lists an item with which he/she is not familiar or during times of a soft economy. I have found some real buys on the Internet for both reasons. The most important advice is to learn by experience and have fun along the way.

Finding items

As I said earlier, it is increasingly tougher to find items "on the street," so to speak, but it can still happen. I use every available technique known to find items for my collections. Every once in a while I get lucky and find a good item for a low price. But it takes work and diligence to be successful. Collectors finding items with the most regularity are not just lucky, they are also industrious. I know one picker who is always finding great things but he is out of bed early, at estate sales to get No. 1, works at least four days a week finding items, etc. Also, he is willing to pay for an item. Many people think that items are out there at ridiculously low prices just waiting to be discovered. Trust me, this is the exception and not the norm. The norm is that an estate dealer prices items fairly, with enough profit margin left for the dealer to also make a dollar or two. Thus, decoys at estate sales are not "cheap," but are fairly priced in most instances.

The point is that I have a real issue with those who do not want to pay a fair price for an item. Sure, we all like bargains if found, but please do not always try to beat down prices when someone has an item for sale.

In the same fashion, if asked the actual value of an item, I believe it is our ethical duty as collectors and dealers to tell the truth the best we know it. If I go to a garage sale and see a string of Masons, not priced but hanging on the wall and ask them if they would sell the decoys, I should also be prepared to tell the value of them when asked. This is not to say that we have to tell people the value of an item that is already priced; this I do not think is necessary.

But if we are relying upon our knowledge and experience and are after something of theirs that is not already priced, we have a duty to be honest about the value. Of course, I am not suggesting it is only fair to pay full retail for an item, only that the seller has a right to know the full retail if asking. Each of us will make our own decisions on how much to pay, but we should be duty-bound to be fair and ethical in all of our dealings. I know that in my own experiences this has only resulted in positive repeat dealings with people and me having access to collections denied others desiring the same access.

How do you find items? Well, a list could be quite long, but to summarize:

1. Dealers
2. Antiques shops and malls

3. Farm and household auctions
4. Sporting shops
5. Advertising in local papers
6. Advertising in regional magazines
7. Advertising in retirement homes
8. Telling each and every friend of your interests
9. Buying advertising space on a billboard
10. Visiting shows dedicated to sporting collectibles/decoys
11. Visiting areas rich in waterfowl hunting history
12. Visiting Internet sites where you can buy/sell/learn about decoys
13. Visiting museums with decoys and related items
14. Going to auctions dedicated to decoys and sporting collectibles
15. Joining every organization related to decoys and sporting collectibles
16. Joining a local organization dedicated to carving decoys
17. Giving lectures on the topic to community service groups and local schools
18. Developing a network of collector to collector exchanges
19. Lots of footwork, phone calling, e-mailing, and other contacts
20. Training and using a quality picker or pickers to assist you

Identification of antique decoys

There are many characteristics of decoys that make identification fairly easy in some cases. A considerable number of decoys, for instance, can be identified as to maker by such simple things as the brands, logo, name or initials on a bird. Many makers can be determined because of a certain style or shape. Many of these early craftsmen had styles of carving, construction technique or painting that were unique. Those make a decoy unmistakably his, even in the absence of other identifying marks. This is also true of some of the factory-produced birds.

For instance, some maker's decoys are all of the same distinctive body shape, only painted differently to represent different species of wildfowl. Others had a distinctive style of carving details such as carved delineation of the mandibles and/or carving separating them from the head of the bird. Others used the two-piece hollow construction exclusively, or all with heads inlaid, or all with the upper and lower hollowed-out pieces joined, always above or always below the waterline. The same type of characteristics can be used to at least allow the collector to determine the school or area of the maker, most of the time. The list goes on: paint styles, painting techniques, method of attaching head to body, position of head, species of bird carved, type of wood used, body shape, size of the decoy, eye types, and shaping of the tail and face carving, etc.

Certain designs are meant to be used in shallow marshes while others are obviously made to be used in deep waters subject to weather. Knowledge of changing migratory patterns can be helpful also. For instance, if you know that there were few or no Canada geese migrating through the Chesapeake Bay area prior to the 1930s, then you know any Canada goose decoy represented as being from there and dated by the seller as being made by a carver earlier than that, is a case of mistaken identification.

This general discussion may lead you to believe it is easy to date and identify the maker of any decoy. Not so. True, there are some that are easy to spot and, with time and experience gained from the easier identifications, you can develop your ability to include identification of other, less obvious examples. The problem is that there are as many types of decoy construction as there are opinions of just what constitutes an effective decoy. For the most part, luckily, carvers within a particular school were influenced by the species of bird hunted in his region and by the local conditions under which they had to be hunted. Therefore, there are common characteristics.

If you are a beginning collector you should not be afraid of what you will find. There seems to be a tendency among novice collectors to pick up in a shop or flea market what is truly a fine decoy that has no documentation or provenance and then let it go.

Unknown Virginia decoys,
$150-$250.

This reluctance is understandable, but if it has the look and feel of a good piece, by all means buy it. Many have an inherent ability to recognize good form and design. If you do not have it, you can develop it simply by handling and examining a few that are known quantities. Again, this is one of the advantages of attending some decoy shows. You can sometimes be fooled, but not often, by today's decorative reproductions.

Brands

The term brand as used in this book, and by most collectors, encompasses just about any markings placed on a decoy (usually on the bottom) by a user, maker or collector. If a collector places his mark on a decoy, it is usually a paper label or a rubber stamp type. This practice is not particularly widespread. Its own distinctive nicks or wear pattern can usually identify each decoy.

User and maker brands can vary significantly in dating a decoy, documenting its maker, and influencing its value. Unfortunately the majority of decoys do not have brands or, at the least, the brand does not mean anything. The latter is particularly true in the case of user brands unless the user can be identified and is of historical importance to collectors.

In the case of a decoy on which both user and maker brand appear, each being known and important, you have a real prize. The importance of either or both brands can have a very positive influence on the value of the decoy. The value can be increased by two to five times, depending on the brand.

What follows are descriptions of some of the most famous and significant maker and user brands that you might find. There are, of course, more than those listed here, but the two lists are of many of those considered most important.

User brands

A user or owner brand can be that of the individual owner or of a hunting club or lodge. It usually appears in the form of a genuine brand such as those used in the cattle business. It was not a particularly expensive proposition in those days to have a local blacksmith fashion a branding iron for the impression of initials or name into a wooden decoy by heated iron or by striking with a hammer. Many owners and makers did not go to the trouble but simply carved or painted their marks.

There may be more than one user brand found on a decoy. For instance, there is a Harry Shourds' Black Duck decoy with three brands on the bottom: H. W. Cain, B C P, A C. The C common to all three brands suggests that H. W. might be gramps, A C might be his son, and B C P could be his grandson. Conjecture, yes, but if so, think how exciting it might be for his family to possess this particular bird. Incidentally, this particular decoy was spotted by a collector in someone's front yard being used as a decoration with a heavy coat of chartreuse green.

Accomac: The name of a hunting club in the heart of the Virginia Eastern Shore about 65 miles north of Norfolk. This brand is found mostly on shore birds. However, it is also on a lot of good duck decoys. A decoy would increase in value about four times if the Accomac brand were present.

Barron: A relatively scarce brand to be found, it is the name of an Eastern Shore Virginia hunting club. The Barron hunters believed faithfully in the Mason factory-made decoys. So far the brand has shown up mostly on Mason decoys, but there have been a few very fine, unidentified decoys found bearing the brand as well. The Barron brand on a Mason decoy increases its value by about 50 percent. When it is present it is usually found in two places, on the back and on the side.

Chateau: Fred Chateau was a game warden who lived in Accord, Mass. His brand has shown up on Joe Lincoln's and some Martha's Vineyard decoys, as well as a good many other New England decoys.

Gooseville G.C.: The Gooseville Gunning Club was another Eastern Shore Virginia club. It went out of existence prior to World War I, so any bird found with this brand can be dated no later than 1917. Most decoys found bearing this brand will bring about twice the normal price.

Hard: The Hard Gun Club brand is found on many good factory decoys such as Masons, Dodge and Petersons.

North Carolina: The North Carolina was one of three well-known gunning scows. Each of the sailboat's rigs of decoys was branded with the boat's name. As in the case of the other two gunning scows, just about any decoy with the brand would be worth at least $500. The North Carolina sank in 1888 on the Chesapeake Bay.

NPW: The initials in this brand are those of Nelson Price Whittaker. He was one of those who cast the heavy iron wing decoys for use with sink boxes.

Ed Parsons: Parsons was a legendary market gunner who hunted only over decoys made by Ben Dye and Captain John Daddy Holly; therefore, if you find a Parsons brand on a bird, it is most likely to be one or the other. The brand was a P within a circle.

Reckless: The Reckless was one of the earliest gunning scows. The brand could make an otherwise insignificant upper Chesapeake Bay Canvasback duck decoy in the $100-$200 range worth $500 easily.

Susquehanna: The Susquehanna was another of the old gunning scows whose brand makes the decoy worth much more than the norm. The Susquehanna sank just before the Civil War so, obviously, a decoy branded with its name pre-dates 1860-65.

Suydam: This brand belonged to a wealthy Long Island family that did much sport hunting in Long Island Sound. The brand shows up frequently on good Long Island decoys.

Maker brands

Few of the thousands of individuals who carved decoys for personal or commercial purposes identified them with a brand, but most of the factory-made decoys did carry brands. The list here is of several of the more important makers who sometimes, often, or always identified their decoys with a brand. The descriptions are of brands only.

Joel Barber: He is one of the big names in decoy collecting. After Barber wrote his book, *Wild Fowl Decoys*, he decided he would try his hand at carving decoys himself. His brand, when present, is very distinctive and readily recognizable.

Thomas B. Chambers: A carver from the St. Clair Flats area of Michigan, he did not always place his brand but when he did it is easy to identify. It simply states, "Thomas B. Chambers, Maker" and is stenciled onto the bottom.

Nathan Cobb Family: The Cobb families were originally New Englanders who migrated south to Virginia. Their products are best identified by construction techniques and style, but they sometimes carved their initials into the bird. Since they did not brand, but carved an initial into their decoys, it is more a matter of interest than anything else. Most of the time you will find only an N for Nathan Cobb, an E or an A carved into their products, if you find any at all.

Elmer Crowell: Crowell, starting around 1915, customarily used the oval brand and the rectangular version is usually associated with his later work and/or his son Cleon's work. Unfortunately, the decoys carved by Crowell prior to 1915, before he adopted a brand, are considered to be his finest work. Collectors should be aware that a few decoys have shown up with an apparently authentic Crowell brand that is known not to be his work.

Lee and Lem Dudley: They were twins who lived, hunted, and carved decoys in the far northern Currituck Sound area of the outer banks of North Carolina. The brand L. D. found on their decoys could be either brother, although the late Bill Mackey stated in his *American Bird Decoys* that probably it was Lem Dudley who carved most of the decoys. Simplest of the brands to forge, it has been known to happen. So it behooves any collector interested in Dudley decoys to get to know their characteristics intimately.

Mitchell Fulcher: Also a North Carolina maker, he, like the Dudleys, identified his decoys with his initials, M. F.

Laing: Albert Laing's decoys are almost always found with his last name branded large and clear on the bottom.

Decorative and reproduction decoys

A discussion of decorative decoys is absolutely necessary in a chapter devoted to guiding the collector in this hobby. Experienced and seasoned collectors are quite cognizant of these products, but some could very well mislead those who are new to the hobby or contemplating beginning a collection of decoys.

Collectively, decorative decoys comprise several types:

1. Decoys carved and painted by craftsmen/artists of great talent. They could be called modern folk artists.
2. Reproductions of classic antique decoys. These are almost always offered in a reduced scale from the originals. Some are offered in a limited edition and all are (or should be) well identified as to exactly what they are.
3. Decoys that are factory-made or hand-made and offered to the public strictly as decorator items. They have no claim, nor do their makers make any claim, to anything other than that.
4. Decoys offered by various companies in kit form for finishing by individual hobbyists or those that are made by individuals for their own use or enjoyment.

The first category is the most important of the four. The carvers of these fine bird sculptures, for that is truly what they are, find their progenitors among the early master makers of the working wildfowl decoy. Many of those early makers just were not satisfied with their product unless it reflected their own high

A Raymond Lead Co. of Chicago lead keel weight was used on Illinois River decoys. This is an Animal Trap or Padco wooden decoy found in Henry, Ill.

knowledge of the anatomy and habit of the living bird. They were truly artists who could not help expressing their talents in the working decoy.

The contemporary carvers are carrying on the active pursuit of this acknowledged original early American folk art. It could be said that the competition of today finds its roots in the first organized competition of decoy makers that was held in Bell Port, Long Island, in 1913. Charles E. "Shang" Wheeler, one of the old master decoy makers, entered his work in this competition and walked away the Grand Champion. Most of these contemporary sculptures in wood are easily recognized by their extreme detail and excellent workmanship. In addition to this attention to anatomical and feather detail, the decoy must also pass a set of strict requirement of floating attitude, etc., taken from both the real birds' habits and those that would be necessary for a working decoy. A few contemporary carvers do work in the old style.

The second group, that of reproductions, is probably the most controversial among collectors. Many seasoned serious collectors look upon these products with disdain, but the fact remains that they exist and satisfy the appetites of many individuals. They are usually done in a smaller scale than the original and are well marked as reproductions. Some are machine-made and some entirely hand-made. Like the originals, however, even the machine-made likeness has to have finishing, carving, and painting applied by hand.

Third is a group of decoys that is factory-made or hand-made for decorative purposes only. The legitimate makers of these decorator items clearly mark their products so that the new collector should have no problem identifying them. Some are strikingly beautiful and can make wonderful additions for those who decorate their houses with early American-style furnishings. There are many carvers in this category that approach the quality of those decoys found in the first category.

The last category is that of the various individual woodworking hobbyists who either create their own designs or finish factory-made kits that are available in various stages of completion. The finished products in this category can vary from crude to wonderfully detailed decorations depending on the abilities of the hobbyist.

Value range of decorative decoys

Do not underestimate the value of these decoys. At the July 2002 Guyette/Schmidt auction, 21 decorative decoys averaged $1,000 each, with a range of $100 to $15,000. It is not uncommon for the miniatures and decorative decoys of known carvers such as Crowell, Perdew, and Schmidt to exceed the value of their working decoys.

A number of duck hunters still make and use their own

blocks for hunting and some also sell their decoys to others for use. Some of these decoys may indeed become very collectible in the future but should not be confused with the older decoys with values already established based upon collector demand.

All have a particular market, from the active collector of the beautiful decoys created by contemporary artisans to the kits and individually made decorative decoys. They were not originally, however, looked upon as a part of decoy collecting. But, as time passes, many of the artist-carved birds representing ducks have gained in popularity and value. They should likely be considered part of the mainstream of decoy collecting. It is only important for the beginning and intermediate collector to keep in mind that the information is presented more for interest. It is especially important for the neophyte collector so that he may not become confused in the early phases of building a collection and learning about antique decoys. The vast majority of current collectors are interested in decoys made and used prior to the 1960s, and many collectors limit their collections to birds made and used in the 1800s or early 1900s. However, again, only the collector has the right to determine his/her own interests in decoy collecting. The future may see even more people adding contemporary carvers to their collections.

Misrepresentations, forgeries and fakes

Fortunately there are very few nefarious dealers in antique decoys and most antiques shop owners and flea-marketers are honest. The latter two, however, seldom know decoys in any detail. These shops and flea markets can be good hunting grounds if you know your stuff. You might find a real treasure for just a few bucks.

However, you may also find plastic heads on beautiful old wooden bodies—and we come to the problem of re-heads. Do not misunderstand re-heads as misrepresentations, fakes or forgeries because the discussion appears here. The majority of old bodies fitted with old heads that are not the originals are legitimate decoys. Remember that bills and heads are usually the parts of a decoy most susceptible to damage in handling, so many hunters had to replace heads from time to time. The ability to recognize a re-head most of the time will come with increased familiarity with individual, recognizable characteristics of various makers. Re-heads represent an altered form of a decoy, hence its inclusion here.

So far not too many outright fakes or forgeries have reared their ugly heads, but it has happened. A few obviously inferior decoys have been found with the easily recognizable oval brand of Elmer Crowell. The most popular forged brand is that of Lee and Lem Dudley, for they simply carved L. D. into their products. Fakes of Mason decoys have shown up. By far the most popular subjects of forgers are the decoys made by the Ward brothers, Lem and Steve. In other words, the more expensive the bird, the more likely someone will attempt to recreate it.

So far, not many of these bogus offerings have turned up. But, as in any area of collecting where some of the items have reached values as high as decoys have, we have to be ready for anything. There are many exceptionally talented craftsmen in the United States today and it would be safe to say that among them are a few bad apples. In addition, with the spate of well-formed decorator decoy bodies and kits for the hobbyist, a dishonest individual would not have to be necessarily endowed with great carving talent, only a degree of ingenuity. Also, more than one dealer has realized that paint may duplicate the aging process by leaving a new decoy out in the weather for an extended time. Most of these, fortunately, are blends of several styles or just simply a talented designer's own creation and are marked in such a way as to identify them as modern. The problem is some of them are not so marked and others are actual copies not marked as such. Most experienced collectors and sellers can readily identify these as bogus, but those of us a little less punctilious might be fooled.

There is yet another potential area of fraud that's important to know about. With the modern CAD/CAM techniques of a small factory, a person can reproduce any such product identical to the original form. Thus, by using a Dodge as a model, someone can reproduce a Dodge in form. Of course, this would still have to be painted correctly. However, you can see how it pays to only purchase rare items when the provenance and authenticity of the items can be verified. All of this comes down to one cardinal rule of collecting: Establish a good working relationship with one or more knowledgeable and trustworthy dealers. Any reliable dealer would back up his/her sale to you with a guarantee of reimbursement if what you were sold turns out to be other than what was represented.

Restoration and repairs

There are always two schools of thought among collectors when the subject of restoration comes up. One is labeled the purist approach: that is the strong belief that the decoy should be left "as is" and no restoration effort should be made. Some collectors of this persuasion will, however, approve of taking the years of working repaints down to what is left of the first or original coat.

In the other group are those who advocate complete or partial restoration. This could run the spectrum from a simple paint touch-up to replacing broken or rotten wood parts and faithfully reproducing the style of painting of the original maker.

What you do or think about restoration is strictly a personal decision made under the circumstances. You should know, however, that probably the majority of serious collectors prefer the decoy to be left as it is. Further, if you do elect to have a decoy restored, it is incumbent upon you to be certain that you say it has been done before selling or swapping the bird. My own opinion goes a step further. Each restored decoy should be clearly and permanently marked as such in an inconspicuous place, preferably on the bottom, then subsequent owners will know exactly what has been done to it. The condition of a decoy can be an extremely important consideration when placing a value on it. A restoration of any sort can have a tremendous influence on its value in either direction. So you must think carefully before having any restoration done and be careful in selecting the person to do the work.

There is presently some controversy brewing about restoring and repairing decoys. While it is easy to be a purist and collect only those examples that are in mint condition, you would find such a collection rather limited by the rarity of such examples, not to mention expensive. Such examples could command rather daunting prices.

The controversy revolves around the value of restored or repaired decoys. Some collectors feel that a beautifully restored decoy should be worth nearly, if not as much as, a pristine example. Others argue that they should be considerably devalued. This is not a problem with any real solution that would cover all cases. It must, of necessity, be a subjective decision and one which

A miniature Mallard drake on a wood base is stamped "Fieldcraft, Inc., Boston, Mass." It was carved by Raymond Stanley for Fieldcraft, circa 1940s, 4" long, **$450.** *Hank and Judy Norman Collection*

must be made personally by each collector. How could you possibly make a sweeping statement covering all cases? How could you, for example, say that an Ira Hudson decoy restored to perfect condition be worth as much as one that is just as nice that had never been damaged at all? Hudson produced a prodigious number of decoys in his career and there are plenty of nice examples out there. There are other makers, such as Shang Wheeler, who made fine decoys, but in limited numbers. In that case, the restored one could conceivably be valued at near or the same as an undamaged one.

Care of your collection

You might think that just because many of your decoys survived the ravages of water and rough treatment by hunters, you do not have to give them any special consideration in display or transport. If you give it just a little thought, millions of decoys were made and used over the years. There can be no realistic estimate made as to how many have survived, but suffice it to say, they are becoming more and more difficult to find in any condition, much less good to excellent condition.

Any wooden object is subject to a number of different hazards. Checking, the splitting or cracking of decoys, is not an uncommon problem. Some of it is due to the maker not using sufficiently seasoned wood. Due to subsequent drying out of unseasoned wood, checking can and does happen. Consider also that a decoy may have lain untouched for years in a boathouse, shed or barn with more or less constant moisture conditions. You find it, add it to your collection in your modern climate-controlled home, which is dry as a rule, and after some months a crack appears. It could be dismaying, but you can do little about the problem unless you have the wherewithal to install expensive systems like the better museums have. This is a problem most of us will have to accept as inevitable, although it does not happen often. There are some precautions you can take to at least retard this problem, and others you can take easily to alleviate the likelihood of damage.

For one thing, make sure that your display is not subjected to direct blasts of heat or cold from a floor or wall register. They look great on a mantel, but that is one of the worst places to display them and if you use your fireplace even just occasionally, do not leave them up there. Heat and smoke will do harm to your decoys. Never let them be exposed to direct sunlight even for a few minutes each day; the cumulative damaging effect of ultraviolet light from the sun can fade the already fragile paint. A little known fact is that continuous exposure to fluorescent light can do the same thing. Try to avoid exposure to either one.

There is also some controversy concerning applying oil or wax to a decoy. Once again, a purist might not like this because it alters the original state of the decoy. This must be an individual decision, but

it is known that proper application of these materials to any wood acts as a preservative by feeding the wood. You would not hesitate to care for a piece of fine antique furniture in this manner, so why not your decoys? Obviously, rigorous rubbing of an already old and fragile paint job may do it irreversible harm, so judgment is needed.

Not too much has been written about termites, powder-post beetles or lyctid beetles and other wood-boring insects, but this problem presents a very real and present danger. If they are in the wood, they can damage or destroy your decoy and also can literally eat your house from around you if they spread to the wood surrounding the infested object.

If you find small piles of fine dust around a decoy, do not panic; just remove it from your collection and isolate it. Recent research has indicated that freezing the piece of infested wood will usually kill the live lyctid beetles, but not much is yet known about the effect of the larvae of the beetle. My advice would be to freeze it for several days and isolate it for about a month, preferably in a sealed plastic bag or tightly lidded metal box. Inspect it periodically for new evidence of the dust-like, powdery spills from the tiny holes made by the beetle. If no new ones are found, you are probably safe.

A most important consideration in the care of your collection is insurance and theft protection. This can be a paramount importance if your collection has grown for some years and represents a sizable sum of money in appreciated value. Additionally, much of it may be irreplaceable. There are some safeguards against these threats, including insurance. I would bet a great many collectors are sublimely comforted by the mistaken belief that their homeowners' insurance covers their collection. They are suffering from a common but risky supposition. Most of these policies specifically exclude such collections. A trusted insurance expert should examine the situation. Also, some collecting clubs now offer insurance programs for specialty collections and this may be an avenue for some to insure their collection.

A careful record of your collection is almost obligatory in its protection. If you have a good record of the items in your collection, it can be of immeasurable aid in documenting your loss in the case of fire, theft, etc. Law enforcement authorities often turn up stolen goods that cannot be claimed by the true owner because of lack of ownership documentation.

It is strongly recommended that you accomplish a detailed listing of each decoy in your collection. A very effective method is to photograph each of them and record any distinguishing characteristics on the reverse of the photo, such as species, maker, marks or brands, size, and any readily recognizable wear patterns, nicks, etc. You should keep this in a safe place away from your home such as a bank safe deposit box. If you wish to have such a record in your home for the convenience of making changes and additions, make sure it is a second set and be certain you make the same additions and corrections to the other set in your safe deposit box.

With this kind of record, in the event of theft and recovery, you should have no problem reclaiming your decoys. It will also go a long way establishing the amount of your loss to insurance companies.

Beginning the search

There are many ways to approach the idea of collecting decoys. There are hundreds of known carvers and numerous factories, even more of each being discovered every year we avidly collect. There are also dozens of species of birds represented, as well as many different hunting areas and major waterfowl flyways. With this in mind, you may choose to specialize in one of the areas. For instance, you might wish to concentrate on decoys that are indigenous to the area in which you live, a particular species of bird, factory-made decoys, decoys of only one factory, etc. Another satisfying way of collecting is to obtain any decoy within your means that pleases you and build a collection around those acquisitions.

There are three major groupings of decoys defined as to maker:

Commercially produced decoys: those carved and painted by hand for purposes of sale to others for use.

Non-commercially produced decoys: those produced by a hunter for his/her own use or a friend's use and not sold, as a rule.

Factory-produced decoys: those made in a commercial facility, usually turned out in great numbers by machine lathes or other mass-production techniques such as injection molding. Not all factories were large; it is the machine carving or molding that makes it a factory.

Most decoy collectors refer to certain geographic areas where decoys were carved and hunted over as "schools" of decoy makers. There are probably 30 or more identifiable schools of carvers in the various flyways. The information and photographs attempt to give you some basic tools that should enable you to look at a particular decoy and at least identify what part of the country it is from.

Information related to valuation of the decoys and other collectibles will be presented as actual valuation when known, related to sales and will also be presented in ranges and, in many cases, widely varying ranges. The value ranges are given merely as a guide and most of them have been derived from auction catalogs and dealers' sales lists.

When using the value ranges in this chapter, you should bear in mind several factors: If, for instance, there is a particularly rare and hard-to-find decoy known to exist only in four or five collections and suddenly, however unlikely, a group of 20 to 25 is found in an old barn loft and offered for sale at auction, the resulting prices realized might be considerably less than the heretofore-accepted value.

Marks on the decoy can also affect value, and condition can have a heavy influence. The values presented are for decoys in good to excellent condition. There is a tendency for collectors to take a book such as this one and use it as the final authority. This would be unwise as it is only one source in many needed to make value determinations. You must use this book in conjunction with your own experience, the word of a trusted dealer, and all the other sources of value information you can get your hands on: dealer lists, periodical articles, sales ads, auction lists, etc.

For now, though, look for those old factory decoys by Mason, Dodge, Peterson, and others that were made up until the end of market gunning. Look for the factory birds that were made in the 1920s and later by Pratt, Herter's, Evans, and others. Look for the mass-produced decoys that survived until much later, such as Herter's, and for the more recently semi mass-produced decoys such as the Ward Brothers and Waterfowlers. Look for the early papier-mâché birds in pristine shape, and for unusual, early or rare plastic decoys from the 1950s. Look for anything else that you enjoy for your own collection. Hopefully, after reviewing this entire chapter, you will be able to better identify decoys, makers of decoys, and your own desires in building a collection. Good hunting!

Early decoys were crude but effective. A very rare Ira Hudson Hooded Merganser hen, circa 1900, is one of the earliest of all documented Ira Hudson decoys, **$10,000-$15,000.** *Gary Campbell Collection*

Individual carvers

This section shows examples of some of the many wonderful decoys carved by individuals in America and Canada. My book, *Warman's Duck Decoys*, shows many more decoys and is organized according to geographical regions, whereas here I show a good sampling to whet your appetite for more. Many of the decoys shown have not appeared before in either *Warman's Duck Decoys* or *Collecting Antique Bird Decoys and Duck Calls*, 3rd edition, and hopefully the serious duck and bird decoy collector will purchase both of those books for further photos, information and history on decoy carving and collecting in America.

Black Duck and anchor. This wooden, glass-eyed decoy was designed for the heavy waters of Lake Huron and was made by Ed Fitzpatrick of Weale, MI, **$800+.**

Black Duck, Art Best, Sebewaing, Michigan, **$300+.** Art also made fishing lures.

Thomas Chambers, Michigan, heavy water Bluebill drake, likely an overpainted Canvasback given the head shape, leather thong, heavy keel, **$500+.**

This Old Squaw drake is attributed to "Os" Bibber, circa 1920, Maine, **$20,000.** *Hank and Judy Norman Collection*

Coykendall Coot, wood, glass-eyed, signed, **$200+.**

Ned Burgess, Churches Island, N.C., carved this Mallard hen. It is very rare, was created in the early 20th century, and has original paint and a small dent in back. It is featured in *Southern Decoys*; **$21,000.** *Guyette & Schmidt, Inc.*

Elmer Crowell, East Harwich, Mass., carved this rare pair of cork-bodied Pintails early in the 20th century. Crowell's oval brand is on the underside of each, with slightly turned heads with wooden bottom board on each. They are also branded "F. WINTHROP." The drake has an inlet tail and both have raised "V" wing carving. Original paint with very minor wear and small chips in cork, **$11,000.** *Guyette & Schmidt, Inc.*

Elmer Crowell, Massachusetts, carved this Goldeneye hen. It has an oval brand, fluted tail, original paint and a few small dents, **$7,500.** *Guyette & Schmidt, Inc.*

A Black-bellied Plover by Elmer Crowell is dated about 1915 and branded "P.W.W." for Parker W. Wittemore of Marblehead, Mass, **$12,500.** *Hank and Judy Norman Collection*

Elmer Crowell's Canada Goose, made using the slat body technique common to that area, is a large goose measuring approximately 42" from bill to tail. It has an oval stamp under the tail, original paint and is strong structurally, **$5,500-$6,000.** *Guyette & Schmidt, Inc.*

Elmer Crowell carved this Black Duck, circa first quarter of the 20th century. It has an oval brand and near mint original paint. Provenance: Chatham Family, **$4,750.** *Guyette & Schmidt, Inc.*

Elmer Crowell also carved this Black Duck in the early part of the 20th century. It has an oval brand, slightly turned head with glass eyes, original paint with nice feathering, small touchup on tail, cracks and shot marks, **$750.** *Guyette & Schmidt, Inc.*

At top left and right is a very rare Ward Brothers, Maryland, Styrofoam decoy produced only a short while in the 1950s in limited production. Bottom left and right is a decoy made by Robert Elliston, Michigan. Both decoys are similar in that they are in the sleeper position. Elliston decoys are fairly rare and made of balsa; the Ward Brothers were premier carvers on the Maryland shore. Ward Brothers: **$500+**; Elliston: **$1,000+**.

Joseph Enright, Ohio, cork bodied, wood head, glass-eyed Black Duck, **$400-$600+.** Enright was a National Decoy Carver winner in the 1940s.

A Golden Plover is by the Folger family of Nantucket, Mass., circa 1870, **$12,500.** *Hank and Judy Norman Collection*

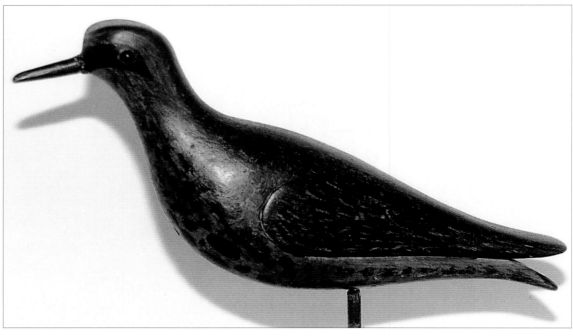

Hen Mallard by Gibradltair or Foote. **$150+.**

Bottom carving details on the
Mallard decoys.

Head details of the Drake
Mallard.

John Kalash Gibradltair
or Jim Foote Drake
Mallard, Michigan,
$150+.

Here is a nice example of miniatures from Wisconsin, circa 1930s. These diminutive little decoys, one of which is featured on the front cover of this book, are only about 5" in total length, with excellent painting, **$300** a pair. *Lewis Collection*

J. E. Kelley miniature decorative decoy, wood, glass-eyed, circa 1983, **$25+.**

Charles Klopping, Ohio, carved this Canvasback drake, circa 1935, **$1,500.** *Hank and Judy Norman Collection*

A Blue-winged Teal by Paul Lipke, Indiana, dates to about 1940, **$4,000.** *Hank and Judy Norman Collection*

A Green-wing Teal made by McAlpin, Illinois River, **$1,500-$2,000.** *Pitt Collection*

A Mallard drake by John McLaughlin, Bordentown, N.J., is signed and original, with excellent condition and details, **$1,200.** *Guyette & Schmidt, Inc.*

Four Canvasbacks by Ben Schmidt, Michigan: three drakes and a hen. The former owner from whom I purchased this string of decoys bought them directly from Ben prior to his use of feathering details. They are similar to a Canvasback by Frank Schmidt, Ben's brother, sold in 2006 by Decoys Unlimited for **$250.** However, Ben indeed made them. Hens are more rare in nearly all decoys and thus worth a bit more; **$300+** each, **$400+** for the hen.

Three photos show an R. Madison Mitchell Bufflehead drake with original keel that dates from the late 1940s or early 1950s. Details in the photos show it can be dated by the one nail both fore and aft as opposed to two nails found on later models, **$400.**
Pitt Collection

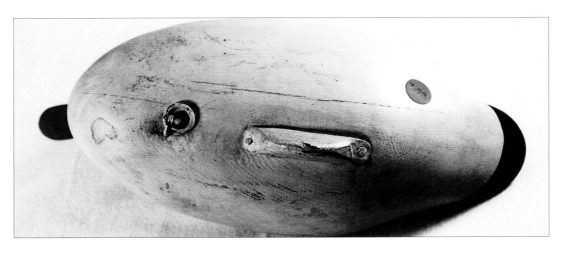

Roger Philip, Michigan, drake Mallard, signed/dated 1970, **$150+.**

Roger Philip, drake Redhead, signed/dated 1988, **$150+.**

An Ed Phillips Bluebill drake in original paint is circa 1930s, Cambridge, MD, **$2,000-$2,500.** *Griff Evans Collection*

A Magnum-size Illinois River drake Mallard, carved by premier early carver Mario Piolotti (1900-1964) of Spring Valley, Ill., circa 1940, **$3,000+.** *Pitt Collection*

C. C. Roberts and J. R. Rheinschimdt wooden, glass-eyed decoy, Canvasback made for heavy waters, Wisconsin. These famous lure makers (Robert's Mud Puppy lures) also made about 200 decoys for family and lure company employee use and this is one of about 20 in my collection. It was sold at auction for **$225+** on April 7, 2007.

Willie Ross, Cheabeague Island, Maine, carved this red-breasted Merganser pair, circa second quarter of the 20th century. They have inlet heads and glass eyes, original paint with some repaint to white areas, peacock plumes normally inserted into back of head are missing, dowel protruding, the hen has a crack in the neck, **$1,950.** *Guyette & Schmidt, Inc.*

Ben Schmidt, Michigan, wooden, glass-eyed Canada Goose showing the feathering detail typical of Schmidt birds, **$500+.**

Ben Schmidt, Michigan, Black Duck overpainted Canvasback drake showing his typical bottom board, red glass eyes and feathering details, **$300+** due to being overpainted, otherwise **$1,000+** for a nice Schmidt such as this. Recent sales have averaged between **$1,000-$2,000** for his better birds.

Canvasback drake, Frank Schmidt, Michigan, **$175+.** Frank is Ben Schmidt's brother.

George Warin, Toronto, Ontario, is credited for this hollow carved Teal. It is an old Belleville style repaint, with a small chip and shot marks, **$450.** *Guyette & Schmidt, Inc*

Frank Brogan bobtail Canvasback drake with heavy Great Lakes anchor and carrying device, **$400+.**

Unknown bobtail Canvasback drake, wood, glass-eyed, keel for heavy water with leather anchor strap, **$300+.**

Len Suzor Bluebill, wood, glass-eyed, Detroit River, Ontario, Canada, **$300+.**

Len Suzor Bluebill drake, wood decoy, glass-eyed, nice details, Detroit River, Ontario, Canada, **$300+.**

Folk-type wooden, glass-eyed decoy circa 1968 made by Keith Van Dusen, Houghton Lake, Michigan, **$50-$75+.**

This Rhodes Truex hollow Bluebill pair, circa 1920s, Atlantic City, N. J., was repainted by Lem Ward in the 1970s, **$600-$800.**
Griff Evans Collection

A Ward Brothers, Crisfield, MD, preening deluxe grade North American Pintail drake is from 1963, **$10,000.** *Pitt Collection*

The bottom of the Scaup decoy shows the Ward Brothers pedigree and details about the deluxe grade decoy.

A Ward Brothers, Crisfield, MD, deluxe grade greater Scaup drake has no date but is found in the Ward Brothers book, **$8,000.** *Pitt Collection*

Beautiful unknown wooden Bluebill drake, long bodied, neck inset about 2" from chest, nice paint, glass eyed, similar to a Stevens, **$150+.**

Unknown Hayward, Wisconsin, area Mallard, glass eyed, natural color, two-piece construction. The only one left from a string of decoys purchased a number of years ago by author, **$300+** (based upon former sales).

Unknown miniature decorative decoy, wood, glass-eyed, **$25+.**

Unknown bobtail type wooden, glass-eyed Bluebill drake decoy with leather thong and circular weight, **$150+.**

A gorgeous pair of Canvasbacks, wood, glass-eyed, deep water wooden keels, nice detailing on beak, likely Lloyd Natzmer from Michigan as the shape of the bottom boards and back carving is very similar to his decoys, **$400+** each.

Unknown Bluebill drake with painted eyes, wood, nice feather painting details, dowel insert for head mounting, branded "OK" on bottom, **$150+.**

Unknown cork bodied with wooden head, glass-eyed Canvasback drake and wooden bottom board, **$125+.** Similar decoys were made by Don Parker and Jack Fletcher in Bay City, MI, and this is possibly a Parker decoy.

A canvas over wire on a wooden bottom board Swan with a wooden neck and head, glass-eyed, unknown but common in Minnesota and the Carolinas, **$100-$200+.**

A Friendship, Maine, area Eider Duck, circa 1900, has an inlet head and original paint, **$6,000.** *Guyette & Schmidt, Inc.*

This upstate New York early Goldeneye drake has a 45-degree turned head, good original paint, some chipping, **$300.** *Guyette & Schmidt, Inc.*

Factory decoys

This section shows examples of some of the hundreds of factory decoys available to the collector ranging from the popular and often very pricey Mason Decoy Factory birds to some of the more affordable papier-mâché decoys made by a variety of manufacturers beginning in the 1930s. Even some of the early 1950s plastic decoys have become popular for collecting even though their values remain fairly low compared to wooden decoys and papier-mâché birds. As the pricing on early wooden decoys continues to rise, you can expect more and more interest in other types of decoys. Photos are listed alphabetically by maker.

Pair of Acme Folding Decoys, Mallards, similar to the ones shown on Page 42 showing how the decoys operated using the little lever on the side of the decoy. Pair sold for **$160** at auction on April 7, 2007.

Acme Folding Decoys from
St. Louis, early 1900s.
Another rare find due to
the box more than the
decoys, **$500+** for box and
dozen decoys.

Animal Trap wooden solid bodied drake Mallard, **$175+.**

Animal Trap wooden decoy with Red Head Tenite head, stamped on bottom of decoy, **$75+.**

A Model D-10 Scaup drake by Animal Trap Co. of America (Victor) shows the cross keel to wrap an anchor rope, developed in the mid-'50s, **$125.** *Pitt Collection*

The General Fiber Co. of St. Louis produced many decoys under the Ariduck brand name. An Ariduk Scaup female, in pristine condition, is a harder decoy to find than the drake, circa early 1950s, **$175.** *Pitt Collection*

An Ariduk Mallard drake is a rarer version that was made for Sears, Roebuck & Co. **$175.** *Pitt Collection*

The bottom of the Ariduk decoy has the Sears brand.

The bill is green on this Ariduk Black Duck, **$125.** *Lewis Collection*

The bottom of the Ariduk decoy has more company details.

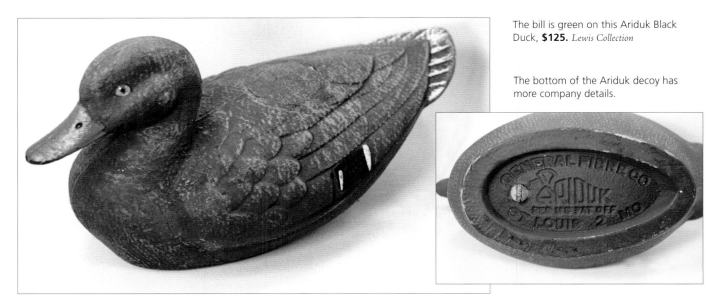

A grouping of 31 decoys by Armstrong Decoys of Houston, Texas, includes two Canada Geese. The rest are Pintails and Mallards, with some tip ups. This is a great sale buy, **$700.** *Guyette & Schmidt, Inc.*

A movable-wing duck made in the mid-1950s by B & J Manufacturing Co. of Chicago, IL, **$250.** Above is the duck with its wings open. *Pitt Collection*

A Superior Grade Model Green-wing Teal drake by Benz Lifelike Decoys of Jefferson City, Mo., has its original paint with small cracking underneath, **$600.** *Guyette & Schmidt, Inc.*

Wood Duck salesman samples from the Italian exporter of Carry-Lite Decoys (Milwaukee, WI) to the U.S.A. All salesman samples are hard to come by so even these plastic ones are of interest. They were purchased online more than five years ago for **$50** each and are now **$50-$75** each. *Lewis Collection*

Carry-Lite Dove decoy, papier-mâché, note clothes pin holder, **$25+.**

Carry-Lite "Dura-Beak" style papier-mâché decoy, hen Mallard, with glass eyes, in near-mint shape. **$50-$75.**

Carry-Lite DECOYS

No. 700
MALLARD HEN

Actual Color
Reproductions
¼ Full Size

No. 700
MALLARD DRAKE

No. 702
BLUE-BILL HEN

No. 702
BLUE-BILL DRAKE

No. 701
PINTAIL HEN

No. 701
PINTAIL DRAKE

No. 703
CANVAS-BACK HEN

No. 703
CANVAS-BACK DRAKE

First introduced to the sporting goods and outdoor trade last year, Carry-Lite Decoys proved an instant, sensational success . . . exceeding our most optimistic expectations in sales. Production facilities were overtaxed, due to the overwhelming demand. For 1941 . . . we are all set to take care of all your requirements.

DEALERS: Order from your regular sporting goods or hardware jobber. Complete stocks available.

No. 704
BLACK DUCK

See Other
Side For
Additional
Decoys

Fall issues of leading outdoor magazines will again carry our Carry-Lite Decoys advertising messages to hundreds of thousands of sportsmen. From Coast to Coast and from the Arctic Circle to the Gulf of Mexico, duck hunting enthusiasts will be clamoring for "Carry-Lites." Be prepared to meet the demand. Stock orders placed NOW, will be put on our "priorities" list.

Carry-Lite DECOYS

MOLDED CARRY-LITE DECOYS

2601 N. 30th ST., MILWAUKEE, WIS.

Carry-Lite also produced goose decoys and some decorator ducks and salesman samples. All of these are more difficult to find. These are some examples of Carry-Lite birds.

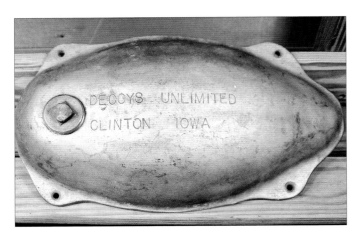

Decoys Unlimited, Clinton, Iowa, decoy examples and mold used to pour the Styrofoam birds. Mold: **$200+**; decoys, **$75+** each.

A very rare Barrow's Golden Eye drake by J.N. Dodge of Detroit, MI, is one of only four known to exist. This is the same bird as shown in the Dodge decoy book; **$10,000+.**
Pitt Collection

A Bluewing Teal drake by Evans Duck Decoy Co. of Ladysmith, WI, bears an Evans stamp, original paint with touch up on the speculums and white area of the head, and filled crack at the factory; **$1,200.**
Guyette & Schmidt, Inc.

Duck-In Decoys, St. Louis, MO, canvas decoy pair with the original Duck-In weight attached, **$100+** for pair and weight.

Stamped wooden Evans decoy in rough shape but a rare decoy from Ladysmith, WI. Sold on April 7, 2007 for **$200+.**

Earlier Herter's wood/balsa glass-eyed drake Canvasback, **$150+.**

Herter's mold for Styrofoam or Tenite heads, **$50+.**

An oversize cork Mallard drake by Herter's Inc. of Wasceca, WI, has a balsa head, circa 1950s, **$125+.** *Pitt Collection*

Tenite head balsa Herter's Bluebill drake, **$100+.**

Tenite head, balsa Herter's drake Canvasback with large bottom board and owner's mark and date of 1971, **$100+.**

Herter's Mallard with nice pear-shape weight. I picked up a string of nine of these Herter's and all have similar paint and weights, made of balsa wood, sold at auction on April 7, 2007, **$75+** each.

Oversize Herter's Black Duck, Tenite head, cork body, wooden bottom board. Wildfowler made similar decoys, **$200+.**

Cork Herter's Redhead, **$50+.**

Tenite head Herter's Mallard drake, balsa body, heavy keel, **$100+.**

Herter's canvas and wooden neck/head Canada Goose with glass eyes and the metal strip holding the stretched canvas over a cork body. These have become very collectible and Harvey Pitt offered me $1,000 for this one just prior to his untimely death. Harvey had a number of ducks but needed a Herter's goose to round out his collection, **$1,000+**.

Wooden Goldeneye decoy with Tenite head, marked "J M" on the bottom, possibly for John McDonald of McDonald's Island, MI. John made decoys of his own from both wood and cork. This is likely a Herter's, **$75+.**

Illinois River Folding Decoys, J. W. Reynolds Company, Chicago, complete dozen of wooden Mallard decoys in original wooden box, circa 1930, rare to find the complete set in this condition. Individual set of three tri-fold decoys average **$250-$300** each; **$2,000+** for entire dozen and original box.

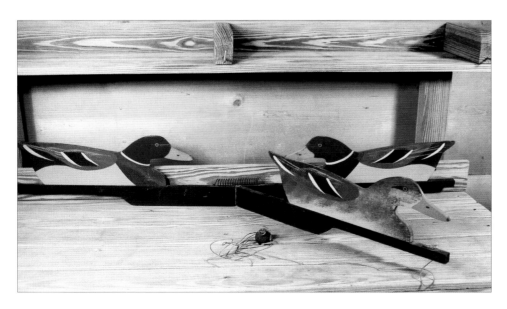

Illinois River decoy repaint, note the typical Illinois River weight used made in Chicago, **$50+.** This is possibly a Pratt, after the company bought Mason's production line when Mason went out of business in 1924.

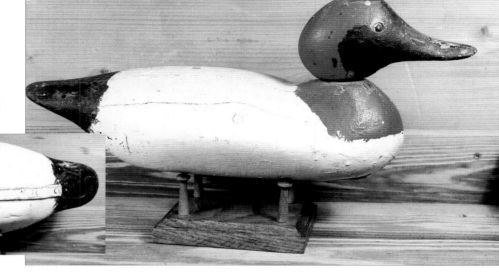

An oversize female Scaup was made by L.L. Bean, **$175.** *Pitt Collection*

A Premier grade Widgeon drake by Masons Decoy Factory of Detroit, MI, is circa 1915, **$11,000.** *Hank and Judy Norman Collection*

Mason Factory Decoys, Detroit, MI, early 1900s, Bluebill drake showing the fine painting details, glass eyes and the beautiful shape that most collectors admire in a Mason bird; **$200+** in this condition. Masons run from **$100+** to nearly six figures.

A Mason Standard Grade glass-eyed White-wing Scoter was used as a confidence decoy, **$800-$1,200.**
Pitt Collection

This is the hen Blue-wing Teal Mason Standard Grade, with glass eyes, **$5,000+.** The second photo shows the decoy's bottom details.
Pitt Collection

A Redhead drake in Mason Premier Grade is the low-head version, **$5,000+.** *Pitt Collection*

Painted eyes mark this Mason Standard Grade Wood Duck drake, **$700-$1,200.** *Pitt Collection*

A Canvasback "snake-head" drake is in Mason Premier Grade, **$15,000+.** *Pitt Collection*

The Mason "snake-head" Pintail drake, in Standard Grade with glass eyes, is a very rare configuration, **$32,000.**
Pitt Collection

A close-up shows the "snake-head" of the Pintail drake.

A Redhead drake is in Mason Premier Grade, **$5,000-$7,500.** *Pitt Collection*

One of the Mason Special Orders is this Seneca Lake Premier Grade Canvasback drake, **$20,000+.** *Pitt Collection*

Milwaukee Museum School
Bluebill drake, note the slat
construction, **$100+.**

Possible Milwaukee Museum
School decoys, at left and
below, showing slat type
construction, quite primitive,
$75+ each.

A Peterson Decoy Factory Widgeon drake, circa last quarter of the 19th century, has original paint, neck filler missing, **$1,200.** *Guyette & Schmidt, Inc.*

A rare Bufflehead drake by William Pratt Manufacturing Co. of Joliet, IL, has its original paint, **$550.** *Guyette & Schmidt, Inc.*

A Merganser drake by Sperry Decoy Factory, New Haven, Conn., is oversized and has its original paint, **$1,100.** *Guyette & Schmidt, Inc.*

Rubber Duraduck decoys from the 1950s, two mallards and a pintail, **$10-$15** each.

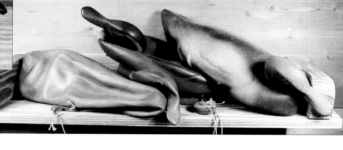

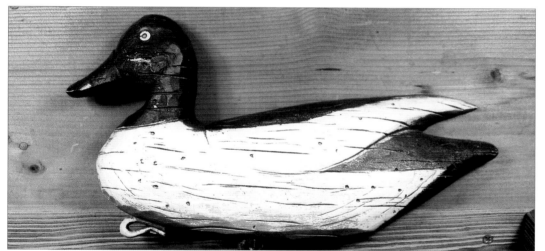

Decorative door mount, fiberglass, Model 7016 made by Syroco, copyright 1966, **$25+.**

Bluebill pair, wood, likely Victors circa 1950s-60s, **$50-$75** each.

Victor wooden Mallard pair, stamped on bottoms, **$100+** each.

Pair of Victor Mallards rigged for heavy waters, stamped on bottom, glass-eyed, wood, made on a lathe showing the lathe marks, **$150+** each.

Overpainted Wildfowler or L. L. Bean wooden decoy, **$50-$75.**

A Wildfowler Decoys Inc. Green-wing Teal hen was made in Point Pleasant, N.J., circa 1970s, **$500+.** *Pitt Collection*

Unknown tin Bluebill and a variety of anchor weights found on decoys on top of the Acme box, **$20** for decoy; weights, **$1-$10** each, a little more for the rare Acme Folding Decoy weight.

Unknown factory Bluebill drakes, each one has a half-weight as shown on the one decoy. These are glass-eyed and nicely painted and are likely Michigan birds. Sold at auction on April 7, 2007 for **$100+** each.

Two unmarked repainted wooden decoys, appear to be Evans, note the weight is common to the Great Lakes area. Sold at auction on April 7, 2007 for **$150+** each.

A second unmarked Minnesota or Carolinas canvas over wire with wooden bottom board and wooden head Swan, **$100-$200+.**

Unmarked wooden decoy, sleeper position, possibly an Evans, sold at auction on April 7, 2007, **$150+.**

Unmarked wooden decoy, found with the Evans above, possibly a tack-eyed Evans or simply a copy made by an individual carver. Sold at auction on April 7, 2007 for **$100+.**

Chapter 2

Duck and Game Calls

The perfect follow-up to duck and bird decoys is to cover calls made and used to lure game birds and other animals closer to the hunter. Early calls were likely as simple as blowing on a blade of grass placed between your thumbs or using two pieces of slate rubbed together to confuse a turkey. Duck and game calls have been collected seriously for nearly as long as decoys but have had far less written about them with only a handful of decent resources available. *Collecting Antique Bird Decoys and Duck Calls*, 3rd edition, mentioned earlier covers both traditional makers and company calls. I have also written a book with studio-quality photos titled *The Art of American Game Calls*, copyright 2005, published by Collector Books, a division of Schroeder Publishing. This 174-page hardcover book covers many more of the traditional makers than were featured in my first book. It is $24.95 and available from the publisher or me.

Calls date back into the 1800s and early calls by Elam Fisher and others are collectible, as are calls by "known makers" such as Charles Perdew (also a great carver of decoys). With the advent of the baby boom generation, such as myself, there has been a growing interest in factory calls from the 1940s-1960s as well. You are far more likely to find a "sleeper" among duck and game calls than with duck decoys. The Charles Perdew crow call in my collection came from a local garage sale for $5. It is not the only call purchased at a bargain; however, calls will bring market price if purchased from a dealer in the know or a collector of calls. But there are still some bargains to be found at garage sales, flea markets and even some antiques stores primarily for the reasons that many of the individual makers did not sign their calls or only marked them with a particular symbol not easily recognized by the casual collector of calls.

Calls are most familiar to duck, goose and turkey hunters; however, many other types of calls exist and one has been made for nearly every type of sporting hunt and the hunting of most prey animals as well. I am not a call-maker but I have used calls for duck, squirrel and turkey hunting. I grew up in an extended family that hunted, trapped and fished and used every possible means of gaining their objective at hand, including the use of calls. As a collector, I became interested in the beauty of the calls and started keeping a few. The next thing I knew, I had well over 100 of them and the calls became a new collection to go with my decoys and fishing lures.

You will see factory calls here that you may not have ever seen

before. The same is true for individual call makers. I have included some brief introductory comments but this chapter is really about the photos. Each one has call identification, value information, and a comment or two about the maker when known. The chapter is broken into two major sections: individual makers and factory calls. Sometimes it is difficult to decide where to put calls as some people made so many they were as prolific as small factories, such as Perdew and Bishop. However, their calls are in the individual call maker section. Then Faulk and Olt were of course at one time "individuals" that became so prolific as to grow to a factory level of production, so they are covered in the factory section.

As a former working anthropologist and folklorist, I am all too aware that much of the data about items such as calls is rapidly disappearing as we lose our current oldest generation. Men and women in their 60s, 70s and 80s are carrying around with them the best information we have on many of the people and calls represented in this book. We need to talk to them now! We need to document as much as possible while it is still possible. The recent passing of Harvey Pitt and the recent illness of Joe Jaroski document this all too well. I wish Joe the best and hope he is again soon making calls for us all.

Individual call makers

This section shows examples of calls made by "individuals." As mentioned above, some of these individuals were nearly mass producing calls but did not quite cross over that line, such as Charlie Bishop. Some only made a few calls, some made a few dozen or few hundred. Some were painters who added their creativity to a call carved by another. Some were famous and some are nearly "unknown" in the collecting world. Many, if not most, of the individual calls are not marked in any way, unlike factory calls that normally are marked. However, the experienced collector can usually identify a maker by his style, materials used, sound or some other attribute. The calls shown are identified when it is fairly certain as to the maker. Any unidentified calls included are so noted.

The development of the art and science of call making has reached high pinnacles. The calling contests and contestants have constantly demanded finer and finer instruments. This has resulted in the high quality, technologically advanced calls produced by makers today. Unbelievably, they are still improving them. The final quality of a call is found, however, in the ability of the hunter to use it. A fine call does not a fine caller make, and used wrong it only lessens your chances at bagging a limit, or any birds at all. Bad calls can, at the very least, make friends unhappy and nearby hunters downright angry. The latter have been known to express their dissatisfaction in most unpleasant words and actions. If you persist in driving the birds away, the friends may become hostile, making it very difficult to find hunting companions.

Although quality and versatility of the sounds capable of being made on a call can certainly have a bearing on its collectibility, this is more important with contemporary calls than with the old ones. Most of the old calls that survived probably were as effective as was needed or required at the time or they probably would not have survived. However, sound quality is something many collectors also admire in a call and they would prefer a quality sound over an inferior one.

Identification and evaluation of calls

Many calls are starting to get a track record of sales. I think it's safe to say that calls by even the lesser-known makers will easily bring $50; others will command several hundred dollars in many cases for highly detailed checkering, painting, fancy or unusual wood or materials. Many calls by makers such as Perdew have brought five figures, and many more calls now sell in the four-figure range. Values have been established and you will have to do further research online and at auctions to keep abreast of the rapidly changing pricing. As with duck decoys, a quick tour of online sales will educate you in a hurry. Also, attending sporting collectible shows and auction sales will increase your awareness of call prices. The only thing for certain is that calls have gone up in price about four-fold, at least, since the mid-1990s. It is likely that game call collecting is currently about where lure and tackle collecting was about 15 years ago. The associations are just now starting to grow and expand in numbers. Awareness of this interesting hobby is rapidly growing nationally.

This growth and exposure will result in increased demand for calls and increased prices. The future is likely bright for this facet of collecting.

Their history, construction and use are, of course, fundamental to appreciating calls, but the beauty and rarity of the fine call is the primary motivation for collecting it. The quality of the sound you are able to produce on the call is of secondary importance in collecting.

Although the sound of a call is the reason for their existence in the first place, sound quality is really of secondary importance since the advances in call making have improved to such a degree as to make many of the old calls pale in comparison. You could argue further that few, if any, makers would go to the trouble of fashioning a call that would nowadays be considered collectible, if he could not produce the requisite sounds with it.

Once you have seen and handled a number of the finer collectible calls, you will begin to be able to recognize what is good and what is not. There is no substitute for experience. You can read this book and study the photographs and it will give you a good basis on which to build, but hands-on is the byword here. There are a number of things that influence the value and collectibility of a call. Here are a few of them:

Maker—This is the most important *factor* in the valuation of calls. Is the maker well known? A recognized and accomplished decoy carver? The second point is important because it then creates double demand by crossover collectors.

Condition—Collectors differ on the importance of this factor, but all agree that calls need to be in decent condition. As with any collectible, a rare example is desirable in just about any recognizable condition. Finish and appearance would weigh heavily here. Also, quality of the wood or the presence/absence of burls and so on may become an important consideration.

Patent model—This is the extremely rare instance where you come across a call that is exactly like the drawing in the original patent application in every detail. Also, some models are available with "Patent Applied For," "Patent Pending" or some

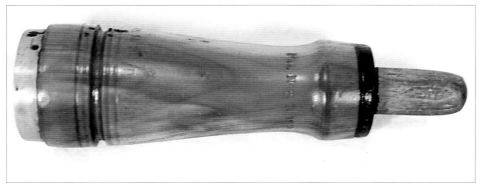

This Charles H. Perdew crow call is valued at **$500.** *Lewis Collection*

An example of an Elam Fisher call from the author's collection, **$200+.**

other such nomenclature, making it special. Then, of course, there are calls without any numbers and ones that have the patent numbers on them.

Special owner—You might encounter a relatively common call that was owned by a famous individual or was used to win a world championship-calling contest or to bag a world record. Whatever the circumstances, a thing called "provenance" comes into very important play. Provenance is a provable record of origin and ownership. It is a written, provable record of an unbroken chain of ownership from the time of the incident of a famous person's ownership. It is not always written, but should have a sound oral history at the very least.

Quality, age, uniqueness, beauty and rarity—All of these factors are self-explanatory.

A history of duck and game calls

Until just a few years ago there was precious little written material with regard to the origins and early history of the development of bird calls in America. What little we have now is, however, a valuable asset to the collecting of these calls.

Primitive times (pre-1850s)

This would be the time before we have any concrete, demonstrable evidence of a man-made object, fashioned expressly for the luring of wild game to within a killing distance by imitating the calls or sounds. At some point in time in early North America, some pre-historic being likely may have successfully mimicked the cry of a wild animal with his own vocal cords and mouth in order to lure it in. It is also likely that early on, primitive man would develop the talent for using whatever might be at hand for imitating game sounds. Certainly the American Indians developed

this to a high degree. They are known to have used whistles and reeds. (Have you ever placed a blade of grass between your thumbs and blown a shrill call?) Certainly any people capable of creating the beautiful decoys found in the Lovelock Cave excavations in Nevada were sophisticated enough to have fashioned some sort of calling device.

Early history (1850s-1935)

The areas of most concentrated activity in this period of the development of commercial call making were the Illinois River basin and the Reelfoot Lake area in Tennessee. There are distinct differences in the style of call from each of these regions.

Collectors and writers have been able to trace production calls back to 1854 or slightly before. There appears to be a Tongue Pincher style of duck call clipped or otherwise attached to the left breast pocket of a hunter's coat in a Currier and Ives print dated 1854. The print is titled "Wild Duck Shooting/A Good Days Sport." It is a stone lithograph of a painting by Arthur Fitzwilliam Tail (1819-1905). It is not clear if this is a European call or an early American attempt at call making.

The earliest evidence of American production of a duck call is a patent issued to Elam Fisher of Detroit in 1870 for a Tongue Pincher type call.

There is a scarcity of information about this period of time, but there was apparently a surge of interest and activity among call makers then, and there seems to have developed some amount of competition among them. There is evidence by the Fisher patent and advertising claims by Fred A. Allen of Monmouth, Ill., and Charles W. Grubbs of Chicago, that each was the first to offer a production duck call commercially. Grubbs claimed in a 1928 advertisement that he did so in 1868. The

Three F. A. Allen calls are from the author's collection. Reed details are also shown; **$125-$200** each. *Lewis Collection*

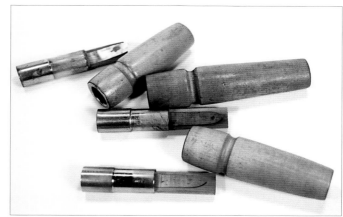

Reed details are displayed from the three F. A. Allen calls.

authors of *Decoys and Decoy Carvers of the Illinois River*, Paul W. Parmalee and Forrest D. Loomis, state in their book that: "Allen's Nickel-Plated Duck Caller" was made for private use in 1863 and "...was considered to be the first duck call to be mass produced in Illinois." Whatever the case, it is ample evidence of commercial call-making activity at that early date. It is important to note here that the Allen call was the first to have utilized a barrel, thus creating a resonant chamber for the call. His Nickel Plated Duck Call is recognized as a significant development in call making and examples of it are highly collectible.

So far as can be determined, it looks as if no one got the bright idea to advertise his or her products until the early 1880s. It seems almost absurd that it would not occur to these folks for 10 or 15 years, but so far a search of old magazines and catalogs has not turned up any ads for calls. They took up advertising with a vengeance from the early 1880s on.

There were some distinctly different styles invented and refined during the Early History period. The Illinois Style and the Reelfoot or Glodo Style were the first to be developed, followed closely by the Arkansas Style and concurrently, the Louisiana or Cajun Style utilizing bamboo or cane (as it is known in the South) instead of wood or other substances. Refer to the Construction and Nomenclature section for details regarding the differences between these styles.

There were many variations and experiments in the development of the styles. One that has survived through the years is that of Victor Glodo of Reelfoot Lake. All the others made contributions of varying importance, but the Glodo or Reelfoot Style is the one that survived intact. Glodo moved to Reelfoot Lake around 1890. Until recently it was thought that Glodo was a French Canadian, but we now know that he came from a call-making family that hailed from the Fountain Bluff Area of southern Illinois. His calls were of the two-piece type using a wooden wedge block, a flat tone board and a curved metal reed. The Glodo and Reelfoot Style of duck call is the most widely used style of metal reed design in call making today. The fact that he was the first maker to decorate his calls (he was the first to use checkering) makes him the father of the American duck calls as a folk art in the estimation of most aficionados.

This important era, the Early History Period, in the evolution of duck call making can be laid out more clearly in the following chronology:

1854-1870

First patent of the Tongue Pincher Style duck call. It was characterized by a straight reed sandwiched between two rounded or curved radius tone boards bound together; no barrel. An 1854 Currier and Ives lithograph possibly illustrates this type. Elam Fisher-1870, Charles Schoenheider-1880.

1863-1870

Early Illinois River Style. This style is characterized by a curved metal reed, a single straight or flat tone board (two-piece stem and insert), a half-round cork wedge block, and a barrel. The first known use of the barrel to create a resonant chamber is attributed to Fred A. Allen. Others making this style call were Charles W. Grubbs of Chicago, who claimed he was making them as early as 1868 and advertised his calls at least as early as 1892, and George Peterson, who was in business in 1873 making decoys and perhaps duck calls. Jasper N. Dodge bought out the Peterson business 10 years later, about 1883. The Early Illinois River Style continued to be made into the 1900s, though the

An early call maker is the Fullers Goose Call, **$200+.** *Lewis Collection*

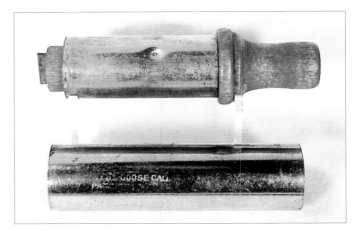

The patent and reed details of the Fullers Goose Call.

variation known as the Later Illinois River Style had been developed and was being used in call making, also in the 1900s. The Later Illinois River Style, however, is more appropriately discussed in the next period of this chronology.

Victor Glodo of Reelfoot Lake originated the Reelfoot or Glodo Style. It is characterized by the use of a curved metal reed held to a straight, one-piece (combination stem and insert) tone board by a wooden wedge block inserted into a barrel. Glodo was the first to decorate duck calls. He used checkering. Herter's calls are more recent examples following in the Glodo tradition.

A lot of eight shorebird and dog whistles are circa 1885-1915 and range from **$100** to **$400** each. *Hank and Judy Norman Collection*

1880s-1920

The Tongue Pincher Style continued to be made into the 1910s by Fisher and Schoenheider. Others who joined in the making of them were the Bridgeport Gun and Implement Co. (B.G.I.) in Connecticut, a company named Red Duck Calls, and the N. C. Hansen Company of Zimmerman, Minn. They all made their calls in the Elam Fisher design. The Hansen Company was still advertising these calls (albeit modified) in the late 1940s. Early Illinois River Style calls continued to be made into this period by Charles H. Ditto of Keithsburg, Ill., (he made other styles also) and James W. Reynolds, Chicago, who became more known for his Double Duck Call patented in 1906. Charles H. Perdew of Henry, Ill., also produced calls in the Early Illinois River Style.

The Later Illinois River Style was developed during this period (c. 1903). This is the era when the hard rubber call and reed were developed. August L. Kuhlemeier of Burlington, Iowa, was the first to patent this, but may not have been the inventor. For some unknown reason, the Later Illinois River Style was characterized by a return to the older rounded radius or curved tone board and straight reed (both of hard rubber, frequently). They also used cork wedge blocks. The call made by Philip Sanford Olt represents this style developed to a high art. His company, P. S. Olt, Pekin, Ill., developed a call dubbed the D-2 that, with some minor changes, has been successfully made and sold since 1904. The company is still in business today. I have included more on the impact of the P. S. Olt in the next section on modern calls.

Reelfoot or Glodo Style duck calls. Victor Glodo died in 1910, but the style he developed was continued by Tom Turpin of Memphis, Tenn.; J. T. Beckhart, Swiftwater, Ark.; John "Sundown" Cochran, Samburg, Tenn., whose son John "Son" Cochran continues to make calls in this classic style and form today; and G. D. Kinney of Hughes, Tenn.

In addition to the classic duck and goose calls of the early years, shorebird and dog whistles make an interesting addition to any decoy collection.

C1920-1935

All of the styles covered so far continued to be produced in various numbers, from few to many, all through this period of time. But there were two more styles that developed almost concurrently. Each is a variation of the preceding style, but with sufficient differences to render them unique. The Arkansas Style is thought to be a modified version of the Illinois River Style. It is quite obvious that the P. S. Olt calls have a strong influence on the construction of the Arkansas Style calls. The calls are constructed of wood for the most part. The one-piece stem has

Weedy's Pin Oak call and details, candy stripe acrylic duck call, **$100.** *Lewis Collection*

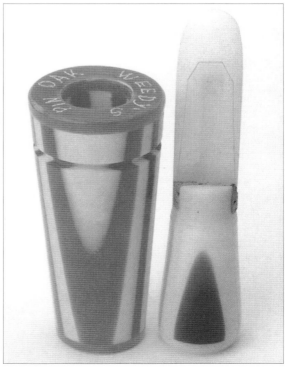

Champion of champions duck call made by Art Beauchamp, Flint, Mich., **$100.** Art is one of many "known" carvers from the 1950s-70s period with a collector following.

a notch cut out at the beginning of the tone board so that the straight reed could be held in, independent of insertion of the stem into the barrel. It is likely that the Arkansas Style evolved around the late 1910s. Presently, it appears that the earliest makers are probably Clyde Hancock and W. T. Lancaster, both of Stuttgart, Ark., followed closely by A. M. Bowles of Little Rock in the mid-1920s and Darce Manning "Chick" Major of Stuttgart in the early 1930s.

Louisiana Style duck calls, or Cajun Style as they are sometimes called, have probably been around as long as the Arkansas Style calls, but for now we cannot substantiate any commercial production before the 1930s.

The earliest names associated with the Louisiana Style calls are Faulk and Airhart. Clarence "Patin" Faulk of Lake Charles is known to have made calls much earlier than the 1935 date generally accepted as when he began making calls to be sold in commercial quantities. Although he produced thousands of calls, it was not until 1950, when his son Dudley Faulk went into business, that we recognized the company as it exists doing business today, Faulk Calls. The other famous name in the Louisiana Style of call making is Allen J. Airhart. He started the Cajun Call Company in Lake Charles in 1944. It is still in business today. Although many are made of wood and other materials today, most classic Louisiana Style calls are made of cane. They are generally of the two-piece design much like the F. A. Allen calls.

The Golden Age 1935-1950

The Early History Era was a terrific growth and development era in call making where everyone was experimenting and perfecting what they thought were the best in effective game calls. But there was not an impetus for large scale manufacturing until 1935. Heretofore using baited field and/or live decoys was common, especially in the Mississippi Flyway. Who needed to produce calls in any quantities when you had the benefit of having a few live English calling ducks, or Suzys as they were affectionately known? Hunters could have the double benefit of live ducks making real live, authentic calls when desired and a few family pets at the same time.

In 1935, two significant things happened that had a profound and lasting effect on the way wildfowl hunters pursued their prey. First, Ducks Unlimited was formed in the interest of proper wildlife management and conservation. Second, the federal government made baiting fields and the use of live decoys illegal. The previous year had seen the birth of the Federal Waterfowl Stamps and the publication of Joel Barber's classic work on decoys. All of these events had an impact on the current hobby of collecting calls and decoys.

A D-2 call made by the P.S. Olt Company with the "world logo." This logo was only placed on calls for a short period of time and is desirable, **$40+.** This is typical of mass-produced calls made during this period.

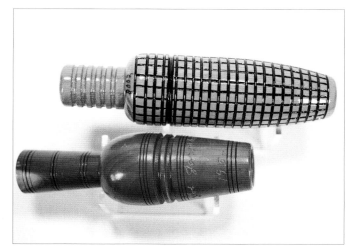

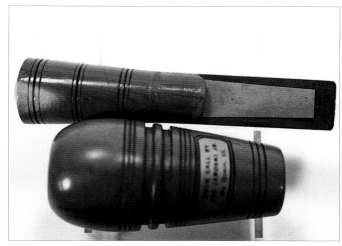

Here is a Joe Jaroski Jr. corn cob duck call from 2000, and a gold label and signed duck call from 1954. Details show the early metal reed on the 1954 call; **$75** for corn cob call; **$150** for the early duck call. *Lewis Collection*

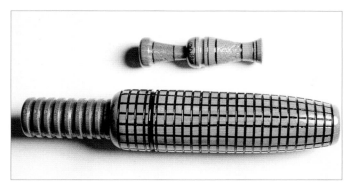

Joe Jaroski Jr.'s corn cob goose call is shown next to Joe's miniature working call. Miniature, **$25**; corn cob goose call, **$100**.

Two fancy Jaroski calls, both duck, are signed and have dates with labels, **$75+** each.

There was suddenly a very good reason for obtaining and learning to use game calls. Thus was born the Golden Age of duck call making. Many of the older call-making operations expanded to accommodate this sudden demand. Call makers began producing thousands of calls and new companies were born, also producing calls in the thousands to meet this demand. Everybody and his brother seemed to be in the call-making business. This included the P.S. Olt Company, turning out several thousand calls a year. Also, decoy makers got into the business. The big sporting goods firms such as Von Lengerke and Antoine (VL&A) of Chicago, Sears Roebuck, H. D. Folsom Arms Company, and the like began commissioning call makers to manufacture calls for sale through their stores and catalogs, some even with their own logos on them. This was also the time when duck-calling competition came into its own.

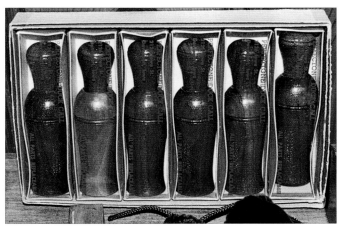

A rare Six Pack of Bishop's Perfectone Calls are all new in package, **$600+** for whole pack.

New Golden Age (1970s-present)

The 1970s saw a renewed interest in all things related to American craftsmen and especially those things that were uniquely American. With this came the now famous explosion of interest in old hand-made hunting decoys and all sorts of other Americana. Good game conservation and management had begun to pay off with rapidly increasing waterfowl populations. Along with these conservation efforts, heavily supported by hunters and other outdoor sportsmen, came a new appreciation for what was almost lost. There was a new appreciation for the sheer pleasure of the hunt. It was a heightened awareness of the experience of the hunt, being outdoors, enjoying it with a friend or introducing a child to the magic. It is a great pleasure and satisfaction to introduce a non-outdoorsman friend or a child to this world of outdoors, knowing that you helped bring it back. You and they will continue to practice good game management to assure it will not be lost. With all of that came the renaissance of the fine duck call. It can only get better.

Ebony duck call with six checkered panels, carved by Joe Jaroski of DuQuoin, Ill., **$300.** Joe started making calls in 1945 and this call shows the beauty and advanced quality of many "current" carvers.

Joyner's Enticer turkey call and the peg box used with it, Joyner's Wood Products, Georgiana, Alabama, **$20+.**

Joyner's Satellite turkey yelper, Joyner's Wood Products, Georgiana, Alabama, **$20+.**

Box call, wood slide on spring rubs against a slate bottom, **$15+.**

Standard Smith box turkey call, **$50+.**

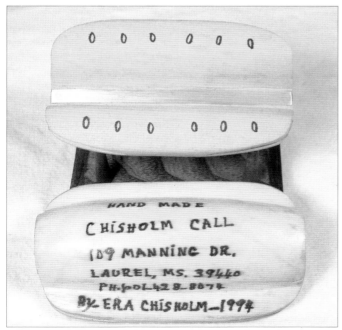

Era Chisholm tortoise shell shape yelper and slate call, Laurel, Mississippi, **$25+** each.

Bone peg and leather holder for rubbing on turkey calls, unknown maker, **$25+.**

Three examples of Smith's Game Calls box calls, made in Summerville, Pennsylvania, left to right: Standard, Model ST-17 Extra Loud and a Sweet Butter Nut, **$50+** each.

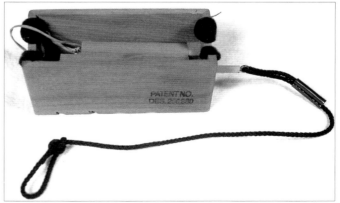

Very simple box call with wooden insert to rub against slate bottom to produce the turkey sound, **$15+.**

ST-17, Extra Loud Smith box turkey call, **$50+.**

Sweet Butter Nut Smith box turkey call, **$50+.**

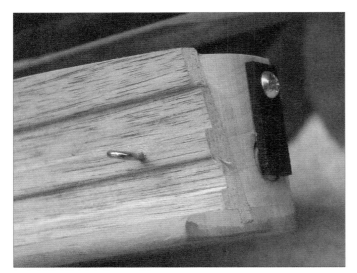 

These two photos show the clever chalk holder placed on the end of all Smith's box calls.

Glass/ceramic box call and original Smith's slate box call on right, **$50+** each.

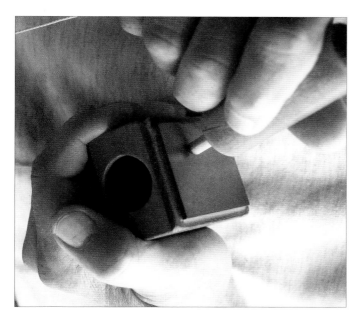

Two photos show the correct positioning for slate call use.

Smith's Easy Squeeze-O-Matic turkey call which can be mounted to the gun on the barrel or fore-end and it makes excellent yelps and purrs, **$50+.**

From left: Three of Mark Weedman's colorful acrylic calls and two of his wooden ones, circa 1970s-80s, **$50-$75** each. *Photo courtesy of Clyde Harbin*

Stevenson's Turkey Talker box call from Wellsboro, Pa., **$50-$75**; and a Kelly Cooper Owl Hooter, **$50+**. *Photo courtesy of Clyde Harbin*

From left: Smith's Crow call; Smith's Two pitch Owl Hooter, Great Horned or Barred; and two of Smith's Predator calls which squeal like a mouse or rabbit, **$50+** each. All of the Smith's call photos were provided by my friend Ron Kommer, user of many Smith's calls over the years.

Smith's Crow call, similar to the calls made by Tom Turpin and nice sounding, **$50+.**

Factory call makers

This section shows examples of many of the collectible calls made by major factory producers in the 1940s-1970s. Some of these factories, such as Olt, are now out of business and that has only increased interest in the calls made by them. Others, such as Mallardtone and Faulk, are still producing calls but many of the calls made in the 1940s-1970s are difficult to locate, especially new in the box with papers. Also, many of the modern calls had small variations which are important nuances to collectors that lasted for only a brief time period of production increasing demand for certain calls. Hopefully, the calls shown in this chapter shall whet your appetite to learn more and help you discover the beauty in even the newer "factory" calls.

This section is meant to complement my emphasis on modern items for the collector. Just as I indicated in Chapter 1 concerning the growth in collecting more recent or modern decoys, the call collector should be aware of modern calls and mass marketed calls while searching for items for his/her collection. Although each of us would love to add any of the calls in the foregoing section of this chapter, it is unlikely for many of us to find or acquire such exceedingly rare calls, at least not more than a few of them.

Mass-produced calls from the 1940s and '50s are still readily available. They can be purchased online, in antiques stores, at flea markets and even in some sporting goods stores if you are diligent in searching. Many of the calls will still be found in their original one- or two-piece cardboard packaging and with package inserts telling how to use the call or little pocket catalogs. These make great additions to a collection and further one's knowledge of a company's products. Even concentrating on just a few of the larger or better known companies can take quite an effort to acquire all calls known to exist. Even some of the calls of more recent 1970s companies, such as Mallardtone, are getting harder and harder to find.

There were likely dozens, if not hundreds, of small mom and pop call companies in the later '40s and early '50s that have yet to be documented. Nearly every small community had a small company operation operating out of a kitchen or a garage. These small companies were cheap to start, but most did not last due to the inability to market the products widely enough. Most of these little companies lived on local sales, direct marketing to sports shops and word of mouth.

A nice selection of three different boxed calls from the early 1950s. All of these are hard to find new in the box, **$50-$100+** each. *Photo courtesy of Clyde Harbin*

Quiet times (c. 1950-1970s)

By about 1950, the wildfowl population had dwindled again. Good efforts were being made at conservation, but it was slow to get started and gain support. It came almost too late. At this point, general interest in hunting waterfowl was on the wane and the number of hunters was declining. There were a good many commercial call-making companies doing business. The decline of waterfowl population and hunter interest, and the ready availability of inexpensive, manufactured duck calls combined to put quite a damper on the business of hand-production of fine duck calls. This depressed situation remained at a status quo until renewed by growing interest in Americana beginning in the 1970s.

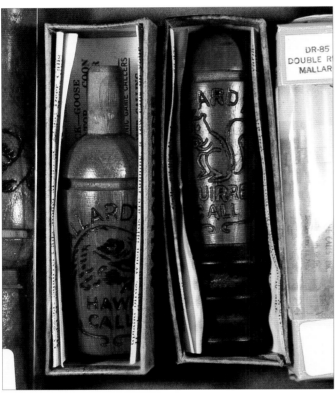

Two Mallardtone calls in boxes, the boxes are hard to come by for these calls, **$50-$75** each. *Photo courtesy of Clyde Harbin*

Two Lohman calls new in boxes from the 1950s, **$50-$75** each. *Photo courtesy of Clyde Harbin*

Not much is known about a Black Duck call that was made in Whiting, Ind., **$35-$50+.**

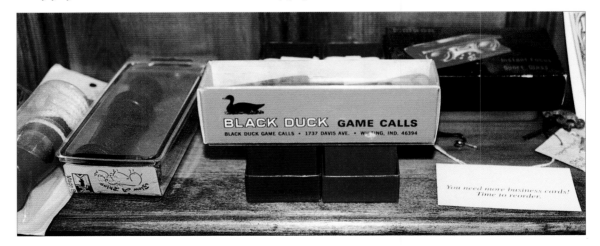

Joe Jaroski Jr. Calls

Joe Jaroski Jr. made his first call in 1945 and another in 1946. He then started making them in greater numbers and selling them in 1947. Jaroski worked as an underground coal miner in southern Illinois and found call-making an excellent creative outlet. He now finds it a way to fill the hours since retirement. Joe has been making calls ever since his first year of production for sale and trade. As with many call makers, he trades a lot of calls and has a fine collection of calls made by many modern makers.

Jaroski has made around 2,000 calls. Price range is from $50 to $400. Among his calls are corn cob calls and some beer bottle calls (see Page 75). Since he retired from mining, his creations keep him busy almost every day. He has a love for call-making and for coming up with different and new ideas. All of Joe's beer bottle calls are working calls, both duck and goose.

Jaroski has won a number of awards, including blue, purple, orange and red ribbons, for call-making from the Callmakers & Collectors Association of America. These include many ribbons for Fancy Call Contest, Checkered Division Fancy Call, Miniature Fancy Call, Matched Sets and more. He also took the Best Exhibit award plaque in 1994 and the Most Outstanding Exhibitor's Booth in 1995 at Reelfoot Lake Callmakers & Collectors Association.

Black Duck calls

All I know is what is in the photo on Page 82. This is a newer post-zip code box with a duck call made in Whiting, Ind. Call-maker Joe Jaroski paid $25 for the call at a meet some time back and the value is likely double that or more today. I did not see any advertisements for the call company in my literature review, but it is indeed an example of modern duck hunting products from the Hoosier state. Of course, Indiana also gave us the famous Hoosier Crow Call.

Burnham Brothers Calls

Burnham Brothers Calls of Marbles, Texas, made a number of calls. They are collectible, not because the plastic calls are unique, but because they came in very nice two-piece cardboard boxes with detailed inserts explaining the use of the calls. Although it did not make as wide a variety as Herter's or Olt, Burnham made any number of predator calls that command up to $60 each if still found in their boxes. I have sold about a half dozen the last few years and always get a good price. I would guess that the calls are worth from $15 without a box up to $100 each for some of the less common models. I am sure we will see these values continue upward as more folks learn about this company.

Duk-Em Duck call, **$75.** *Lewis Collection*

Duk-Em Duck Calls

"The Shooter's Bible" for 1947 lists two of these calls for sale: the Pull-Em Crow Call and the Duk-Em Duck Call. Both calls use the phrase "Tone Tested" in their call names as well. I have shown a Duk-Em wooden duck call but do not have a crow call example.

The advertisement read as follows: "…are of hand made quality, each one individually tested for tone by an expert in the art of calling…sounding mechanism…will not fall apart when removed from the receiver." It goes on to say they are very easy to use with little effort and that they are made of hard wood and hand-rubbed satin finishes to show the grain. One thing interesting about the ad is that the Lohman type calls do fall apart when removing the "sounding mechanism," which is frustrating to the uninitiated in calling. It takes a little skill to place a Lohman reed back in the correct position and my guess is that this advertisement was capitalizing on this fact.

This company also advertised a duck decoy as shown in some of the same advertising. It is a nice call and does indeed make a nice sound. Either of these calls would bring about $75, more with the box as shown.

Dye-Call Company

This company of Seattle, Wash., is listed as a supplier of both game calls and decoys. Harry Dye of Dye-Call produced a nice looking wooden call named Dye's Mallard Call and a 45-minute L. P. record of calls. He also offered a six-hour class on duck calling in various western states. I have not found a catalog of his items.

The Mallard Call is a rounded shoulder call with a straight stem with two groves in the end and a slight shoulder near the stopper entrance. The call barrel itself is widest at the stem end with a lathe groove about one-quarter of the way down. The call has a straight, not flared, mouthpiece. The call is marked on the side as Dye-Call in one line with Mallard underneath it. It appears the wood is two-toned. It is similar in design to a Faulk's, but more rounded on the stem end.

Faulk's

This company began commercial call production in about 1935 in Lake Charles, La. The company made a number of calls in the 1940s, '50s and '60s. Any of these would make nice additions to a call collection, especially the ones still in their original packaging with package inserts. As a general rule, the presence of original packaging tends to at least double the value of an item such as a game or duck call.

One dating technique on Faulk calls is its own use of advertising on the call labels, the boxes and the paper inserts. Faulk Calls won a number of competitions and liked to list the years in which it won on the call labels, boxes and inserts. However, an interesting thing is that the years often did not match, showing that Faulk would use calls on hand, boxes on hand and place updated inserts into the box. One call clearly shows the box as a 1959 model, the call as a 1961 model and a paper insert dated 1963. Thus, the call is really from 1963, likely made in 1961, and placed in a box on hand from 1959. So, when you get a Faulk, look at all the dates to determine the likely date of your item.

Another possible dating technique is the box design and/or color. I have shown three boxes from the '50s and '60s. The earliest one is red, then orange, then yellow. The design on the box stayed the same, but the colors changed. Also, all of the ones shown from this period are the plastic slide top boxes. Earlier boxes would have had plastic lids over cardboard or would have been two-piece cardboard boxes. Later boxes may have a cellophane insert as seen on some later Olt boxes shown in the Olt section. As collector attention is placed more and more on these factory calls, we will learn smaller distinctions in box types to help us date the items.

The more unusual calls to find would be the gift set, the turkey call (just beginning to get popular in the northern states in the early '80s), the expensive professional duck call (wholesale was $12.45, retail was $22.95) and the calls for the more unusual species. Most of the calls listed were in the Faulk line for a number of years, allowing the collector to amass examples from different time periods. A most unusual Faulk item is its Faulk's Big Duck Call, Model FGD (Faulk's Giant Duck). In 1970, Cabela's offered this item for $15.95. It is a giant working call measuring 11-3/4 inches overall, but actually properly tuned to work. It was meant as a gift for the sportsman with everything already, a nice item for the duck blind or bar.

On Faulk's CH-44 goose call, the box is marked through 1959 and the call itself is marked through 1961, as explained in the text, **$40+.**
Lewis Collection

Faulk's WA-33A, adjustable duck call is in mint condition, **$40.**
Lewis Collection

A second Faulk's WA-33A adjustable duck call shows reed details and cork insert, **$30.** *Lewis Collection*

A Faulk's Model PW-70 Pintail whistle/call came in an orange pre-zip code slide top box, **$50+.** *Lewis Collection*

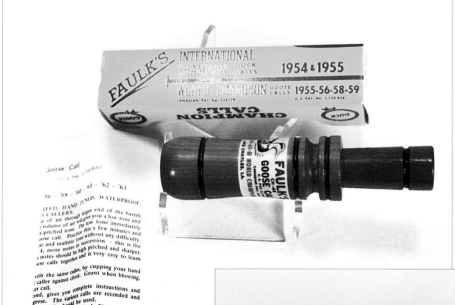

A Faulk's Model CH-44 goose call is in a yellow pre-zip code slide top box. This one shows a 1959 box, a 1961 call, and a 1963 paper insert, **$60.** *Lewis Collection*

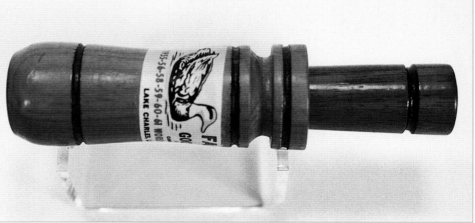

Faulk's Model WA-11 (walnut) duck call from 1959 came in a red pre-zip code slide top box, **$50.** *Lewis Collection*

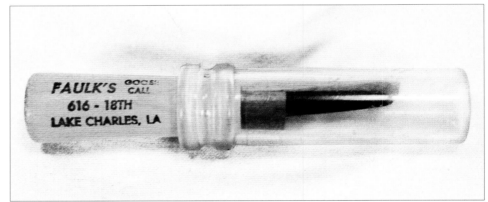

Faulk's Clear Goose Call, circa 1970, is shown in 1970 catalogs, **$25+.** *Lewis Collection*

A Faulk's duck call and an unmarked Faulk's-type adjustable goose call, **$30** each. *Lewis Collection*

Fetch-It

Although not a game call, I thought this was the best place to illustrate a great duck retrieving item and the beautiful advertising graphics that went with it. This nifty little "retrieving lure" attached to the end of your fishing rod. You simply cast out and reeled your dead duck in to you. I am not sure how handy it would be to carry along a rod and reel in a duck blind, but it may have actually been handy for those of us shooting ducks on farm ponds. It is amazing the contraptions that various companies present to us for consumption. I would not want to use this item, but I am glad I have a couple in my collection. The item was new about 1947-48, according to advertising.

A Fetch-it duck-retrieving lure, with a two-piece cardboard box, is made of wood with a metal loop. It was made in Hayden Lake, Idaho, for duck hunters who would rather carry a fishing pole to the pothole than use a dog, **$65** or more. *Lewis Collection*

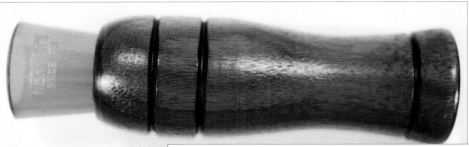

A modern Herter's Indian Glodo duck call and box, **$70.** This is one of the Herter's calls marketed by the company that bought Herter's in 1977. It was likely made prior to 1977, with the marketing material updated when distributed.
Lewis Collection

Herter's Inc.

Herter's, Inc. of Wasceca, Minn., was documented in Chapter 1 on decoys. However, Herter's also made nearly every imaginable call for game, ducks, and geese and needs to be covered in this section as well.

Most of the calls follow the Glodo style and are so called by Herter's. The Herter's specialty catalogs detail the calls nicely, but even the general Herter's catalogs list all calls available from the company: duck, goose, any imaginable flying game bird, crow, deer, elk and predator, to name just a few.

Not all calls were available for the entire 40 or so year span, so you need to study catalogs to precisely date calls, but this is affordable with Herter's catalogs.

Maybe just pick up a catalog for every five-year span to check out the model continuity. Of course, since Cabela's purchased Herter's, we will need to see what future collectibles may be in the offing.

The previous owner of Herter's still marketed the famous Glodo Duck Call in an old Herter's two-piece cardboard box, so make sure you can tell the old ones from the newer ones, the package being the best guarantee.

I have included a shot of the newer one, showing the packaging to look for. The oldest Herter's calls had brass rings and bring hundreds, if not thousands, of dollars each. However, for the most part, the new collector is more apt to find nice old Herter's calls from the '40s or '50s than one of the very early calls.

Hoosier Crow Call

This fairly common and successful crow call was made in Delphi, Ind., and advertised nationally in sporting magazines. It sold well. It is an attractive, well-made call that brings $45 loose, and $60 or more in its cardboard box. One early advertisement indicated that the company also made some decoys, but I do not have any examples of them (see photo on Page 81).

A KumDuck Duck Call made in Beaverton, Ore., circa 1955, **$50+** due to rarity. *Lewis Collection*

KumDuck Calls

This green plastic duck call with a plastic reed is manufactured similar to an Olt in style. It is marked with a patent number of 2,711,614 and location.

According to the patent data, the call was made in circa 1955. The patent was applied for on May 5, 1952, and granted on June 28, 1955, to Gordon E. Hallsten of Beaverton, Ore. According to the patent application, the main purpose was to construct a call that took little effort to blow and used a straight reed construction. The call is all plastic, the material of the hour in 1952 when the patent was requested. This is another good example of our modern era calls.

The company is again in business and the calls made are beautiful and work well. Learn more by going to www.kum-duck.com. The call is now black and is packaged in a great and handy carrying case. Thanks to the new owners for sending me an example.

Lohman Calls

Lohman Calls was located in Kansas City and Neosho, Missouri, and marketed its calls directly through wholesalers to sporting goods dealers. The calls also were carried in many major publications such as Stoeger's. The photos show some Lohman calls in boxes and some without. If the calls themselves are not marked, usually the reed holder inserts were marked. See the two crow calls on Page 90 for two different examples showing two different dates, with the Kansas City 27 being the earlier of the two.

Values on Lohman calls depend on rarity and condition, boxed or loose. I would rate the boxed calls at $25 minimum, up to $100 for some of the rarer calls in boxes. The loose calls would bring about 50 percent of that value for the most part.

A Lohman Model 103 duck call includes the box and pocket catalog, the box is pre-zip code, **$50+.** *Lewis Collection*

A Lohman Model 112 goose call from Neosho, Mo., includes the call, box and instructions, **$35** due to rough shape of call. *Lewis Collection*

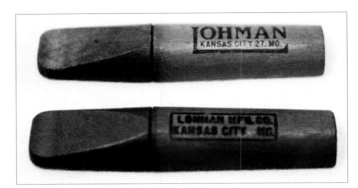

Shown are two Lohman crow calls and a Lohman duck call, with the oldest crow call on top, **$25-$40** each. There are also markings on stem inserts. *Lewis Collection*

A Lohman duck call from Neosho, Mo., has a mark on the stem insert, **$40.** *Lewis Collection*

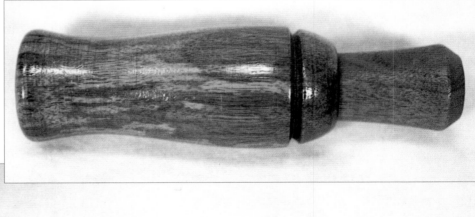

Mallardtone Game Calls

Mallardtone Game Calls are some of the most recent calls in this section. Most of them appear to date from the 1960s or even '70s. I did not start finding advertising for the calls in wholesale catalogs until that time period. One magazine advertisement from 1962 indicates that the company won the National Crow Calling Contest in 1962, both first and second places. You can infer the company had been around a few years as it indicates winning "…numerous other championships with duck and goose calls." The address given in 1962 was 2100 Stadium Drive, Dept. 962, Rock Island, Ill. The calls were also distributed in Canada by Canadian Sauer Ltd. of Toronto.

In 1962, the company offered crow calls, predator calls, squirrel calls, duck calls, goose calls, deer calls and pheasant calls. In addition, Deluxe model duck and goose calls were available for $10. The other calls were all $2.95 each. An instruction record was also available for $2. All calls came with an unconditional guarantee.

However, like other modern calls, you do not often find these calls in pristine condition in their packages. I have most of the Mallardtone calls and do not have a package. Possibly they were marketed in bulk through wholesalers in addition to being individually packaged. I know this was the case with some of our less expensive fishing lure lines.

I like the calls and find them well made with excellent finishes. Also, the engraving gives them a nice distinction from other mass-marketed calls. The advertising for them in Buckeye Sports Supply said: "Made of finest materials available. The barrel (or body) of each call is American Black Walnut, assuring beauty and lasting durability. All calls are hand tested by an expert."

A mint Mallardtone deer call, **$50.**
Lewis Collection

Mallardtone duck, goose and fox calls are shown, along with a Wisconsin miniature Mallard pair. Calls are **$50** each; ducks, **$300**.
Lewis Collection

A Ken Martin goose call, **$200.** Note the beautiful burl on the one side of the call. *Lewis Collection*

Here is the Natural Duck call in open and closed positions; **$700** if mint, **$300** or so in this condition. *Lewis Collection*

Ken Martin Calls

Although not as prodigious as some of the larger companies, Ken Martin marketed beautiful duck and goose calls through a number of outlets. The 1970 Cabela's catalog offered his Model KMG (Ken Martin Goose) call for $10 and his Model KMD (Ken Martin Duck) call for $5.

Both of these calls were clearly marked on the barrel so the collector will have no trouble identifying them. This is an example of a vintage call maker responding to mass-marketing pressures to sell his calls.

The Martin calls are very collectible and would command at least $100 each, likely more. Martin is deceased and his calls will continue to appreciate in value.

Natural Duck Call Manufacturing Company

A unique and desirable call from the 1930s was manufactured in St. Paul, Minn. The call has a nice sound and details are shown, with the call in the closed and open bill positions. The call was patented in 1932 by Francis J. Muchlistein. There are early calls that are simply marked "Patent Applied," so be aware of this variation.

Perfectone calls

Charlie Bishop lived from 1912-2001. He made calls during many of his 89 years, and produced a highly collectible call of fine quality, including a unique store advertising piece, a large Perfectone call, to hang in the sporting goods store as an advertising gimmick.

These large calls were often carved by call makers who marketed their wares locally or regionally. I have also shown a rare Perfectone Duck Call six pack in the Jaroski call section earlier. These would sell for $100 each new in the packages due to pristine condition. The six pack would bring a premium over this amount due to rarity (see Page 75).

P. S. Olt

Like Herter's, Inc., P. S. Olt was also mentioned in the section on vintage calls. That shows the age of the company located in Pekin, Ill., which only recently ceased production, circa 2005. The biggest challenge to an Olt collector is dating with accuracy any of the hard rubber calls. There are some clues in addresses, model numbers on calls, logos on calls, shape of stoppers, etc. However, even many fairly recent Olt calls command more than $50 if still found in the original packaging. An individual could, and many do, concentrate on just Olt calls and never get bored looking for a new one.

Olt, like Herter's, made every conceivable call. Some of the calls are harder to find than others. They also made "Junior Models," not for kids, just smaller-sized calls that are more difficult to find. The Olt calls were plentiful because they were excellent calls and still are. In addition to hunting ducks, I have been an avid squirrel hunter from when my now departed dog Bandit treed his first squirrel in 1983 until his death in 1996.

Bandit "loved to hate" those pesky little devils that used to bug him in our back yard. One day, I discovered the Olt Perfect Squirrel call shown in black and brown. I picked up the black one at a farm auction for a song but it turned out to be quite an old model sold from a now defunct Detroit sporting goods store. I used the black one for nearly 20 years with success each time I went to the woods. The calls are shown with the stopper purposely stuck in on the black one to show the operation of the automatic caller. Just push in on the one end and the call sound is made automatically. It provides a little chatter that nosey squirrels just cannot resist due to their territoriality.

Most Olt calls are affordable but there are some rarer ones out there commanding more than $100. However, most of the calls will bring between $25 to $75 loose, maybe double that with clean, crisp boxes and any inserts that came with the call.

The values given are obviously a general "range." You must remember there are some short production run calls that will

An ad for Philip S. Olt in the *Sporting Goods Dealer* catalog announces, "Nine great calls for 1950," including another "black hard rubber" call.

command premium prices. There are also color variations, logo variations, presence of lanyard ring variations and many other items to learn about with Olt calls, all of which affect valuation. I am certain that there are some Olt calls that will start commanding some premium prices once we have documented their rarity and once the demand increases even more with additional collectors entering the hobby. A person could concentrate on just Olt calls and keep very busy indeed building an exemplary collection from early call-making through the modern era. Now that Olt is out of business it will be interesting to see how values change in the near future.

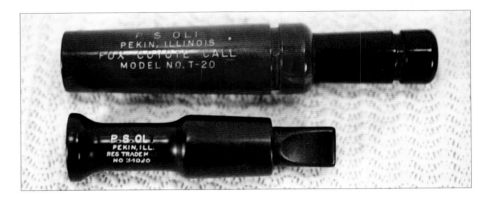

An Olt brown barrel Model T-20 fox/coyote call is shown with a difficult-to-find Junior Duck Call by Olt; T-20, **$40**; Junior, **$100+**.
Lewis Collection

An Olt Perfect Deer Call, Model No. R-25, **$50.**
Lewis Collection

The Olt M-9 Crow Call is new in package, **$50** in package. This packaging was being advertised as early as 1970. *Lewis Collection*

An Olt Model Perfect No. A-5 Goose Call, **$50-$75.** *Lewis Collection*

An Olt Perfect Squirrel Call with a brown barrel, **$100.** *Lewis Collection*

An Olt Chukar Call of wood/rubber has worn lettering, **$40.** *Lewis Collection*

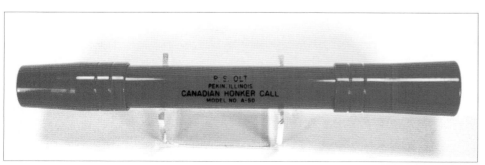

An Olt Canada Honker Call, Tri-County special issue is numbered 142, **$75.** *Lewis Collection*

Scotch game calls

These are a neat invention for those of us not wanting to learn to call with our own wind. They are calls constructed in the fashion of a regular wooden call, shaped similar to many Lohman calls, with a rubber bellows then placed over the mouth piece of the call for air inlet. When the bellows move and emit air, the call sound is produced. Yes, they really do work. One issue is that they call anytime one moves the bellows, including while walking or moving around if not careful. This could be an unwanted noise emitted at just the wrong time in the blind.

However, it is a neat idea that was apparently new in commercial production about 1955. An advertisement for the duck call (Patent Pending) appeared in the October 1955 *Outdoor Life*. The call was available for $7.50 and only duck, goose, and crow calls were available at the time. The Detroit address was 173 Victor Avenue, Dept. L10, Detroit 3, Mich. The L10 likely stood for the advertising source (e.g. Outdoor Life, October with the code L for *Outdoor Life* and 10 for October) to track sales similar to how Pratt Decoys used different names in advertising.

I have shown a Scotch Predator Call No. 1503 new in its box, a Duck Call No. 1401, and Goose Call No. 1605. It also made a Crow Call No. 1707 and a Squirrel Call No. 1911. A wholesale catalog also listed a Deer Call No. 1809 advertised in 1968 that must have been short lived indeed. The interesting thing that I noted on the predator call shown is that the call itself is imprinted with a Detroit address and so was the box originally. However, on the box, Detroit was lined through and the New York address added without a zip code. The booklet inside the box had the New York address with the zip code. The duck and goose calls shown have the New York imprint on them. The calls were invented in Detroit and produced there briefly. Thus, the Detroit calls are harder ones to find. I have owned all but the squirrel call and do not see it listed in as many wholesale catalogs.

If you remove the bellows, the calls function just fine if you know how to blow them. The value on these is between $25 and $60, depending on age, box type, and condition. The 1970 Cabela's catalog offered all five models at $4.75 each. The 1982 Buckeye Sports Supply wholesale catalog still offered the duck, goose, predator and crow calls for $7.55 to $8.95 each wholesale. They also offered a double or single Scotch Lanyard at that time. Retail on these calls was an average of about $12.50 in 1982, so expect to pay double for even one of the early 1980s models. As noted already, the squirrel call did not appear in the 1982 wholesale catalog so it is likely more difficult to find.

"Scotch" duck and goose calls and some details of them. These are both marked Oakfield, N.Y. The goose call is No. 1605 and the Duck is No. 1401, **$40** each. *Lewis Collection*

A "Scotch" predator call, Model 1503, was made in Detroit, but Detroit is marked out on the address on the box and corrected to 60 Main Street, Oakfield, N.Y., in the lower left corner of the box. The paper insert also includes the zip code of 14125 but it is not on the box, demonstrating the call must be from the era when zip codes were first being used. The Detroit calls would be earliest and most difficult to locate, **$50+.** *Lewis Collection*

Thompson Calls

Like Ken Martin, Tom Thompson made vintage calls and then marketed his calls nationally at a later time. He made calls using both wood and plastics, and his plastic goose call is excellent. Most of his earlier calls from Illinois bring from $50 to $150 at this time. He was first located in Illinois and later moved to the high country of Idaho.

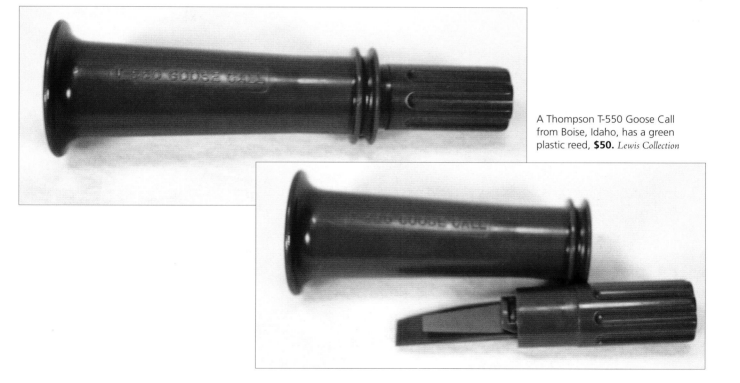

A Thompson T-550 Goose Call from Boise, Idaho, has a green plastic reed, **$50.** *Lewis Collection*

Trutone Calls

Some of the most beautiful modern calls were made by this Oak Park, Ill., call-making company headed by call maker L. G. Larson (1888-1947). Many of these beautiful calls were made with curly maple, special burl walnut, or a combination. The calls were normally marked on the top of the sound barrel in lettering in an arc stating on the top line: "TRUTONE" with "Oak Park, Ill." underneath it.

A beautiful TruTone call, circa 1930s, **$700.** *Lewis Collection*

Unknown calls and newer calls

I am unsure about a couple of calls shown. They are all without markings and/or I could not verify them in advertising literature or other texts.

This wooden goose call with plastic end is similar to many modern calls.

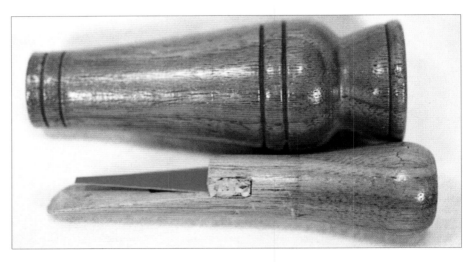

A wooden duck call has five grooves in barrel, a cork holding red plastic reed, and rounded Louisiana/Arkansas stem style. It could be a Faulk's, **$75.** *Lewis Collection*

New Ron Benson Game Calls include a deer bleater, Muskegon, Mich., circa 1998, a gift from a good friend.

Weems Wild Call

The Weems All-Call Lot 100 shown is a neat little package from the Weems Wild Call company of P.O. Box 7261, Fort Worth, Texas. This is a pre-zip two-piece cardboard box and is likely from the mid to early 1950s. It is also a Pat. Pending box, making it more valuable. This was basically four calls in one with a squeaker that could be used for squirrel or chukar, a coon call insert, a cottontail insert and a jack rabbit insert. A person could predator-hunt a variety of animals with the squeaker as well. The unusual thing about this call is that it is complete and virtually new in the box. I am sure most of these found in the field are missing most of the inserts.

A Weems All-Call Lot 100, new in box, **$125.** *Lewis Collection*

Chapter 3

Fishing Lures

I have been interested in the beauty and art form of old wooden fishing lures since I was a young child when I began admiring the display of a few hundred lures on my neighbor's pegboard in his garage. My neighbor Nick was a retired industrialist with considerable wealth and his lures were for fishing, not collecting. He and I used them often, casting primarily for large mouth bass and sometimes for northern pike on either his lake, Big Clear, or our family lake connected by a channel called Little Clear. Both lakes were deep spring-fed glacial pothole lakes with considerable depth and a wealth of game fish.

As a youngster, Nick gave me three Creek Chub Plunkers and that set the stage for a lifetime of love of both lures and fishing. I was fairly poor, especially by Nick's standards, and could not afford the Abu Ambassadeur 5000 that I wanted nor the Heddon line of lures available in the early 1950s. But today I have managed to collect a few thousand lures, rods and reels to make up for lost time as a child. I shall discuss lures in this chapter and save rods and reels for the next.

With all of my writing of lures, eleven books on lures to date, you would think I may be out of words to say about them. No such luck. As a baby boomer, I am interested not only in the very old "vintage" wooden lures with glass eyes and paint jobs making them true art forms, but also the wonderful plastic lures introduced in the early 1950s replacing the wooden lures of days gone by. Plastic lures were of course experimented with as early as the 1920s and became quite common in the late 1930s and truly took hold after the invention of Tenite II during World War II. But it has become common knowledge that now an

entire generation of lure collectors in their 40s and 50s are changing the way lures are collected with as much or more emphasis being placed on lures of our youth than of our grandfather's.

Recent sales at upscale auctions such as Lang's Antique Tackle Auction held on November 3 and 4, 2006, only further document this trend. I consigned some of my "high-end" vintage Heddon lures to the auction, along with some reels discussed in Chapter 4, only to find prices were about 30 percent lower than five years ago, sometimes even lower. Reel prices were as strong as ever, but lure prices for "vintage" lures were simply not as strong primarily because collectors are showing more interest for some of the 1940s-1960s lures in today's market. Also at the same auction, I paid $560 for a Heddon prototype Preyfish due to the interest in this rare 1980s Heddon lure. Production models of the Preyfish often command $100 or more if mint.

This is surely not to say that interest in "vintage" lures is dead; far from it. It is simply that the market has now created an equally strong interest in "modern lures" from the 1940s-1960s and those prices are stronger than five years ago by far more than 30 percent. It is not uncommon for me to sell a "modern" collectible lure for $100 and that was unheard of in 1995.

As with duck decoys and other sporting collectibles, you should not collect fishing lures for the mere investment potential of said lures. Of course, in general, lures have gone up over the past 10 years with certain peaks (2000) and valleys (2004) but the true value of a fishing lure is its intrinsic beauty and design. Also, some of the lures with a few pike teeth marks in them could tell some great tales if only they could speak and that, too,

The Creek Chub Plunkers that led to a lifetime of love for lures and fishing, **$20+**, but priceless to the author!

can add value for some collectors. But for the most part, as with duck decoy collectors, lure collectors want their lures to be in the best condition possible and paint loss, marks, missing parts, rusty hooks and other blemishes lowers the value rapidly of even a rare lure.

My wife, Wendy, and I have always called fishing lures "little pieces of art" and for that reason they are a joy to collect. Add to that all of the nostalgic memories of a calm night on a small lake casting for bass with a Jitterbug or Crazy Crawler and it is no wonder folks such as myself enjoy the collecting of Jitterbugs and Crazy Crawlers with the same passion that older collectors hunt for early Heddon 210s.

The lures shown in this chapter are just enough to whet your appetite. No single lure book, not even Carl Luckey's 7th edition of *Old Fishing Lures & Tackle*, Krause Publications, to which I contributed about 25 percent of the photos and text, can feature all lures. I have included a mix of "vintage" old wooden lures and what I refer to as "classic" plastic lures and newer wooden lures to give the general collector and dealer a sense of values. For more detailed information, refer to any one of the following works I have written on fishing lures: *Classic Fishing Lures* and *Fishing Collectibles: Rods, Reels and Creels*, both published by F+W Publications and available from either Krause Publications or myself. In addition, I have written an entire series of five volumes (nearly 2,000 pages) on *Modern Fishing Lure Collectibles: Volumes 1-5*, published by Collector Books from 2002-2007; all books are available from either me or the publisher. I have also written two specialty books on *Heddon Catalogs* and *Heddon Plastic Lures*, also published by Krause Publications. Finally, my *Field Guide to Fishing Lures*, 2005, is a handy little guide to both vintage and classic lures and is available from me.

Information is the basis of knowledgeable collecting and this photo shows most of my own works related to this book. Also shown are some Montague reels, a Michigan 1929 small game license button, some Marlin matches, my trademark lure, a Fin-Dingo and some other fishing items. Values are given in this chapter for the fishing items. It always shocks me when people do not want to spend a little money on books, for they can save you hundreds, if not thousands, in mistakes made in buying and selling collectibles.

A general shot of a few items in my own lure collection. Many of these items are detailed in this chapter and later ones. Value for most would be **$12-$30** with some of the better reels and lures reaching **$150** each.

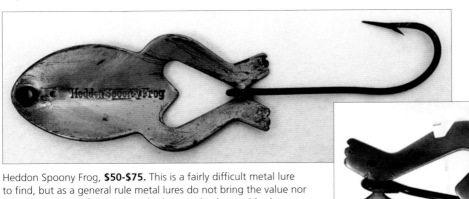

Heddon Spoony Frog, **$50-$75.** This is a fairly difficult metal lure to find, but as a general rule metal lures do not bring the value nor have the collector following as do the wooden lures with glass eyes and other early wooden lures. Some metal lures are very valuable, e.g. early Chapman minnows, the Haskell minnow at **$125,000+**, etc., but most are worth only a few dollars.

Even these 1970s-'80s lures from Rebel (Pradco) are collectible. The Rebel natural series of lures is in demand and many examples have been sold for more than $40 each by the author in recent years, **$15-$40+.**

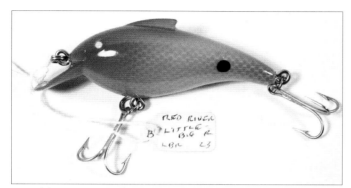

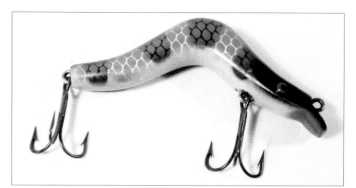

One of the most successful of all modern lures is Cordell's Big-O. It has been copied by dozens of companies and here is an early 1980s example by Red River of its Little Big R lure similar to a Big-O but with a fin added, **$10-$15**; more if boxed.

An interesting lure from the 1950s is this Pulverizer lure, **$10+.**

Plastic lures are also very collectible and some need not even be very old to demand interest. This one is a "classic" plastic lure that is indeed fairly rare, a Paw Paw Platypus lure from the late 1940s-early 1950s, **$100+.**

One of the most successful lures of all time is the CCBC Pikie and it, too, has been copied and the Radtke Pikies are very collectible and in demand often bringing well over **$50** each. These were made in Markesan, WI, in the 1960s, **$40-$75** each.

Recent fishing items sold at Lang's by the author, November 3-4, 2006

The following items include rods, reels, lures and miscellaneous items consigned to Lang's Antique Tackle Auction in Boxborough, MA, November 2006, and sold on the floor of the auction and on eBay Live. The prices represent the actual sale price plus the 20 percent buyer's premium. In addition, buyers had to pay shipping which made the item cost even a bit more. In my opinion, prices were a bit down for some of the better items. I believe one reason is that it was a huge sale with multiple examples of fairly rare items, such as some of the Meek reels I sold. Also, the pricing on the lures in general seemed to be a bit soft, with beautiful Heddon and Pflueger three- and five-hook models bringing about half of what they normally have brought during the past five years. But the prices sold are shown and that is all someone was willing to pay on that particular day for that particular item. But please keep in mind the variations in sale results depend on the time, market, availability, rarity and the number of items released for sale at any given time.

I also sold a large number of lots in the "Discovery Auction" Nov. 2, prior to the sale of the catalogued items at Lang's. The 55 lots sold in the Discovery Auction fetched an average of $85 per lot and consisted of lots of five to 10 lures, tackle boxes, bobbers and floats, creels, Fenwick glass rods, split shot and a rough Horton-Meeks #4 reel on an old steel rod that brought $125.

All in all, the sale at Lang's was a success for me and overall was a huge success setting records again for the gross amount of antique tackle sold. Some items brought a disappointingly low price and I will always especially miss those items, but a wonderful 1800s cast iron trolling reel brought an excellent price and shows how just one item in a sale can at least partially make up for a few others. One thing for certain is that Lang's is a professional auction and John and Debbie Ganung treat sellers well in their dealings with them. I recommend the experience to anyone parting with items that are in excellent condition and a bit on the rare side. I also wish to thank John and Debbie for providing the images for the Lang's sale items shown here.

These items could be shown in each separate chapter on fishing items, but this is an ideal overview of the fishing collectibles desired by most collectors. It is also an ideal place to show an overview of this chapter, as well as the next few chapters of the book.

Condition key: EX is excellent; VG is very good.

From the top: Shakespeare 3-hook minnow in Kingfisher trademarked box #100, **$240.** Heddon 209B L-rigged surface bait in frog, circa 1920s, EX-, **$150.** Pflueger bulldog logo unfinished EX-, 3-hook minnow in Canoe box, **$240.**

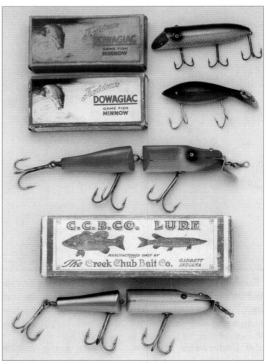

Heddon "Head-On" Basser in box and #5009D green scale Tadpolly, **$174.** Creek Chub Bait Co. Rainbow Fire Pikie and blue-back Rainbow Pikie, both EX, **$210.**

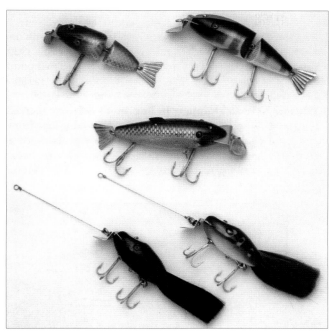

From the top: CCBC Wigglefish, EX+, and Baby Wigglefish, EX-, **$180.** Fluted tail CCBC Fintail Shiner in VG+ condition, silver shiner color, **$150**. EX solid black and EX+ frog spot CCBC Dingers, **$210.**

From the top: Two Creek Chub Beetles, both stamped in gold on belly, EX, **$270.** Scarce pike-colored Husky Dingbat by CCBC w/tiny pointers, EX-, **$150.** Two Pflueger Neverfail hardware five hook minnows, EX and VG, **$240.**

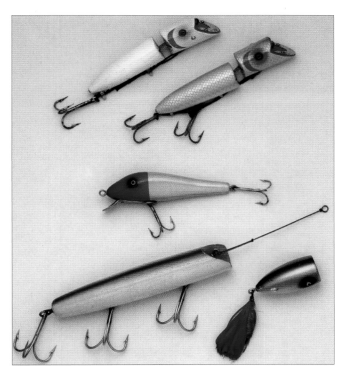

From the top: Heddon King Zig Wag lures, 5", white is EX-, yellow scale is EX, **$186.** Paw Paw Sucker Minnow, tack eyes, EX- condition, **$117.** South Bend Troll Oreno early no eye and Plunk Oreno, 6-1/4", both VG+, **$162.**

From the top: Two Heddon Depression-era lures, Stanley Flipper and Crab Wiggler, **$180.** Heddon L-Rig fat bodied 150, VG+, in VG 151 upward bass box, **$180.** Heddon L-Rig thin body 100 and 150 in frog scale, both VG, **$420.**

From the top: Heddon 100 Rainbow (VG+) and intro box/tag with #1800 Crab (VG), **$252.** South Bend #903 and Panatella Minnow, both VG+, marked props, GE, **$162.**

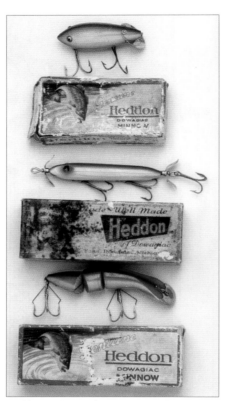

Heddon Crab Wiggler, Torpedo and Game Fisher, Rainbow, VG+ to EX, **$180.**

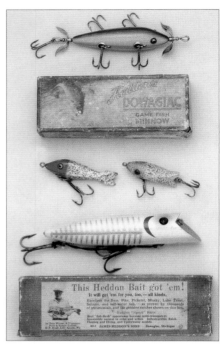

From the top: Heddon 150 rainbow in unmarked downward bass box, EX-, **$150.** R/W GE Heddon Little Joe, VG+, and GE Heddon Wee Willie, VG/VG+, **$162.** Heddon GE #8569PLXB King Basser, EX- in correct Brush box, **$180.**

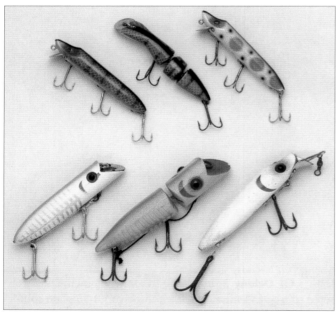

Heddon 1920s lures: 7500 pike (EX), spotted (VG+) & 5500 (EX-), **$126.** Heddon Salmon lures, all glass eyed, VG to EX- condition, **$210.**

From the top: Heddon Batwing decoy in rainbow finish, rough condition, **$300.** Pre-1900s Pflueger Muskellunge Minnow, 7", some chipping, **$270.** Heddon Four Point fish decoy Model 409L, paint wear/chipping, **$120.**

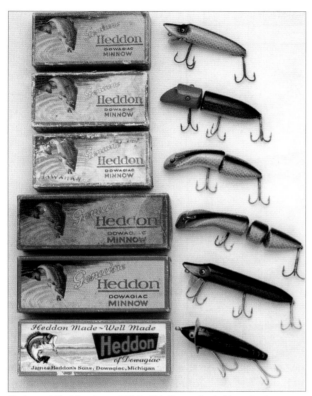

Six boxed Heddon lures, VG to EX, Green Scale Vampire is beautiful, **$360.**

Heddon Spin Fin SS six pack and Heddon Deep-6 345 dozen, **$270.**

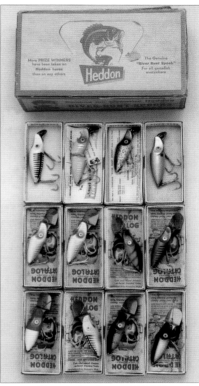

Rare Heddon dealer dozen of 1947 Spooks, **$330** (previous sales: **$1,000**).

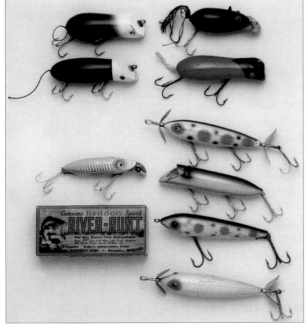

From the top: Four Mouse lures: two Shakespeare, one Paw Paw and one unknown, **$104.** Five Heddon lures: two Flippers, and one Basser, Zaragossa and River Runt, **$420.**

From the top: Rare Heddon unfished black/yellow Bubbling Bug flyrod lure, **$180.** Rare Colorado Moth flyrod lure, EX, **$270.** Heddon wood Runtie flyrod lure, Shiner Scale, EX, **$240.** Heddon wood Runtie flyrod lure, Pike Scale, EX, **$270.**

From the top: Eight Heddon flyrod lure grouping, VG to EX, **$174.** Fifteen Heddon Spook flyrod assortment, VG to EX, **$270.**

From the top: Three Heddon Yellow Flaptail flyrod lures, VG+ to EX, **$91.** Heddon Wee Tad flyrod lure x 2 both EX or better, **$120.** Heddon Widget flyrod lure grouping, VG+ to EX, **$180.**

From the top: Five Heddon Pop-Eye Frog flyrod lures, VG+ to EX, **$120.** Four Heddon Runtie Spook flyrod lures, EX- to EX, **$162.** Six Heddon Wilder Dilg flyrod lures, VG to EX, **$120.**

Nine Heddon flyrod lure boxes, five EX or better, **$180.**

From the top: Three Shakespeare mouse flyrod lures, VG to EX, **$78.** Heddon Punkie Spook and Wee Tad lures, both EX, **$150.** Six Heddon Bass Bug Spooks, all EX, **$132.**

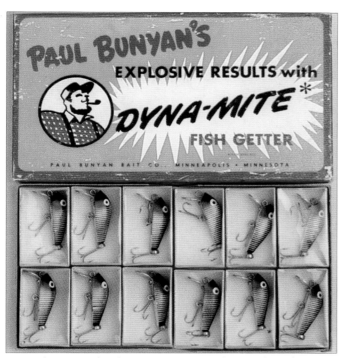

Dealer Dozen of Paul Bunyan Dyna-Mite Fish Getter lures, **$180.**

From the top: South Bend R/W GE Panatella Minnow, EX-, in correct VG box, **$150.** South Bend cup rigged GE underwater minnow, EX, **$180.** Pair of SB Minnows: early VG+ Surf Oreno and EX- five-hook, **$210.**

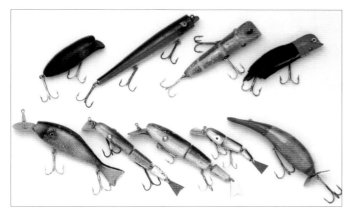

From the top: Carter's Bestever, unknown, 4" unknown wobbler (SB?) and Hula Hula, **$91.** Five Bud Stewart lures, Surface Chub, Hammer Handles, Wiggler, **$65.**

Three Carl Christiansen fly rod lures, new in boxes, **$104.** See Page 215 for more of Christiansen's work.

From the top: Pflueger Rainbow Minnow in EX- and Slate Minnow in VG, **$162.** Shakespeare Evolution Minnow, later vintage missing tail hook, 3", **$78.** Shakespeare PE Egyptian Wobbler EX-, and a GE Bass-A-Lure, EX, **$117.**

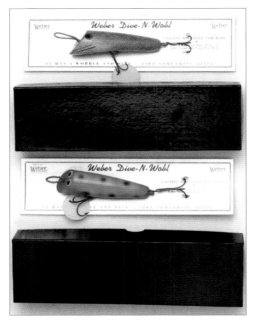

From the top: Weber Dive-N-Wobl Mouse new in box (MINT), rare lure, **$150.** This Dive-N-Wobl is new on card but has small rub, frog finish, **$104**.

From the top: Keeling, Winchester and Ed. Vom Hofe 7" "Sam's" spoons, **$117.** Wilson/Hastings Fluted Wobbler, EX-, and Moonlight Little Wonder, VG+, **$180**. Seven very early Delany spinners and blades, "W Delany Coburg," **$300**.

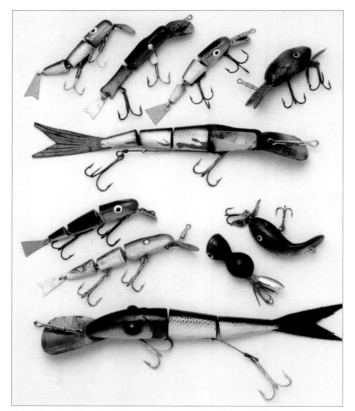

From the top: Five Bud Stewart: Hammer Handles and Convertible Crippled Wiggler, **$104.** Five Bud Stewart: Hammer Handles, Wiggler and Pad Hopper, **$104**.

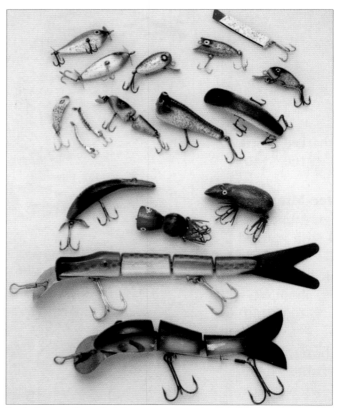

From the top: Silver Flash lure assortment, **$52.** Five Bud Stewart lures: Crippled Wiggler, Pad Hopper, Mouse, Pike, **$210**.

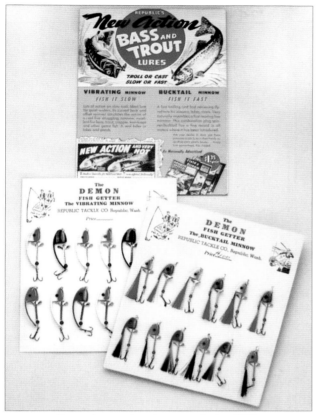

Demon lure cards and counter display, **$250.**

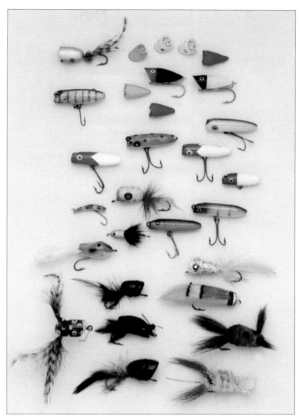

Assorted flyrod lures (22), VG to EX, **$144.**

Three Bethel fish decoys, Minnesota, **$65.**

From left: Duane Sosseur Native American Wisconsin fish decoy, **$91.**
Mark Brunning fish decoy, Michigan, **$150.**

Four Carl Christiansen fish decoys, Michigan; top two: **$300**; bottom two: **$360**. See Page 215 for more of Christiansen's work.

Rare Abercrombie & Fitch Passport Rod in leather case and an A&E fly box. This is my favorite of all fiberglass rods from the 1950s-60s. The A&E Passport Rod breaks down into many small sections for travel (e.g. Passport). I have only seen two of them (this one and my own recently sold at Lang's,) in the past 10 years so I know they are scarce; **$750** for mine sold at Lang's; **$500+** for any found in decent condition.

Top: Ambassadeur 3-screw #5000 and rare unmarked left-hand model, **$420.** Bottom, from left: Ambassadeur reels, red #6000, black #6000C and silver #2500C, **$210.**

Goodwin Granger 8-1/2' Champion Trophy bamboo rod, **$270.**

Early Hardy, circa 1920s, bamboo fly rod, **$91.**

Heddon Expert Bamboo Rod in sock and tube. This is a Model No. 125, 8-1/2' 3/2 rod in F-HCH-D weight made by Heddon in original sock/tube, condition is excellent; **$240** sold at Lang's, but one sold for **$400** online in 2005.

Orvis 7-1/2' Battenkill bamboo fly rod, **$270.**

Three Julius Vom Hofe casting reels, one with V. L. & A. markings, **$117.**

Top: J. A. Coxe casting reels, Models 25-N, 25 and 60-C in box, **$117.** Bottom left: J. A. Coxe Model 25-2 and 25-3, both with cork arbors, **$104.** Bottom right: James Heddon's Sons Model 3-35 German Silver reel, **$180.**

Top, from left: "Cozzone" German Silver/Hard Rubber salt water reel, **$150**; Edward Vom Hofe 6/0 Size, Model 621 GS/HR salt water reel, **$450.** Bottom, from left: Neptune German Silver reel in two-piece box, Model #53, **$210**; Heddon Chief Do-Wa-Giac #4 and B. F. Meek #33, **$132**; Heddon Pal P-41 about mint in correct clean box, **$144**.

Top, from left: Four Brothers "Delite" hard rubber fly reel, 100-yard, **$270**; Four Brothers "Delite" hard rubber fly reel, 60-yard, **$270**; Carlton "Gem" side mount 2-1/4" fly reel, **$98**; unmarked, likely Pflueger, HR/GS 80-yard fly reel, **$270.** Bottom left: tiny 1-1/2" unmarked brass reel and a Meisselbach #150 reel, **$180**; bottom right: two early brass fly reels, John Kopf patent 100-yard and a 40-yard, **$240**.

Bullard & Gormley "Green Lake" and "Brook" casting reels, **$264.**

Top: Heddon Model 57 new in box and Yawman & Erbe key wind, **$180.** Bottom: Orvis "Battenkill" and Sealey (England) "Flyman" in box, **$85.**

Top, from left: Ogden Smith (England), early Pflueger, Allcock & unmarked reels, **$300.** Bottom, from left: Meisselbach #260 "Featherlight" and an "Expert" model #19, **$78.** Meisselbach "Featherlight," Winchester #1235 60-yard & Carlton "Ideal," **$150.**

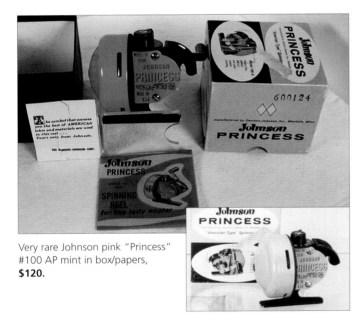

Very rare Johnson pink "Princess" #100 AP mint in box/papers, **$120.**

Pflueger "Supreme" #1573 w/case and Heddon "Heritage" in case, **$120.**

C. Farlow & Co., London, marked "Holdfast" Salmon reel/case, **$390.**

Gladding Cormorant Cuttyhunk full line spool in two-piece box, **$52.**

Pair of Hardy (England) reels: "Viscount" 140 in box and Marquis, **$120.** Another view of the pair is at right.

Heddon "Winona" #105 and a MARC Indiana style reel, **$104.**

James Heddon's Sons Model 45 baitcasting reel, **$210.**

James Heddon's Sons Model 3-15 baitcasting reel, **$450.**

Horton No. 3 Bluegrass reel complete with two piece box/bag, **$660.**

Rare B. F. Meek & Sons No. 2 Kentucky reel, **$840.**

B. F. Meek & Sons No. 2 Kentucky reel (Horton Mfg.), **$660.**

B. F. Meek & Sons, Louisville, Kentucky, No. 33 Bluegrass reel, **$111.**

B. F. Meek & Sons, Louisville, Kentucky, No. 25 Bluegrass reel, **$180.**

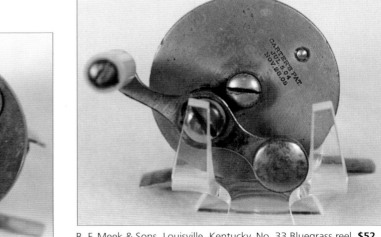

B. F. Meek & Sons, Louisville, Kentucky, No. 33 Bluegrass reel, **$52.**

Two Yale skeleton fly reels, 2-7/8" diameter, one wide spool, **$117.**

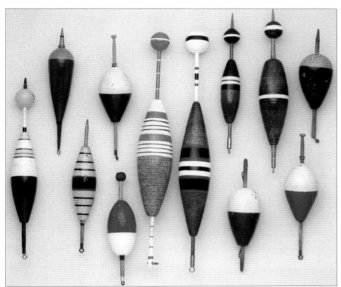

Outstanding assortment of a dozen bobbers, 6" to 13", most EX, **$450.**

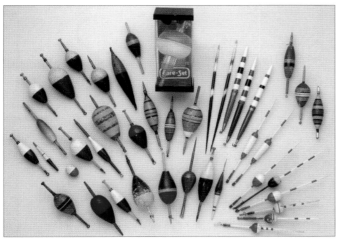

Assortment of bobbers (42) up to 9" long, G to EX, **$270.**

Rare cast iron trolling rig, circa late 1800s, used on Great Lakes, EX, **$780.**

Additional vintage and classic fishing lures

There are truly thousands of lures I could show as examples but for this book I am going to concentrate on the "big six" lure companies. I have attempted to expose you to a wide variety of items, but balanced with enough detail on the better companies to be valuable. As with all general introductory books, my primary goal is to show a good sampling of lures in a limited amount of space. I have included both vintage lures and some of the collectible modern lures which I refer to as classic. For a complete rundown on many dozens of additional companies, see *Classic Fishing Lures*. For the most complete reference on modern lures, consult *Modern Fishing Lure Collectibles*, Volumes 1-5. For the complete "bible" of lures, consult Luckey's 7th edition of *Old Lures & Fishing Tackle*.

Creek Chub Bait Company

Creek Chub Bait Company, originally of Garrett, Indiana and later of Sioux City, Iowa, now owned by Pradco, is normally considered one of the "big two" in vintage bait collecting circles. The company contributed many fine lures and also painting techniques (earliest scale pattern) to lure history. You cannot think of CCBC without thinking of its famous Pikie Minnow or my favorite, the Creek Chub Plunker. Literally millions of Pikie Minnows were sold and the Plunker also sold well. In addition, CCBC made numerous other significant baits and offered them in a wide variety of color schemes and also had some important hardware variations.

As with all lures, color variations are important and color rarity often drives the value of a lure as much as age. To familiarize yourself more with CCBC, or if you want to specialize in this one company, I cannot recommend a better source than the complete history of CCBC written by Harold Smith and published by Collector Books. Dr. Smith does a fine job detailing the history of the company and showing guides to lure colors

and nearly all of the many lures made by the company, including an extensive treatment of Shur Strike.

I would recommend that you remember the following about colors for CCBC: Pikie is common and seldom of great value on most lures, Perch is next in line for most lures. Blue and white is rare, as is black and white, especially on Pikie minnows and crabs. Frog is also rare on many CCBC baits, especially the wooden versions. Also, some of the limited metal baits made by CCBC are hard to find in any condition. There are many rare variations on colors and some of the rarest are even in the modern era, e.g. post-1940 and include better plastic lures such as in the Rainbow Trout pattern shown on Page 122. *Modern Fishing Lure Collectibles*, Volume 1, details the post-1940 era of Creek Chub in some detail and shows many of the modern lures that are in demand but some of the newer lures are shown here as well.

In the past research conducted, it became obvious that the Wiggler and the Pikie lures dominated the early history of CCBC. However, the most common lures to be found in the field today consist of Pikies, Plunkers and Injured Minnows. You actually find fewer CCBC plastic lures from the 1960s than the wooden Pikies, Plunkers and Injured Minnows. These lures made up the success story of CCBC. Shown following are a number of CCBC lures. Dating techniques for these lures include eye types, whether or not the lure is stamped on the back, lip dates (or none), body shapes, and many other techniques. A complete study of Dr. Smith's book will assist in this area. I have included in the captions some basic data on dating lures as well.

Note that most measurements given for lures are actual measurements I took to the closest 1/16 inch and not just what the companies advertised. All lengths given are "body only," unless otherwise stated. Also keep in mind values are given for lures in excellent condition.

The beginnings of Creek Chub: the famous Wiggler lures. The chub scale color is 3-1/2" long, wood, glass eyes, double line tie model, patent date on lip, note that it is fatter than the other one and the hooks have likely been replaced. Also, its diving lip is upside down. The blue scale is also a double line tie, patent on lip model in glass eyes but it is 3-5/8" long with hand-soldered hooks; **$100+** for most Wiggler lures and up to hundreds for some of the early versions in unusual scale colors in mint condition.

CCBC Dinger lures, glass eyes, patent date on lip, marked plate and back, Model 5600 made from 1934-54, natural frog and black, 2-1/4", **$150+** each.

CCBC Fin Tail Shiner, no patent date lip, glass eyes, metal fins and spinners, cup hardware, one belly weight, silver shiner scale, 3-1/2". Lure made from 1924-47, **$300+.** However, the ones with fiber fins and spinners trade for up to **$1,500** each easily if all parts are still intact.

CCBC Beetles, 2-1/2" and 2" models. Beetle marked on bottom, patent on lips, pearl spinners, cup hardware, gold/greenish color, made from 1931-54. Beetles are very collectible and bring a premium price, **$300+** each.

CCBC Husky Dingbat, made from 1938-46, heavy-duty cup hardware, glass eyes, no markings on body or lip, pikie color, Model 5300, 2-1/2" long, **$250+.**

CCBC Baby Wiggle Fish, golden shiner color, made from 1925-33, 2-3/4", **$250+.**

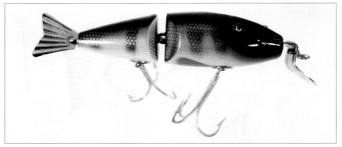

CCBC Wiggle Fish, reinforced lip with patent date, single line tie version, perch color, made from 1925-57, 3-1/2" long, **$300+.**

CCBC Narrow bodied wooden mouse, red/white, carved eyes, cup hardware, belly marked, rope tail. This is from the period in the 1950s when CCBC owned Shakespeare and is basically a narrow Shakespeare Swimming Mouse design. Mouse is 2-3/4" long, **$25+.**

CCBC Beetle Display, includes both standard Beetle and Baby Beetle sizes in black with different eye colors and white (factory paint stick color) with eyes and spinners added. These came from a former CCBC employee and were finished with parts on hand when the factory closed. White was never a production color but only the color used as a primer, **$50+** each.

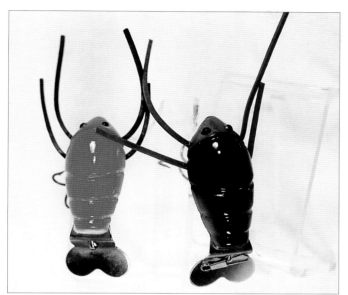

CCBC Narrow bodied wooden mouse, red/white, carved eyes, cup hardware, belly marked, rope tail. This is from the period in the 1950s when CCBC owned Shakespeare and is basically a narrow Shakespeare Swimming Mouse design. Mouse is 2-3/4" long, **$25+.**

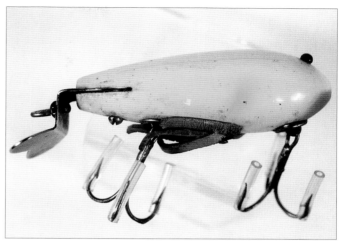

CCBC Crab, wood, plain lip (not painted), marked, white, feelers present, 2-3/4", **$50+.**

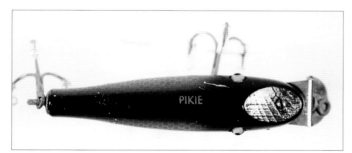

CCBC straight Pikie, golden shiner color, glass eyes, cup hardware, patent date on lip, Pikie in gold letters on back, 3-3/8", **$25+.**

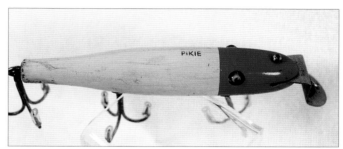

CCBC Pikie, same details at the golden shiner at left, but red/white color, 4-1/4", **$25+.**

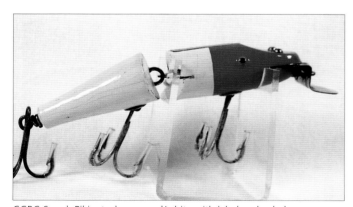

CCBC Snook Pikie, tack eyes, red/white with label on back, heavy hardware, 5", **$35+.**

CCBC Baby Dingbat, wood, golden shiner color, gold letters on back, patent date on lip, 1-1/2" long body, **$75+.**

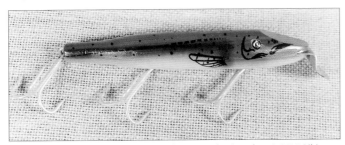

CCBC Model 700P rainbow trout color, rare plastic color, 4-1/2" Pikie lure, slide top box, name stamped on lure as on most CCBC plastic lures, **$75+.**

CCBC Pikie, wood Model 700, gold lettering on back, glass eyes, patent date marked lip of 9-27-20. As any CC rainbow, these are highly desired, **$75+.**

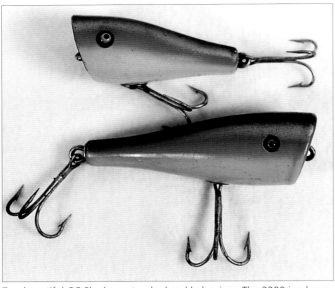

CCBC Model 3201, Plunker, wood, perch color, very common but this is the early brass cup hardware, glass eyes, correct label box. This nice combination of box/lure is not that hard to find but still nice in such clean condition, **$50-$75.**

Two beautiful CC Plunkers, standard and baby sizes. The 3200 is a brass cup, glass eye and the baby is the same. This is a very collectible color and has at least two variations in the rainbow patterns, plus Fire Plug and Rainbow Fire, **$75+** each for any of the standard rainbows. The others (not shown here) bring a premium price of **$125**.

Two straight plastic Pikie lures, 2-5/16" in pikie and silver flash colors. Both are very common colors, **$10+.**

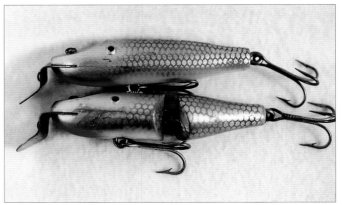

Two Pikies in a better color. Straight Pikie is 2-5/16" and Jointed Pikie is 2-7/16" long. This is a light or mint green scale pattern, **$20+** each.

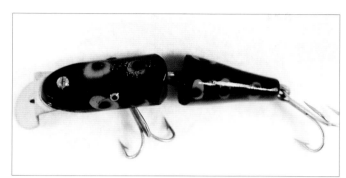

Jointed Pikie in frog, 2-7/16", **$20+.**

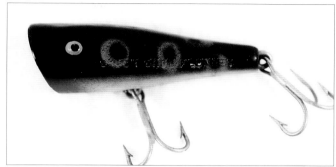

Plastic Plunker in frog, 2", **$20+.**

Two versions of the CCBC silver flash pattern in plastic Injured Minnow lures, 2-5/8", **$15+** each. Note larger flakes of silver on one version.

Pikie, silver flash, wooden lure, tack eyes, date on lip, single line tie, Pikie in gold letters on back, 3-1/4", **$25+.**

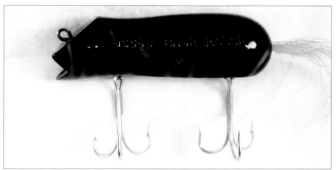

CCBC Mouse in tiger color, plastic Model 65772, 5/8", **$20+.**

Two versions of the 3-3/8" CCBC Jointed Pikie, wood, glass eyes, single line tie, gold stamping on back, **$20-$30.** Note the color variation in the white.

A beautiful little wooden red/white Pikie, only 2-1/4" long, Pikie stamped in gold letters, screw hardware, date on lip, single line tie, gold eyes, **$40+.**

A smaller version Injured Minnow, a bit harder to find, 2-1/8", **$20+.**

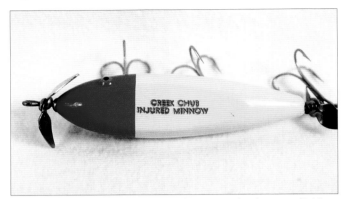

Beautiful wooden Injured Minnow, tack eyes, cup hardware, red/white color, gold stamping on lure, 3-3/4" long, **$40+.**

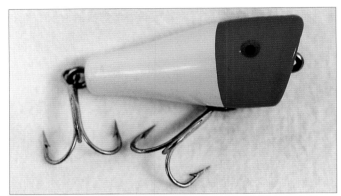

Nice little 2" wooden Plunker in cup rig with gold decal eyes, no markings on lure. Beautiful little lure and hard to find, **$35-$50+.**

Harder to find Viper in plastic, Model 8800 shown in three colors: blue scale, chrome and silver flash. The blue scale and chrome are harder colors to find in CC plastic lures. The Viper has the model number and name stamped on its belly as shown, 3-1/8" long, **$30+.**

Premier CC lure, a Crawdad with a painted diving lip, bead eyes, all feelers present, green/brown with a white belly. These lures are in demand and this one is near mint, **$100-$300** for most of them in great shape.

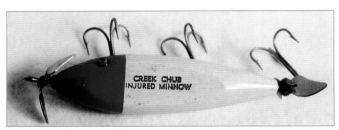

Beautiful set of CCBC Model 1502 Injured Minnow in wood with labeled box. The lure is 3 5/8" long, cup hardware, glass eyes, name stamped in gold letters. The glass eye version is worth more and so is the labeled, as opposed to stamped, box, **$75+.**

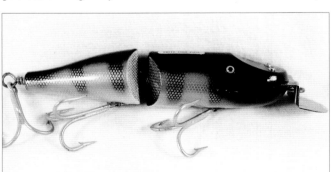

Large 5-7/8" (catalog lists it at 6") wooden Model 3000 Jointed Huskie Pikie with the newest type of label on the back, a sticker. Tack eyes, reinforced diving lip with no writing, heavy-duty hardware, common perch color but a harder lure to find, especially in excellent condition, **$50-$100.**

Prototype CCBC Pikie, **$100+.** A gentleman purchased this Model 2600 type lure in the early 1950s from the board of lures in the Creek Chub plant in Garrett, Indiana, where the lures were made. I purchased it from him. It has brass cups, lip and line ties. The hooks are hand soldered and the eyes are hand-painted circles with the pikie scales also being hand done. The lip is unmarked and it has double line ties. I do not know if it is a prototype for sure but I do know it came from the factory and is unique to say the least.

Older CCBC Pikie Model 701 on top in pikie color and a Model 702 in perch. Both wooden, cup rig and glass eyed. Some of the older Pikies will fetch **$100+** if in the early finish and hardware, even in Pikie color. However, these two colors are fairly common unless an early one, **$30-$50** for most.

The Jointed Striper Pikie version of the wooden pikie with heavy-hardware, reinforced lip, cup hardware, glass eyes, gold stamping on back and box. Sold online in early 2004 for **$50+**; normally this should have sold for **$60-$75**.

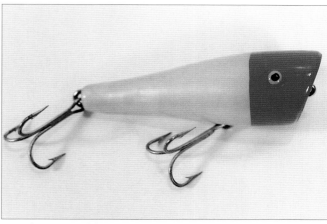

One of my personal favorites, the Model 3200 Plunker in plastic but in rare pearl/red combination. Lure is marked Creek Chub Plunker Model 3200 on its left side. Recessed screw hardware, molded eyes, rare color. I paid $65 for it at a lure show in 2003; **$75+** today.

Dingbat in silver flash color, glass eyes, line tie present, feathering in good shape, all important items to the collector, **$75+.**

One of the few metal bait offerings by CCBC, the Cohokie, **$75+.**

A couple of packaging types used by CCBC in the 1950s-60s, **$5-$10**, unless a box for a very rare lure color or type, then more. These boxes are very common and plentiful for the common lures.

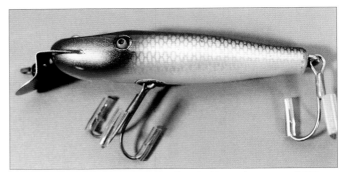

CC Baby Pikie, glass eyes, a rare colored white scale pattern, **$400+.**

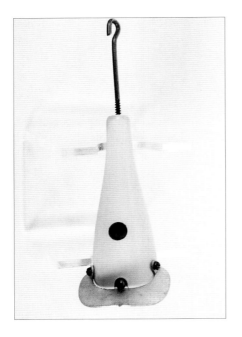

Rare find: a Pop-N-Dunk paint stick from the factory, **$200+.**

Silver Scale Injured Minnow made for Wards. This is a CCBC product made for distribution by Wards. Companies made lures for Wards, Sears Roebuck, Western Auto and other companies. They also sold to and/or made lures for some other large hardware chains. This beautiful Injured Minnow is worth **$100+.**

Model 3008 Jointed Husky Pikie Minnow in correct label box in nice Rainbow color, glass eyed, **$300+.**

Very rare CCBC Fireplug color Beetle with original box and hang-tag, **$3,000+.** *Tom Jacomet Collection*

Heddon lures

Heddon is second only alphabetically but most definitely first in collector appeal. I dedicate 70 pages of about 300 to Heddon in my Volume 1 of *Modern Fishing Lure Collectibles*. The late Clyde A. Harbin, Sr., "The Bassman," wrote extensively about Heddon for years. Collector Books recently published a book on Heddon lures. Prior to Clyde's passing, I revised his book on *Heddon Catalogs: 1902-1953*, 2004, Krause Publications. I also wrote the book, *Heddon Plastic Lures*, 2005, Krause Publications. This is just to give an indication of the popularity of Heddon lures. I cannot recommend more highly my and Harbin's recent book for a complete treatment of the small nuances in lure design and the dates of lure introductions.

James Heddon made some lures for sale in 1901 and published his first two catalogs in 1902. Harbin and others sometimes claim Heddon began in the 1800s but I believe we should use the dates a company begins commercial production of its lures for a beginning point.

By 1903, the company was in full production selling wooden lures that have become known to collectors for their quality of paint and manufacture. The Heddon 100s and 150s from this period (3-hook and 5-hook lures) are some of the most in demand on the market. One such lure sold for more than $30,000 online in 2003 but this is very rare (copper color 1904 Heddon 150) and most of these lures trade for about $100 to $300 on average, as my lures recently consigned to Lang's did. Many are worth more and some worth over a thousand, but they are available and some are still found "in the field."

The vintage Heddon lures are all collectible but the earliest ones command the higher prices in general. Heddon also has many collectible plastic lures, due to the company's early experimentation with various substances. Early examples include the Luny Frog of Pyralin, Stanley Pork Rind Minnows first in Celluloid and then of Pyralin and the early "Spook" baits, the Vamps, Dowagiac Spooks and early River Runts. The earliest River Runt Spooks were made of an unstable Tenite 1 material and it is not uncommon to find them in pieces in boxes. However,

Tenite 2 was more stable and most of those lures are just fine, as are many of the Tenite 1 models.

The earliest Spook baits had two-piece hardware and are easily differentiated from the surface hardware that became popular by the 1940s for most Heddon lures. Some of the rare Heddon River Runt Spook colors command over $100 each. Most River Runt Spooks sell for between $5 and $20 depending on condition; new-in-the-box versions average about $20 to $40.

If interested in Heddon, make sure you re-read the phrase on condition again! Beat up Heddons are not worth much more than beat up Woods or Clarks, or anything else. Yet dealers and collectors seem to think they are made of gold if marked Heddon. This is not true; beat up Heddons are just beat up lures of little value.

One nice thing about Heddons, and I think this has driven up the prices accordingly, is that almost all Heddon lures are marked. Some of the earliest 100s, 150s, 300s, etc., are not marked, not even the propellers. However, eventually Heddon advertised that "All Genuine Dowagiac Minnows have 'Heddon & Dowagiac' Stamped on the Metal." They then started marking lures on the belly or diving lips and continued to do so through the production of most plastic lures as well. This assists dealers and collectors in identifying Heddons and has resulted in more people knowing what they have for sale, increasing the values accordingly.

Collecting only Heddon plastics from 1940 and on is an admiral goal and would give an endless variety to collect. To amass a major Heddon collection of vintage wooden lures from the 1901 to 1940 period will take much time, patience and money. However, from an investment perspective, if things hold true to the past, you cannot go wrong with the goal of collecting Heddon lures.

It is impossible to show all Heddon lures here, and nearly impossible in a full length book simply on Heddon, but the following selection is meant to represent lures often found in the field that are of value. Good luck on your quest.

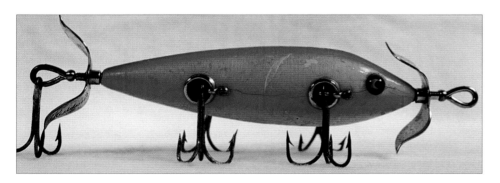

When you think of classic Heddons, usually the Heddon 100s and 150s come to mind. Here is a nice Heddon 150 in rainbow. This one comes in a "downward leaping bass" box, has three hand-painted gill marks, glass eyes, L-rig hardware, a body length of 3-3/4", names on both propellers and the box has the April 1, '02 patent date; **$400-$1,200** for most rainbows with a box if in excellent condition. Some will bring more if needed to fill a particular type in a collection.

Heddon's first lure made of man-made materials other than metal was a Heddon-Stanley Pork Rind Minnow, first made in 1924 of Bakelite and then changed to Pyralin within a couple of years. This is a rare find as it has the papers, box and lure. The one shown is a Model No. 79M, pike scale. Note the chipping on the lure's rear, which is common on these lures. The lure is 1-1/8" long with glass eyes. It came either with or without a weed guard; **$75+** with box and papers, **$35-$50** for loose lures.

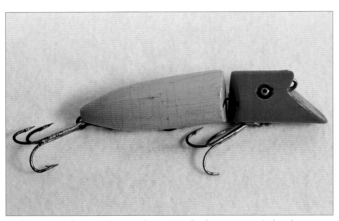

Heddon Model 8300 Zig-Wag lure, wood, glass eyes, L-rig hardware, marked on bottom, 4" long, **$40-$70.**

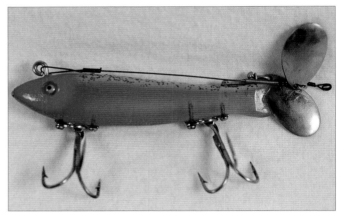

Heddon Dowagiac Super Spook lure, Model 9100, harder to find than regular Spooks, 3-3/4" long, **$50-$75.** First offered in 1930 and in an early "Spook" material, not Pyralin but not the Tenite of later years either. This one is Amber with red head and gold sparkles, marked in red letters on belly, glass eyes. This one also has "toilet seat" hardware (later replaced by "flap rig").

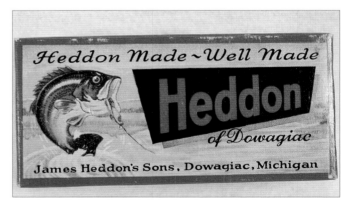

Model F 4000 Heddon Meadow Mouse, wooden, 2-3/4", bead eyes, leather tail and ears, belly marked, black back stripe, L-rig hardware, "upward leaping box" from after 1940, **$75-$125** range for most. This box type follows the "Brush box" and precedes the cardboard bottom/plastic top boxes. It was used primarily during the war years and into the early '50s. Mice are highly sought after by both Heddon and mouse collectors.

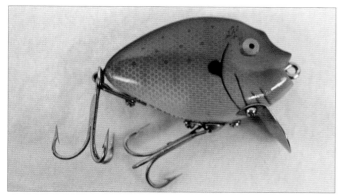

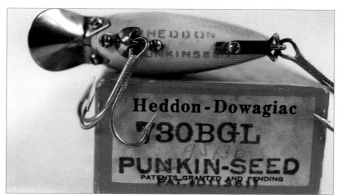

A pretty 9630 BGL plastic Punkinseed found in a Model 730 Brush box, type 2. This plastic Punkinseed has transitional hardware, e.g. surface on bottom and two-piece on tail, gold eyes, and Heddon marked in gold stencil. There are dozens of variations in eye colors, stencil colors, hardware types and small color nuances in plastic Punkinseeds making them one of the most desirable of Heddon plastic lures. Plus, they are, as my wife would say, "super extra cute." The box is named for the photo of the gentleman on the top; **$75-$125** boxed, **$50-$75** loose for common colors. Red/white, yellow or black shore bring from **$125-$300** as the colors are rare, especially black shore and red/white.

Heddon Punkinseed, wooden, Model 740, bluegill, painted gold eyes, line tie under chin (some are in mouth), flap rig two piece hardware, this was the larger floating model only made in wood, 2-1/2" long. The 730 became the plastic 9630 model. The Model 740 is one of the most desirable of all Punkinseed models and is highly sought after by collectors, **$75-$250** and up. The Rock Bass box alone for this model has sold for **$400+** on at least two occasions. A 740 in a rare color will command a King's ransom, e.g. red/white shore. Most will trade for around **$125-$150,** however, without a box. Add at least $50 for common box colors, e.g. bluegill, sunfish, and crappie. Due to the war years, not too many of these were made prior to being replaced by the plastic version of the 730, the 9630 Model.

Heddon Tiny Punkin Spin, rarest of the Punkinseed plastics from recent times, introduced in 1974 and gone by 1978. These lures were only offered a couple of years and are seldom found. I have over 100 Punkinseeds and only two Punkin Spins. It is a Tiny Punkinseed body with the tail hook removed and a spinner added, **$75+.**

Heddon Tiny Punkinseed in bluegill, a pretty little plastic lure from the '50s-'60s, **$40-$75** for most.

Heddon 210 Surface lure new in two-piece box from the '40s-'50s. Painted gold eyes, surface hardware, belly stencil, frog pattern. The 210 is a famous Heddon lure dating back to the early years and usually commands a premium price, even some of the plastic 210s which are actually quite scarce. Frog is a very good color in most lures and Heddon collectors seem to really like it also; **$125+** with box; **$75+** loose.

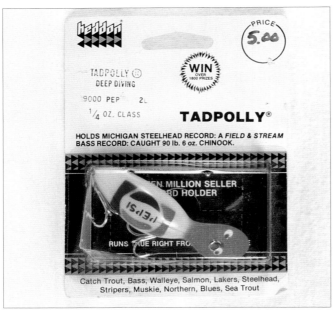

The "green diamond" blister pack was used from 1980-84 and is the last pure Heddon packaging until the Heddon/Ebsco cards of 1984. The lure shown is a 3" Tadpolly Spook in the rare Pepsi pattern. This lure came in two sizes and is quite hard to find for such a recent lure, **$75+.** The blister packs alone have little value but a lure still in the package is worth considerably more than one by itself.

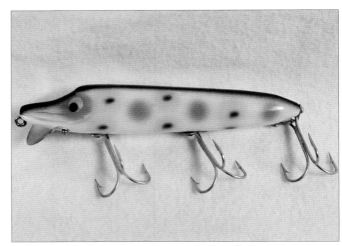

Heddon "Original Wood Vamp," reintroduction of wooden lures in the 1960s version, gold painted eyes, surface hardware, beautiful strawberry spot in high demand by collectors, 4-1/2" long, **$35-$50.**

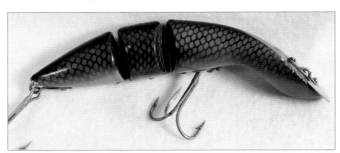

Heddon Game Fisher, a true classic, 4-3/4" long, two joints, marking on lip says Heddon and Game Fisher below it, L-rig hardware, green scale, fairly common in Game Fisher lures but still pretty; **$50-$125** for this color.

Heddon Game Fisher in red/white/red, also 4-3/4" long and same as above in details, **$125+** for this color.

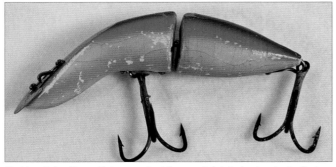

Heddon Baby Game Fisher, marked lip, one joint, L-rig, harder to find than regular size, rainbow pattern, common color for Game Fisher lures, wood, 3-3/4" long, **$125+** (one color has sold for over **$1,200**).

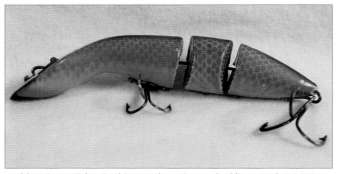

Heddon Game Fisher in shiner scale, L-rig, marked lip, wood, 4-3/4" long, **$125+.**

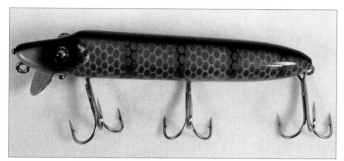

Heddon Vamp, glass eyes, wood, L-rig, unmarked, tack in nose, pike scale with green blush around the glass eyes on face, 4-1/2" long, **$125+.** Vamps are very collectible and have many variations.

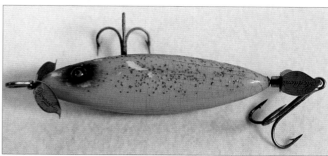

Heddon SOS lure, wood, glass eyes in silver flash color, both props are marked Heddon Dowagiac, 3-1/2" long, **$100+.** The SOS lures are fairly hard to come by and highly desired; the Flipper is even more difficult to find.

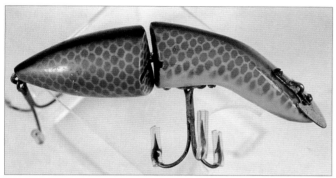

Heddon Baby Game Fisher, one joint, L-rig, shiner scale, 3-3/4" long, **$125+.**

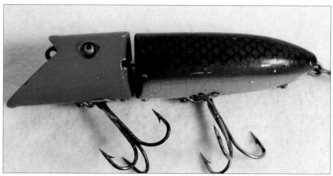

Heddon Zig Wag, Model 8300, made from 1928-early 50s, wooden, one joint, glass eyes, L-rig, red head/green scale, 4", **$50-$75.**

Heddon Zig Wag same as above but in shiner scale, **$50-$75.**

Heddon Walton Feather Tail, Model 40, marked prop, glass eyes, one belly weight, feathered of course, pike scale color, 2-3/16" long, **$125+.** This is the only one I have ever had indicating a fairly rare lure, it is also fairly early only being made from 1924-26.

Heddon Darting Zara Spook lure, plastic, gold eyes, red/white shore pattern, surface rig, a nice collectible Heddon plastic lure, 3-1/4" long, **$50-$75.**

Heddon Crazy Crawler, Model 2100, white with black wing pattern, three-color eye (a sign of an early one), flap rig hardware (also early). This lure is to me "THE CLASSIC" Heddon, as it was introduced in 1940 and it is a lure I grew up with fishing for bass on our own lake in Michigan. Many baby boomers feel the same, as the prices on these lures can be quite high. There are numerous eye color, hardware, and stenciling variations through the years and it is replace by a smaller plastic version in the 1950s. The lure's actual measurements are 2-5/8" long even though the catalog lists these as 2-3/4" long. The common colors are black/white, red/white, red/yellow, frog and mouse. Any of the other colors are harder to find and include silver shore, yellow shore, black shore, glow-worm, luminous red/white and chipmunk. The chipmunk, glow-worm and luminous versions will bring at least triple the value of a perfect mouse: **$75+** for red/white, yellow/red, and black/white; **$100+** for frog and/or mouse; **$300+** for any of the rare versions, with chipmunk bringing even more.

Heddon 150 minnow, wood, glass eyes, L-rig, one belly weight, marked props, solid red. Red is a collectible color for early Heddon minnows but beware of repaints. This one is original and is a field find for me (along with rare Tiny Runt colors shown at right). I have sold red 150s for **$500+** that now trade for up to **$5,000** in the rare cup rig models. Although not perfect, at least we know this one is authentic; **$400+** for L-rig models; cup rig will bring up to ten times as much.

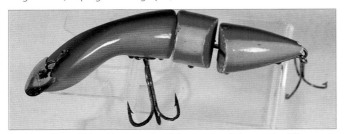

Heddon Game Fisher lure, wood, rainbow color, L-rig, marked lip, 4-3/4" long, **$125+.**

Heddon Crazy Crawler, Model 2100GM, gray mouse, 2-piece hardware, red bead eyes, leather tail, no ears (a few are found with leather ears), actual measurement is 2-11/16" instead of 2-3/4" on this one. This would be the lure for the 2-piece cardboard box for a 2100GM; **$100+** for lure; add **$25-$50** for boxed lure.

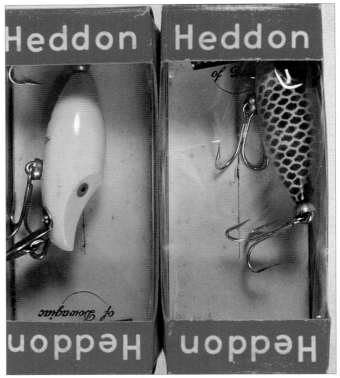

Rare Tiny Runt colors by Heddon. The Model 350 Tiny Runt was introduced in 1952 by Heddon and listed as a 2-1/8" lure in plastic. These lures are all rare colors for Tiny Runts (or any River Runts) and all came from one estate with the red 150 at left. These are also all in the Introductory box for the Tiny Runt. Models shown include the 350 BR (brown), 350 W (white) and the 350 SF BR (brown with silver foil insert). As a general rule, Tiny Runts are not in as much demand as other River Runt models; however, these would garner a lot of collector interest for certain, **$100+** for any of these; most common Tiny Runts sell for **$10-$20**, a little more with boxes.

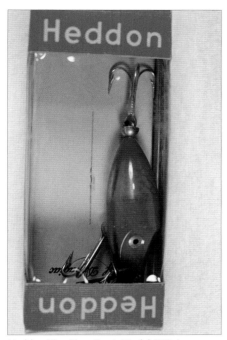

Heddon Tiny River Runt, Model 350, in introductory box from 1952, yellow shore color. This is an example of a common Tiny Runt color compared to those just shown. Box is rough but lure is mint in box; **$20-$30** for this common color.

Some early Heddon lures and a decoy. The fluted wobbler is a prototype from 1908 based upon the type of cup hardware used on it. It was never produced due to similarities with competing lure companies. The small lure is an Artistic Minnow, 1-3/4", wood, made only from 1905 to about 1910 (this one has some wax buildup from being cleaned). The four-point fish decoy is not as desirable as the batwing version but is still an early and rare piece: **$500+** for prototype; **$250+** for Artistic Minnow; **$700+** for decoy.

Heddon Model 151 (rainbow 150) and correct box, L-rig, name on both props, fat body, 1915-30 era, glass eyes, wood, **$400-$1,200.**

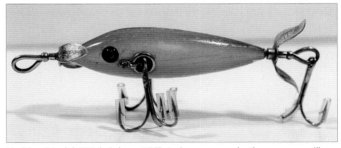

Heddon Model 101 (rainbow 100), L-rig, name on both props, no gill marks, **$400-1,200.**

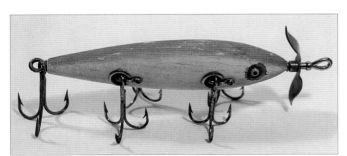

Heddon Model 150, L-rig, no gill marks, glass eyes, single prop with name, **$300+.**

Heddon 100 in highly desired green crackle back color and a very rare color in a 150, brown frog-scale. The Model 100 is a fat body type, name on both props, L-rig, glass eyes, two hand-painted gill marks. The Model 150 has name on both props, also L-rig, glass eyes, name on belly; **$500-$1,500,** with the frog-scale being the more valuable of the two lures shown.

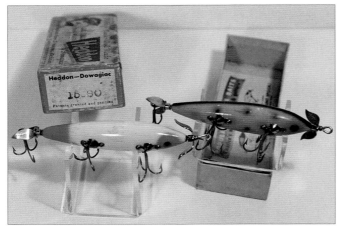

Late 1940s-early 1950s versions of the Model 150, gold painted eyes, wooden, names on props, surface rig, one belly weight, bottoms marked, and a box for the spotted orange version, **$100+.** These two sold for **$95+** for the red/white one and **$110+** for the spotted orange one in early 2004 online.

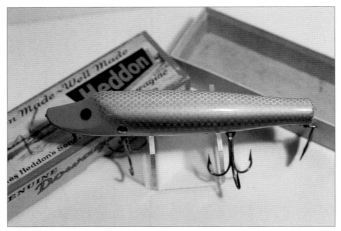

Beautiful Heddon Flaptail Model 7050 PAS (Allen Stripey color), wood, painted gold eyes, heavy duty hardware, gold stenciled name on belly, 5-1/4", made from 1935 until the 1950s, in correct box; **$75+** for painted eyes, up to **$150** for ones with the large "Teddy Bear" glass eyes.

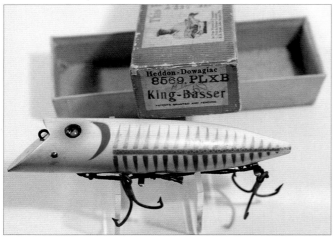

Heddon King-Basser lure, Model 8569, color PLXB, wood, large Teddy Bear eyes, heavy duty cloth hook hangers/hardware, 6" long (King Basser also came in 4-1/2" and 5" versions). Correct Brush box named after H. R. Brush and his 17-pound bass. These are not found too often in the Midwest but are more common on the West Coast; **$75-$125,** maybe a little more for colors such as the yellow shore.

Midget Crab Wiggler, Heddon Model 1950, wood, glass eyes, single line tie, rainbow color, "U" collar, downward leaping bass box, 2-1/2", **$125-$200.**

Three beautiful rainbow Heddon lures in boxes. The Torpedo is a Model 130 RB with glass eyes, surface hardware and marked props; the box is the upward bass box. The wood catalog offerings disappeared in 1936 but this must be a bit later with the upward bass box. The two Game Fisher lures are both rainbow with the weedless treble model in downward leaping bass box and the other one in an upward bass box. The one with weedless hooks is fairly hard to find. Torpedo, **$100-$175;** Game Fisher in box, **$150+**; Game Fisher in early downward bass box with weedless hooks, **$200+**.

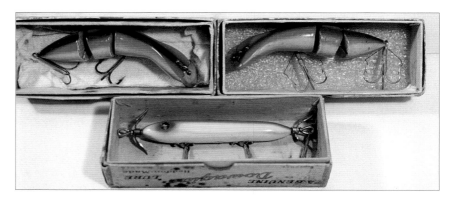

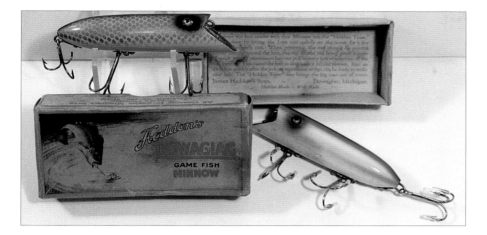

Two fine Heddon Bassers in wood. Bassers came out as Model 8500 in 1924 and for only two years had stamped on the diving plate "Head-On Basser." These lures are great demand by collectors. The scale pattern in the downward leaping box is such a model from 1924-26, glass eyes, L-rig, 4" long. The rainbow is also unique as it has the small toilet seat hardware but it is not the 1924-26 version, a bit later still with glass eyes. These are truly classic lures and in demand: **$200+** for early boxed versions; **$125+** loose. Later versions not saying Head-On on lip will bring **$100-$150** easily in excellent condition. Even the painted eye versions and the "Original Wood Bassers" introduced in the mid-60s command **$50-$75** for most models.

Heddon Punkinseed Spook, Model 9630-SD (shad) new in box with a pocket catalog from the 1940s. Note that collectors will find at least two variations of shad colors, one greener such as this one, **$125+** (I sold it online early 2004).

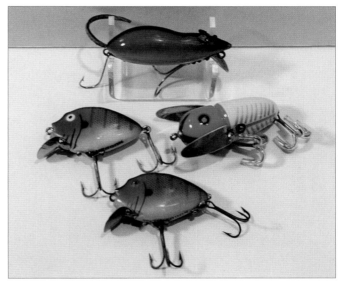

More '40s-'50s lures. The same Meadow Mouse and Model 2120 Crazy Crawler from above (both wooden lures) compared with two of the 9630 plastic Punkinseeds in sunfish color. One has a white eye which is 1950s and other has an earlier gold painted eye. Mouse, **$75-$125**; Crawler, **$50-$75**; Punkinseeds, **$75+**.

Rare Model 2120 Chipmunk Crazy Crawler, **$400+.**

Heddon Bass Bug Spook on left and Bumble Bug (or Bubbling Bug) on right; **$125+** for Spook and **$400+** for Bug.

Heddon Punkie Spook in Shad and Runtie Spook in Shiner Scale. Both are very rare plastic baits by Heddon. Punkie Spook, **$150+;** Runtie Spook, **$125+.**

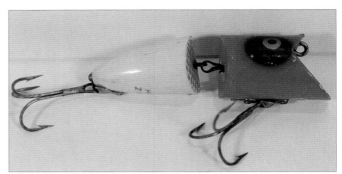

Heddon Zig-Wag Jr. wooden lure. Red/white, gold painted eyes with black blush, surface rig from 1950s, **$25-$35.**

Heddon Bass Bug in downward leaping bass box, very rare. Some have sold for nearly **$1,500,** but the usual range would be about **$300-$1,500.**

Trout size Wilder-Dilg lure in downward bass box, **$400-$800.**

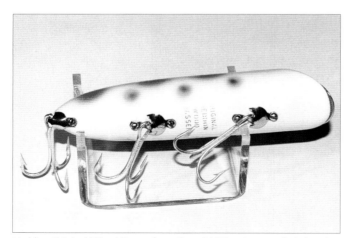

Heddon Original Wood Basser from the mid-60s release period showing the surface hardware typical found on newer Heddon lures. This one is in strawberry spot and thus in high demand, **$50-$75.**

Heddon Model 2120 Crazy Crawler, with surface hardware and eye style of the later models in yellow/red pattern, wood, **$50-$75.**

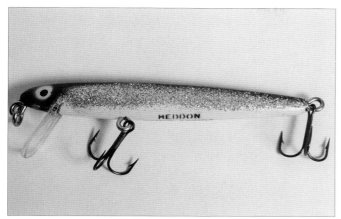

Heddon wood Cobra from the '60s-'70s in black/silver fleck, painted white eyes, marked belly and simple screw hardware. Cobra was Heddon's response to the importation of the successful Rapala lures from Finland. I fished both when younger and I found the Cobra to be a great lure. However, apparently most people preferred the Rapala given sales history of the two lures! It is just recently that collector interest has grown for these lures, coming in a variety of patterns, some with spinners, **$10-$30** for most.

Heddon Scissortail, gold eyes and surface hardware, perch color, **$35+.** The Scissortail was added in 1953.

Heddon Vamp Spook, Model 9750 L (perch). The lure is in a 1950s to 1962 box and sports white eyes and surface hardware. Vamp Spooks are a little harder to come by than most River Runts, **$50-$75** new in box.

Model SCK-4 Sonic Kit with four Model 385 Sonic lures in common colors, new in box (and cardboard shipping container). None of the lures are unusual as they are the same colors sent to wholesale houses and jobbers but the kits are very hard to find in new condition, **$100+** for kit.

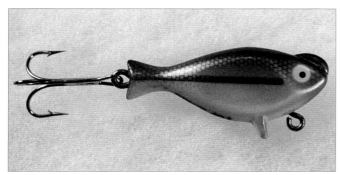

Heddon Top Sonic, toughest of the line to find, in Barfish pattern, **$30+.**

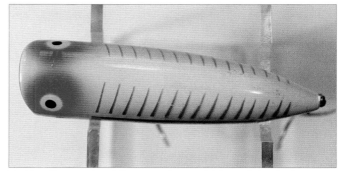

Heddon Chugger Spook in XRW color, Model 9540 dating back to 1939, **$50+**; more than **$100** for better colors. This one is a surface rig version from the 1960s. Chugger Spooks aare highly desired by both American and Japanese collectors, driving the price up some.

Heddon Cousin II lure (note the big loop, Cousin I models had small line tie). This lure was introduced in 1973 but advertised as "New" yet in 1974, **$30+.**

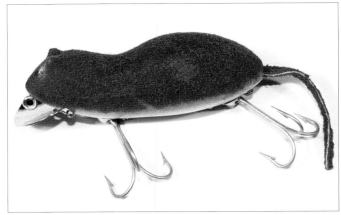

Heddon Meadow Mouse with leather tail, plastic, brown flocked, **$25+.**

Heddon Tiger Cub, small model reintroduced in 1980s and made for only a short period, **$25-$40.**

Heddon Preyfish in smaller size introduced in 1982 so only made for two years at most. These are the rarest of all Heddon plastic lures and command a premium price, **$75-$125.**

Display of mostly wooden Heddon Crazy Crawlers, both 2100 and 2120 Models. The display has some older and newer and rare and common models; **$50+** for most wooden ones; **$100+** for rare colors; **$25+** for most plastic ones.

Heddon Tiny Stingaree in red/white. This 1-1/2" lure in plastic was introduced in 1957 and has gold painted eyes and gold stenciling, **$15-$20** for most colors, a bit more for some others.

Rare Preyfish, new in box. This was purchased online in 2003 for **$75+.** They trade regularly for **$75-$100** each, even loose. As stated earlier, they are very rare and were not made for long.

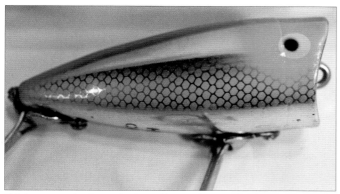

This is a rare color for a plastic Heddon and very collected. It is nickel plate yellow, better known as yellow chrome to collectors. It is rare in Sonics and Chuggers, too. This is a nice new-in-box example found online in 2003. It details also a Daisy/Heddon box from the Victor Comptometer era. I bought this online for more than **$75** in 2003.

Herter's Heddon River Runt sold by Revelation. This is a fun find that adds mystery to lure collecting. It appears similar to a Herter's copy of a River Runt and is marked Japan on lip. It was sold by Western Auto under its "Revelation" brand name. Copying is the ultimate form of flattery and here we have a two-way example: Western Auto selling a lure likely made by the same folks in Japan that made the Herter's examples after copying a Tiny Runt by Heddon, **$35-$50** new in box.

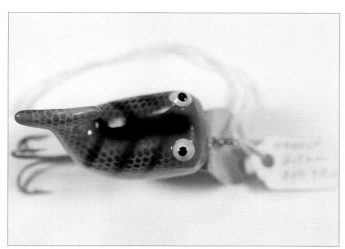

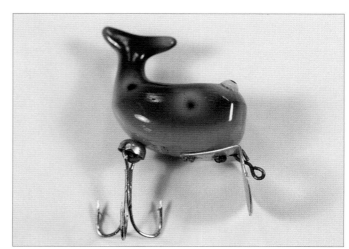

Heddon Hi-Tails are one of the cutest lures from the 1960s and collectors love them. Anglers did not like them, though, as the hook would get pushed up into the lure when a bass hit and could not be hooked easily. But fishing failure has led to collecting success, as the lure is fairly rare due to poor sales. Also, there are some unusual advertising versions and colors to be found. Shown are perch and frog versions of the lure; **$50-$75** each, or more for some other colors.

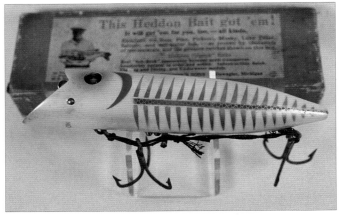

Model 8569PLXB King-Basser lure, **$300+.**

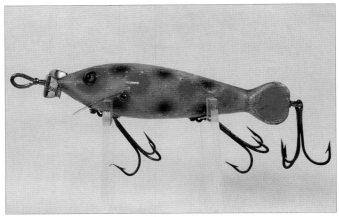

Rare Heddon Spin-Diver in pretty Strawberry Spot, **$500+.**

Some rare Heddons. The center has a very rare find, the Heddon Artistic Minnow in sienna yellow AND its external weight AND its box, which is nearly unheard of, and today's value would be **$2,500** +/-. Above the Artistic Minnow are two nail-eyed Model 20 Baby Dowagiac Minnows, **$150-$250** each. The top has a perch scale Model 130 Torpedo, **$200-$225**. Top left is the very rare Model 1500 Dummy Double, **$1,500-$2,500**, and top right is the rare cup rig Model 100 in green crackleback, **$1,000-$1,500**. On each side of the box is an example of the hard to find Model 9500 Vamp Floating Spook, **$225+**. Bottom left begins with the very rare Model 9409GW, glow worm color in a Floating River Runt Spook with two-piece hardware, **$300+**, followed by two Model 8850 Salmon River Runts, **$350-$500** each, and ending with a fairly common Model 7050 5" Musky Flaptail, **$150-$250**.

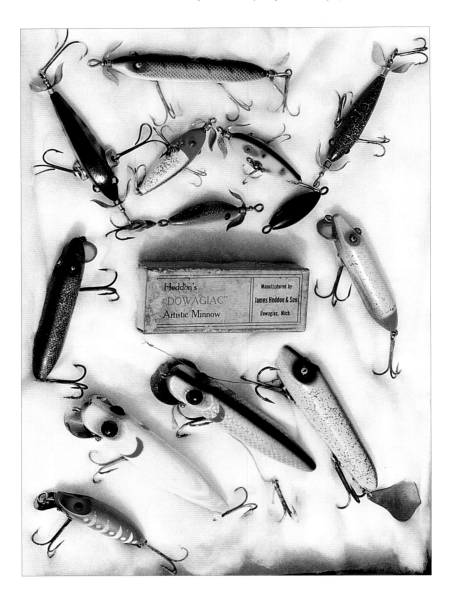

Paw Paw lures

Michigan is also home to the Paw Paw lure company, located originally in Paw Paw, Michigan, not too far from Dowagiac, home of Heddon. When I first became actively involved with trading lures with people in the NFLCC and elsewhere about 10 years ago, any lure not recognized was often said to be "a Paw Paw." Of course, this was not true but indicated something about the company. Paw Paw made many quality lures, most unmarked, that looked similar to ones by Heddon, South Bend, Shakespeare, or some other company. Thus, if a collector could not identify a lure with certainty, it became "a Paw Paw."

Paw Paw lures evolved from an earlier company known as Moonlight Bait Company of the same town. Early Moonlight lures are desirable, as are many early Paw Paw lures. Paw Paw also was a pioneer, selling plastic lures.

What has made it difficult for collectors is that Paw Paw was primarily a seller to the jobber/wholesaler market and did not produce catalogs for the public in the same numbers as did most other major companies. Paw Paw lure listings are harder to find and usually only discovered in wholesale catalogs. I am certain that my Volume 1 was the first book to ever publish any Paw Paw lure listings as to color and catalog numbers and names, at least in color.

Paw Paw eventually sold out to Shakespeare and in the mid-'70s, a few unique wooden lures were manufactured under the Paw Paw name by Shakespeare and are beautiful examples of earlier Paw Paw and Shakespeare lures. Many of these lures were made in Hong Kong and are even so marked. Many are not marked at all. During the same period, Shakespeare also produced a Heddon Super Sonic type lure made in Heddon molds called the Klatter Kat, an example of a fairly recent plastic lure nearly impossible to find.

At any rate, today the Paw Paw name is just another trademark owned by Shakespeare and no lures are produced at all under its name. The last run of lures was in the 1970s and the most collectible lures are from the Moonlight to Paw Paw transitional period with some from the mid-70s being highly sought after, too, due to the short production runs and some of the colors.

PP wooden serpentine pattern tack eyed Torpedo lure, cup hardware, 4", **$75+.** This is one of my favorite Paw Paw patterns and lures.

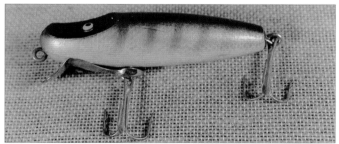

PP River type lure in wood, Model 9300, 3-1/4", **$15-$25.** There are many versions of this plug and also the Lippy Joe and Lippy Sue lures similar to a Shur Strike River Master. This one has an unmarked lip, tack eyes and is in dace.

PP Wotta-Frog wooden lure, Model 73, in yellow splatter finish with feathered trebles, 3-3/4" long, **$75+.** These lures were new in 1941 and are found with and without feathered hooks and in green splatter and yellow splatter.

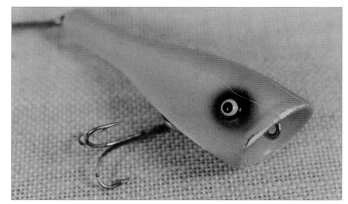

PP Plunker, wood, tack eyes, in "baby" Gantron paint colors, 3-1/8" long, **$75+** due to unusual color.

PP Gray Mouse, wood, green eye blush, unmarked lip, 2-5/8" long, **$50+.**

PP Gray/green Mouse, wood, green eye blush, unmarked lip, 2-5/8" long, **$50+.**

PP Green scale River type, Model 900, tack eye, unmarked lip, wood, 2-1/2" long, **$15-$25.**

PP Model 901 yellow perch River type, tack eye, marked lip, wood, 2-5/8" long, **$15-$25.**

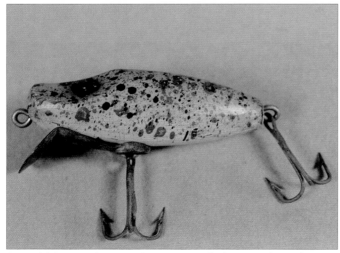

PP Model 9100 or Lippy Joe River type, wood, glass eyes, frog splatter in yellow, better color with glass eyes, 2-5/8" long (both 9100 and 6100 models were same length), **$75+.**

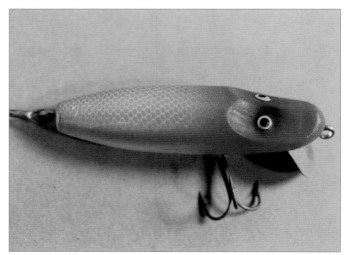

PP Model 6300, Lippy Joe River type, in silver scales with red side, tack eyes, wood, marked lip, 3-1/8" long (Model 9300 was 3-1/4" long), **$50-$75** for this color.

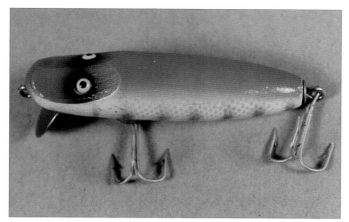

PP Model 6300, Lippy Joe River type, in red back with silver scales and vertical silver bars, tack eyes, unmarked lip, 3-1/8" long, **$50-$75** for this color.

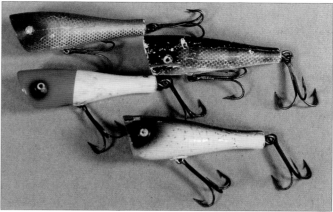

Various PP Poppers, Model 2200, wood, all with tack eyes and cup hardware, 3". Note the slight body shape differences in them. Perch was Model 2201, White/Red Head was Model 2202, Pike Scale was Model 2207 and the Silver Flitter was Model 2212 according to a 1950 catalog; **$35-$50** for most common colors.

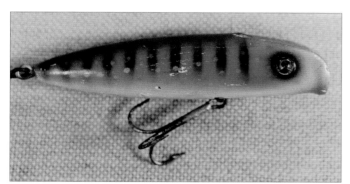

PP Groovehead Wobbler, wood, tack eyes, grooves as diving plane, cup hardware, screw tail hardware, 3-3/4", 1/8" shorter than the frog version. This has a beautiful green background with black vertical bars and small gold dots and a red diving mouth, **$75-$125.**

PP Little Jigger lure, Model 2600, color 2644, red scale, tack eyes, wood, 1-5/16" long, **$15-$25.** This lure is identical to the Jig-a-Lure, Model 2700, with a feather added, and similar to a Shakespeare Dopey lure.

PP wood Sunfish type without spinners, one belly weight, tack eyes, unmarked, white/red head (color #4), 2", **$25-$50.**

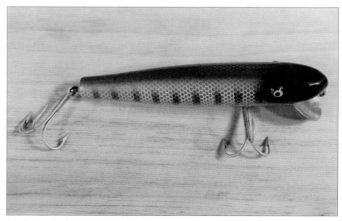

PP Green Scale Pike lure, also known as "Piky-Getum," tack eyes, unmarked lip, 4-3/8", **$25-$50.** The catalog listed it at as 4-1/2", but lengths vary a little. This is color number 3, green scale, making it Model 1003.

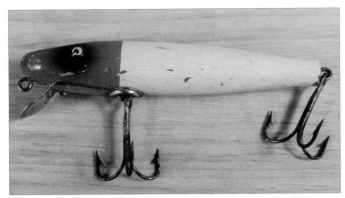

PP Model 1604 Pike lure, white with red head, tack eyes, wood, two hooks instead of three like the later Piky-Getum lures and an unmarked diving lip; listed in the 1950 catalog as 4-1/2", but this is 4-3/8", **$25-$50.** Note the lip is narrower than on Piky-Getum lures. I believe this narrower lip is from the early 1950s Model 1600s.

PP Junior Size Pike lure, Model 1401, yellow perch, tack eyes, two trebles, 3-3/4" long, catalog lists at only 3-1/4", but Paw Paw widely varied standard lure lengths, **$25-$50.**

PP Famous Pike Minnow, Model 1007, pike scale, Paw Paw marked on lip, tack eyes, three trebles, wood, 4-1/2", **$25-$50.** In 1950 this was called the Famous Pike Minnow and had grooves in its mouth; by 1960 the grooves were gone and the name changed to Piky-Getum lures. The model numbers remained the same at Model 1000.

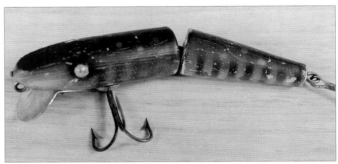

PP Model 1700 Jointed Pike, wood, tack eyes, two trebles, circa 1950, great color of green with vertical lines and gold dots, Paw Paw on lip, 4-1/2", **$25-$50.**

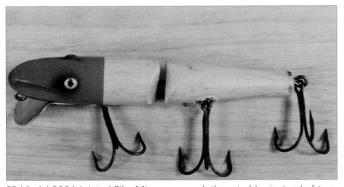

PP Model 2004 Jointed Pike Minnow, wood, three trebles instead of two as Model 1700 just shown, 4-1/2", **$25-$50.** Both lures are circa 1950 but the Model 2004 (4 is the color) has the fluted mouth, tack eyes and marked diving lip.

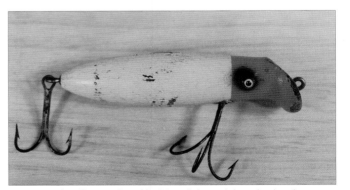

PP Bass Seeker, first produced by Moonlight and dates back at least to 1928. The lure was listed as 4" and 3-1/4", but this one and the one featured next vary from those lengths. This one is red/white and 3-7/8" long, wood, with tack eyes and only two trebles, **$75-$125.** It has a flat mouth unlike the one at top left of Page 145. Please note that this lure could also be a Best-O-Luck (South Bend's less expensive lure line) model from the '30s-40s. Its Model 943 was very similar and supposed to be 3-3/4" long. This details an issue with these companies, as we know that Paw Paw made some lures for South Bend under contract and this could be an example of either.

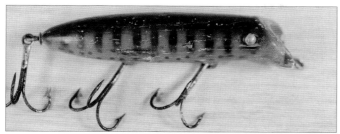

PP Bass Seeker in the same spectacular color shown earlier on a Pike lure, green with black vertical lines and gold dots, 4-1/8" long, **$75-$125.** This one has a scoop mouth, tack eyes and three trebles. It also has the line tie extension standard on these lures.

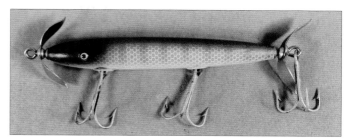

PP Aristocrat Torpedo, Model 2407, pike scale, wooden, two unmarked spinners, painted cups typical of Paw Paw lures, 4" long, **$75-$150.** The lure came in both floating (no belly weight) and sinking (belly weight) models. This is one of Paw Paw's prettiest lures in my opinion.

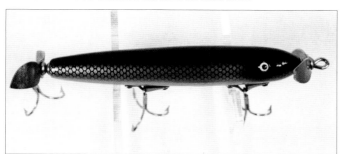

PP Torpedo (also called Slim Jim at times) in black scale, Model 2433-S (sinking), wood, tack eyes, surface hardware, one belly weight, not marked, 4" length, **$75-$150.**

Moonlight Little Wonder from 1925, Series 2100. This great looking wooden lure has painted eyes and is in red scale color with an exceptionally long wooden diving lip and one trailing treble hook mounted with simple screw hardware, 3", **$200+.** It is similar in shape to some early Silver Creek and Moonlight baits.

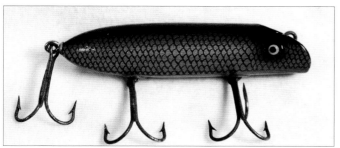

PP Old Faithful Model 4400 in copper scale, tack eyes, painted cup hardware indicating an earlier version, circa 1940s or before, **$75+.**

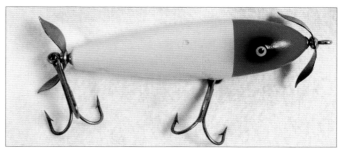

PP unmarked Surf-Oreno type, two unmarked spinners, wood, white with red head color, tack eyes, 3-3/4", **$50-$75.**

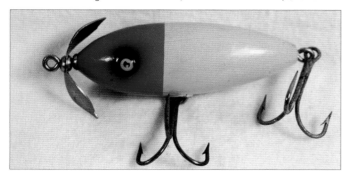

PP unmarked Surf-Oreno type, one unmarked spinner, white with red head color, wood, tack eyes, 2-3/4", **$50-$75.**

PP Model 1300 Sunfish lure, two spinners unmarked, tack eyes, one belly weight, color #4 white with red head making it Model 1304, 1-7/8" standard catalog length, **$50-$125** for better colors such as rainbow (#5) or frog (#8).

PP unmarked double spinner floating surface lure, painted eyes, yellow with black stripe and silver flitter, wood, 1-7/8" long, **$40-$60.**

PP Caster Bait. This series of lures includes numerous versions and most collectors call them all the Trout Casters even though there are many different types. This model is wood, in perch color, tack eyes, marked diving lip, 2-3/4" long, **$75-$175.** The Caster series was introduced around 1940 and also known as "Nature Baits" because they look like little fish. These baits sell very well and are highly desired by all collectors. I sold one rare color for **$227+** in 2002 in an online sale.

PP Floating Jig-a-Lure, no belly weight, painted eyes, green with silver flitter color, unmarked, 1-1/2" long, **$15-$30.**

PP Model 9300 River type, wood, tack eyes, marked gold color diving lip, color is 9307 pike scale, 3-1/8", **$25-$50.**

PP Clothes Pin Lure, Model 2300, salt-water lure, red/cream color with a silver sparkle, unmarked, made of wood, painted eyes, medium size at 2-1/2" long (large was 3-5/8"), **$20-$30.**

PP Jig-a-Lure Model 2701, regular perch color, wood, tack eyes, one belly weight, unmarked, 1-5/16", **$15-$30.** Often sold on a card with an assortment of six standard colors.

PP Midget Underwater, Torpedo type without spinners. wood, one belly weight, unmarked, red/cream with silver flitter (same color as Clothespin shown at top right), 2", **$30-$50.**

PP Model 900 Series, color 903, green/gold scale, unmarked lip, tack eyes, tack in nose, **$25-$50.**

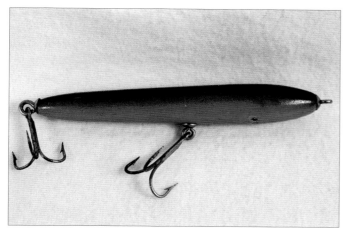

PP Pencil Plug, dark green and cream color, wood, believed to be a Paw Paw based upon hardware type, 3-3/4", **$10-$15.**

PP Grooved Plunkers. The blue/white one is 2-1/4" long and the yellow/black one with diagonal stripes is 2-1/2" long, **$10-$15** each. I believe they are Paw Paw lures based upon the hardware type and lack of detailing.

PP Old Flatside Model 1500, color 5 (rainbow), wood, tack eyes, painted cups, correct color for box, Model 1505, 3-1/8", **$50-$75.** This beautiful lure was found new in a nice Lucky Lures blue box.

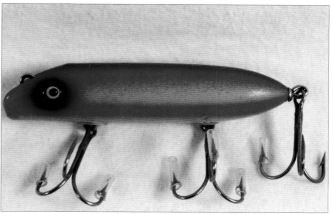

PP Old Faithful Model 4405, beautiful rainbow color in a cup hardware version of this classic Paw Paw 3-3/4" wooden bait. Three trebles, tack eyes, painted cups, **$75+** for cup versions in excellent condition.

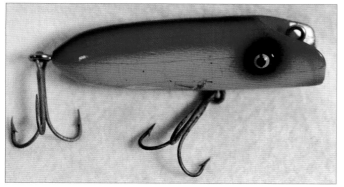

PP Old Faithful Junior, Model 4200, tack eyes, wood, rainbow color, simple screw hardware, 2-7/8" long, **$20-$40.**

PP Underwater Minnow Model 3300. This beautiful little lure was only shown in the 1939 catalog as a 2-1/2" wooden lure in cup rig. This one is 2-5/8" long and has cup hardware, one belly weight, tack eyes, unmarked props, green back with red/yellow scale sides, **$250-$400** based upon limited sales figures.

PP unmarked Jointed Pike Minnow, tack eyes in rainbow, wood, Model 1705 with only two trebles and an unmarked diving lip, 4-1/2" long, **$25-$50.**

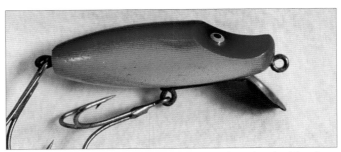

PP Lippy Joe, wooden river type, tack eyes, extra large hand-soldered hooks, rainbow color, 2-1/2", **$15-$30.**

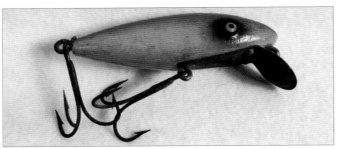

PP Model 900 type or Shur Strike type lure. This unusual green/orange/ yellow colored wooden lure has tack eyes and a Lippy Joe type lip, but it is 2-11/16" long. This may be an Arnold version, as Paw Paw bought out Arnold circa 1960 and many lures were produced by Paw Paw under old Arnold colors and shapes, **$50+.**

PP Wotta-Frog lure. This lure was listed as a standard size at 3-1/4" and a Junior at 2-1/2" in 1950, Models 73 and 72 respectively. However, this later version with surface hardware is 2-3/4", likely the Junior grew a little! So I am guessing it is Model 72, Wotta-Frog Jr., circa 1960. This one has a reversed diving lip and no feathering on trebles and is in a dark green splatter finish, **$75+.**

PP or Moonlight Plunker, unusual grooved mouth popper-type lure, wood, cup rig and tack eyes, rainbow color is similar to earlier Moonlight lures, 2-1/2" long, **$75+.**

PP Model 905 river type, 1/2 oz, wood, two trebles, tack eyes, unmarked diving lip, 2-5/8", **$20-$40,** maybe a little more for a rainbow.

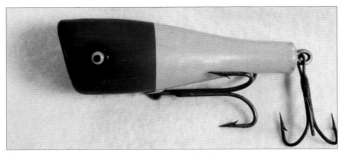

PP Model 2204 Popper, **$35-$50** for most.

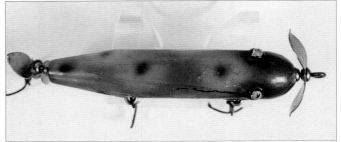

PP Old Flatside injured minnow lure in frog, wood, three trebles, larger of the two varieties of Old Flatside lures, 3-1/2" long, **$20-$40.**

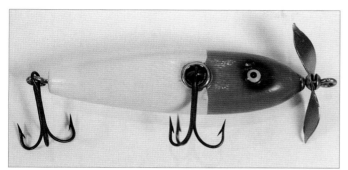

PP Old Flatside Junior injured minnow in white with red head, one spinner, tack eyes, earlier cup rig version, **$30-$50.**

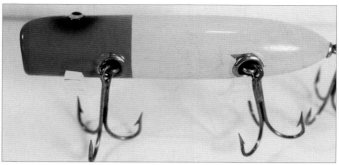

PP Old Faithful Model 4400 in white with red head, color 4304 in cup rig with tack eyes, wood, 3-3/4", **$20-$40.** Also known in Paw Paw listings as the "standard grooved head wobbler."

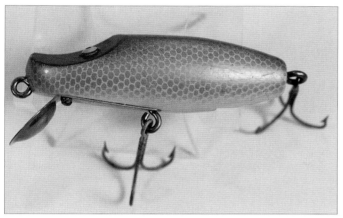

PP Lippy Joe in green scale pattern, wood, tack eye, simple diving plane attached by one screw and the belly hook hanger, **$15-$30.** Shur Strike and Arnold also used this type of hanger on some lures.

PP Flap Jack in rare Aztec pattern, has markings on belly, **$65+.**

My personal favorite Paw Paw, an absolutely mint in box 9300-J Paw Paw Series river type lure. This is one of the Allen Stripey type color variations found in Paw Paw lures. One reason it is my favorite is because I found it in an antiques shop in Pacific Grove, California, in 2002 for only $25. The box and lure are as clean as the day they left the showroom floor; **$75+** for this boxed combination in this nice color.

Old style Moonlight Mouse, wooden ears, wood lure, cloth tail, tack eyes, **$100+.**

Pflueger (Enterprise Manufacturing Company) lures

Of all of the big six, this is without doubt the oldest of the companies and one that produced many fine collectible baits from the 1800s. In addition, many of the wooden baits made from the early 1900s until the 1950s are of great interest to collectors. Also, Pflueger made early minnows of rubber in the late 1800s that are very valuable. Ultimately, Pflueger was purchased by Shakespeare and lure production was of little significance to the company after the early 1960s.

Early Pflueger Never-Fail (a hardware type) Minnows and Monarch Minnows are among the most collectible of all wooden baits. Some of the hammered metal spoons of the 1800s are worth hundreds of dollars, as are the vintage 1800s rubber minnows. The Pflueger Mustang and Pal-O-Mine lures were popular Bass and Muskie baits that are highly collectible. Also, a more recent lure named the Frug is also collectible. The photographs here show a variety of Pflueger lures desired by collectors commonly found in the field.

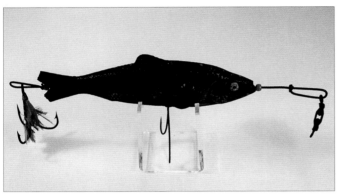

Pflueger Muskellunge Minnow from the mid-1890s. This 7" hard rubber lure is very rare and trades very high, but I found it in an antiques booth not far from a fishing tackle booth! It has gold painted eyes, hand-painted gill marks and gold scales. The two tips on the tail are normally broken off as shown here; **$2,000+** for an example in excellent to mint condition.

Pflueger underwater Never Fail Minnow, three hooks, has the "Never Fail" hardware that is like a corkscrew in holding in the cup on the sides, glass eyes, early rainbow color, **$125-$250** for Rainbow, as it is common in this lure. Some colors fetch nearly a **$1,000** and many bring **$400-$600** in excellent condition.

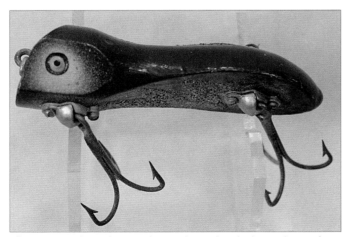

Pflueger Wizard Wiggler, wood, carved eyes, has the heavy duty surface hardware, 1/2 oz, black with silver lightning flash color, 3", **$60-$125.** Pflueger switched to carved eyes in the late 1930s.

Pflueger or folk? These two Surprise type lures are likely folk art but I thought they were interesting and looked like a Pflueger enough to show them. I bought them from an elderly lure collector in 1997 and he had them for 40-plus years, **$75+.** Maybe they were Zig-Wag and Game Fisher copy attempts that Pflueger decided they better not produce!

Pflueger Globe Copy. This lure has been found primarily in the northern Wisconsin and western Upper Peninsula of Michigan region since the 1970s. They were apparently made in the region in the 1970s after Pflueger quit making lures. It is very similar to a Globe, **$40+.**

Pflueger Card. You will find many Pflueger metal baits and spinners on cards as they made far more metal baits and spinners than wooden or plastic lures. This is a 1-5/8" Colorado Spinner on the earlier "Bulldog Card," Model 2223, Size 4-0 with a suggested selling price of 30 cents. The spinner blade itself is also marked 4/0 and Pflueger, as most of its spinners were; **$15-$25** for new on card items; spinners bring very little loose unless a rare version.

Pflueger Pilot Fly Dealer Display. This unusual find is a Model 1823 Dealer Display for a dozen Size 4 Royal Coachman Pilot Fly lures. This version of the Pilot Fly is newer as can be seen by the round plastic bead instead of the "cut" version; **$75+** regardless of lure numbers; add about **$10** per lure, so **$75-$150** is fair value for whole unit.

Pflueger Pal-O-Mine lure, beautiful Golden Shiner, surface hardware, glass eyes, marked lip, 3-1/4", **$100-$175.**

Pflueger Venese Fly, older size 4-0 bucktail fly, had its card but the staple holding it on was loose, Model No. 362, 2-3/4" long, **$25+.** This is how most fly companies packaged their flies until at least the 1960s. This is an earlier Bulldog version, circa 1940s. Flies do not trade very high as a general rule but a fly collector would pay a premium for an on a card and this would also have some appeal to a Pflueger collector.

An older Pflueger Pilot Fly, marked on prop as to size (3/0) and company (Pflueger), Royal Coachman color, nice hackle and an earlier cut bead. These little flies sell quite well and are in demand by collectors, **$20-$30.**

Pflueger Pal-O-Mine lure, Pikie Scale, surface hardware, glass eyes, marked lip, 3-1/4", **$100-$150.**

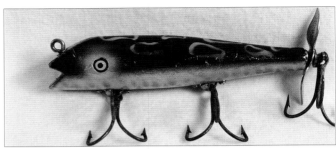

Pflueger Tantrum lure, beautiful frog pattern, carved eyes (pressed eyes), wooden, marked spinner on rear, fairly uncommon compared to Pal-O-Mine and Mustang lures from Pflueger, 3-7/8" long, **$75+.**

This is the famous Canoe Box and classic Pal-O-Mine lure in wood, No. 5073 size one Rainbow, 2-3/4", **$175-$225** for new in the box models is not unusual.

Pflueger Mustang lure, wood, marked lip, carved eyes and surface hardware, Strawberry spot with two gill marks, 4-1/4", **$40-$75.**

Pflueger Mustang lure, wood, marked Hong Kong, lip in blue mullet scale, carved eyes, surface hardware, 4-1/4", **$30-$75.**

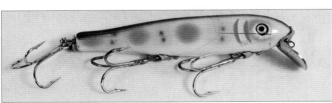

Pflueger Pal-O-Mine lure, Size Three, wood, pressed eyes, surface rig and an unmarked diving lip in perch scale, 4-1/4", **$40-$75.**

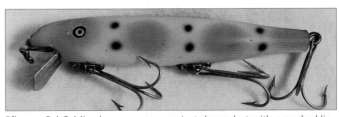

Pflueger Pal-O-Mine lure, same as one just shown but with a marked lip, strawberry spot color pattern, **$40-$75.**

Pflueger Pal-O-Mine, Size Two, wood, pressed eyes, heavier version of the surface hardware, silver flitter pattern, marked lip, 3-1/4", **$40-$75.**

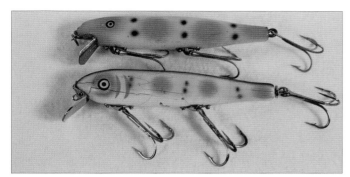

Pal-O-Mine and Mustang lures. The top lure is a 4-1/4" Size Three Pal-O-Mine in strawberry spot and the bottom lure is a 4-1/4" Mustang lure in the same color with gill marks and less yellow on the body; **$40-$75** for pressed eyes, a little less if Hong Kong and considerably more for glass-eyed versions.

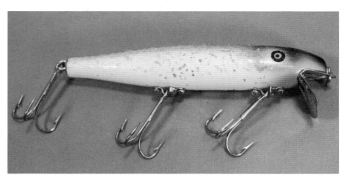

Pflueger Pal-O-Mine, surface rig, pressed eyes, silver flitter, 4-1/4", **$40-$75.**

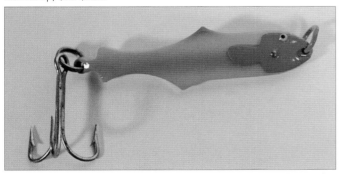

Pflueger Mustang Musky size, pressed eyes, white with red head, two metal plates are standard on this lure, three heavy hooks and hardware, marked lip, **$50-$100.**

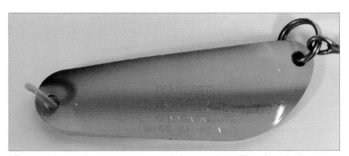

Pflueger Limper Spoon, gorgeous rainbow, paint still on line tie ring, mint, 1-11/16", **$25+** due to color/condition.

Pflueger Pippin Wobbler, shaped like a Pippin Fly Rod bait but heavier for ultra light fishing or spinning, paint still on the line tie ring, mint, fairly uncommon, 1-11/16", **$25+** due to color/condition.

Pflueger rarities: Monarch Minnow, **$500-$1,500;** three Surprises, **$400-$1,000;** and two Catalina Minnows, **$400-$700**. *Photo courtesy of Tony Zazweta*

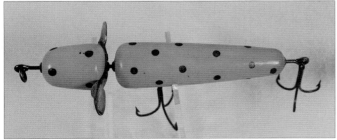

Musky Globe in common color showing details of the lure including the Bulldog trademark on the propeller, **$100+.**

Frug, a modern era collectible in Frog; note the modern trademark, **$20-$40;** more if boxed.

Shakespeare lures

Shakespeare, another Michigan company, dominated the rod, reel and lure industry for years and is still in operation with its headquarters now in South Carolina. Shakespeare is likely most famous for its reels and later its glass rods; however, they also have a long and storied past in lure production. But, by the early 1950s they concentrated on the production of the new glass rods and reels and lures were less important in its production. At one time in the early 1950s, Shakespeare was owned by CCBC and then again became independent.

Eventually, Shakespeare made some great acquisitions in buying Pflueger, Paw Paw (including Arnold) and others. Since the 1960s, Shakespeare has really only concentrated on the production of rods, reels and terminal tackle, with the brief exception of the mid-70s discussed previously under Paw Paw. However, early Rhodes Minnows and Egyptian Wobblers are just two of the most collectible Shakespeare baits, along with others shown. What the collector will most likely find in the field will be lures from the 1940s and 1950s with a good sampling of Genuine Shakespeare Swimming Mouse lures to be found. It seems the most common are the Dopey, the Grumpy, the Swimming Mouse and the Darter known as the Dalton Special (rights were owned by many companies on this lure throughout history). Occasional vintage Shakespeare lures show up but not too often.

Rare items found only in Wisconsin: Marty's Silver Streak, a silver flash Darter type jerk bait and a Marty's Mighty Mouse, a red/white wooden Shakespeare #6580 Swimming Mouse. Although you can find these more often in the northwestern region of Wisconsin, they are quite rare outside of the area and even scarce in the Eau Claire area. These are carved-eye Shakespeare lures and make a nice addition to any Shakespeare collection. The two Marty's lures were a sales promotion idea conceived by Martin Motors, an outboard motor division of National Pressure Cooker Co., of Eau Claire, Wis., in the 1950s to help him sell motors. The Swimming Mice were presented in a colorful one-piece plastic top cardboard box with a picture of a pipe-smoking "Marty" on the red and white box sides. The older Silver Streak was sold in a 2-piece cardboard box. The lures in their original boxes are scarce. Mouse in box, **$40+**; loose, **$20+**. The Silver Streak is less common and may bring up to **$70** in two-piece box.

This "Genuine Swimming Mouse" lure is the typical Shakespeare find by collectors. Shakespeare mouse lures sold very well and most of us baby boomers fished with one. This is a pressed eye wooden Tiger pattern in cup rig, appropriately marked on the belly and 2-3/4" long; **$25-$40** for the 1950s-60s versions and more than **$100** for any of the early glass-eyed slim-bodied versions. Creek Chub owned Shakespeare for a brief time in the 1950s and produced a similar mouse without markings, or marked Creek Chub. Also, Arnold Baits produced a similar one, as did Paw Paw after they purchased Arnold circa 1960. The earliest Shakespeare mice have a longer and slimmer body, glass eyes and a thicker rope tail; this lure is missing its thinner rope tail. A number of colors were available and a number of unusual older colors show up from time to time. I have a beautiful black and red one with glass eyes that must have been a limited production or a prototype, for example. The most common colors seem to be gray, black, tiger and red/white. As they are common, condition is especially important in these lures.

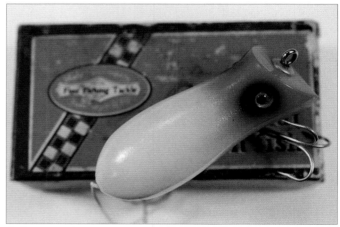

Shakespeare Glo-Lite Mouse, Model 6570, most widely known fish getter with a permanently luminous body, molded into the Tenite, 2-3/4", 5/8 oz, **$25-$40.** Shakespeare also made the Pup lure in a Glo-Lite Pup by 1951.

Shakespeare BRI Dopey; a second Dopey without a box in the same color as above, also 1-3/8", as Shakespeare lures were more standardized than the Paw Paw line, **$25-$40.** Also note it has painted eyes. Dopey lures should have one belly weight under the diving/wobble plane that serves also as the belly hook hanger. This one is unmarked but is a Shakespeare due to length and little solder addition, as well as the color.

Shakespeare Midget Spinner, Model 6601, wood, two marked props, one belly weight, cup rig hardware in silver flitter pattern, 1-3/4", **$75-$100.**

Glo-Lite Mouse Model 6570 G in early 1950s orange/blue box, **$50+.**

Shakespeare box and Dopey lure, Model 6603 BRI, black with ribs, 1-3/8", **$60-$90** for one new in box; loose Dopey lures sell for far less. Shakespeare Dopey was one of the standard wooden lures of the 1950s for this company and this box is from that period; it is newer than the two-piece orange box. Note the details to tell these from the copies made by Paw Paw: In addition to color differences, the Shakespeare Dopey had a soldered "stop" on its front hook hanger to keep the hook from fouling on the cast. This is the first thing to look for if you find an unmarked Dopey type lure, as Shakespeare failed to mark all of them.

Shakespeare Midget Surface, wood, two unmarked props but a Shakespeare pressed-eye pattern and color, simple screw hardware, red scale color, 2-1/4", **$75-$100.**

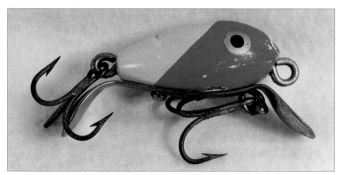

Shakespeare R/W Dopey; a third Dopey lure also in an unmarked version. Note again the soldered addition to the hook hanger, painted eyes and standard color, **$25-$40.**

Shakespeare Midget Floater, unknown model to me, two unmarked props with Shakespeare pressed eyes and a standard color for the company, silver flitter with the bars on the green back, 1-1/2" version, **$30-$50.**

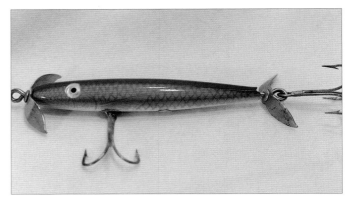

Shakespeare Slim Jim (underwater), photo finish, one belly weight, two marked props, wood, pressed eyes, 3-3/4" long; **$75-$150** for pressed-eye versions, and double to triple for glass-eyed models in excellent shape.

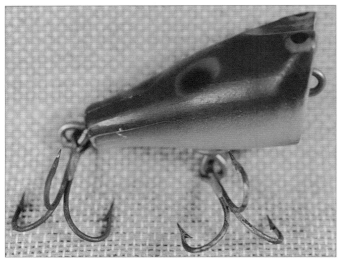

Shakespeare Pop-Eye Junior, wood, lunker or popper type, 1-7/8", **$20-$40.**

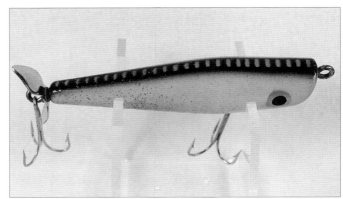

This Dalton Special was originally made in Florida; Shakespeare bought the rights or licensing rights to it, made a ton of them, and then the rights reverted back to a Florida company and are now owned by Luhr-Jensen and Sons of Hood River, Oregon. I show this early cup rig version here as it is the typical color produced also by Shakespeare in the 1940s-50s when they sold so many of them. Shakespeare made it in a 4" and a 3" version; this one is a 3", **$25-$50.**

Shakespeare Evolution, early hard rubber bait, **$500+.**

South Bend lures

The Luhr-Jensen and Sons Company of Hood River, Oregon, currently own the famous Oreno line of lures. It was previously owned by the famous line company, Gladding, and by the Glen Evans company of Idaho, famed maker of fly rod baits. The South Bend Corporation is still in existence but is primarily an importer of terminal tackle and a distributor of products made under license; however, the lure line is not owned by South Bend any longer.

The company takes its name from the original location, South Bend, Indiana. So you can see that five of the six major lure companies were located within about 100 miles of one another.

The most famous of all South Bend lures is undoubtedly the Bass-Oreno family. Millions of lures have been made and sold in this style: Bass-Orenos, Babe-Orenos, Spin-Orenos, etc. Luhr-Jensen still produces the lure for fishing. Also famous was the Nip-I-Diddee surface bait with front and rear propellers, it, too, is still in production. My favorite of all time is the Fin-Dingo made only for a short while in the 1950s after buying the rights from the Ropher Tackle Co. of Los Angeles in 1951.

Some of the early South Bend lures are very valuable and include the 3- and 5-hook minnows, the Vacuum Bait, and a variety of casting lures. Many of the Surf-Orenos are especially in demand, as are rare colors of Bass-Orenos. However, a red/white Bass-Oreno is much like a CCBC Pikie in pikie color: only of value if in mint condition. A red/white Bass-Oreno was the most common color pattern of the most common South Bend lure. However, early no-eye versions are still difficult to find in mint condition.

South Bend lures have increased in value greatly the past 10 years but still lag behind CCBC and Heddon in collector demand. I realize that it is a subjective comment, but the paint on South Bend lures does not appear to be as resilient to age as paint on Heddons and CCBC lures. However, South Bend made many beautiful lures in beautiful paint schemes and a mint South Bend is a beautiful thing to behold. But, condition is likely even more important on the more common South Bend lures than on the others due to paint issues.

Shown are a variety of South Bend lures to assist the collector in identifying finds. Again, a thorough knowledge will only be gained by studying hundreds of lures and as many reference books as possible.

This is what made South Bend rich and famous for a long time: the Model 973 RH Bass-Oreno lure in its correct box, **$50+.**

SB Minnow 999, a "classic" South Bend wooden lure with glass eyes, circa 1930, metal tail cap, brass cup hardware, belly weight 4-1/4" long, **$125-$175.** This minnow is fairly hard to find but still is found in the field by collectors. Most I have seen have fairly poor paint, as they were not apparently primed real well.

SB Bucktail Weedless lure, weighted, 1-1/2", **$50+.** I have found four of these in the past 10 years so a few must have been made.

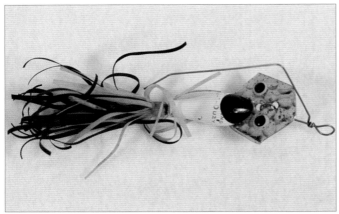

SB Spin-I-Duzy, black and white, one of many South Bend offerings for spinning and spincasting, 3/4", **$5-$10.** This is not of much value unless excellent to mint, but is still an attractive little lure.

SB Dive-Oreno Model 952 in box, perch scale, wood, cup rig with tack eyes and South Bend Dive-Oreno marked on the back, 2-1/8" long, **$40-$60.**

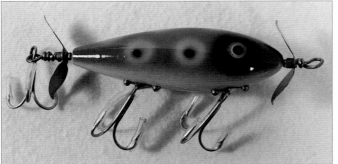

SB Surf-Oreno Model 963 F, wood, frog color, surface rig hardware, carved eyes and two props, 3-3/4" long, **$40-$75.** It comes in a nice plastic top box from the 1950s that advertise the Bass-Oreno line on the back of the box. Earlier Surf-Orenos were cup rig, some with through body hardware, and glass eyes. There is high collector demand and appeal for these lures and the prices go up accordingly. The earlier lures normally command premium prices, especially if boxed. Tack-eye models, **$60-$90**; glass-eye models, **$100-$200.** Boxes will add value and rare colors such as blue/white will bring double the values stated, such as **$400+** for some glass eyed Surf-Orenos in boxes. I think the one shown would sell for **$75** based upon others I have sold recently.

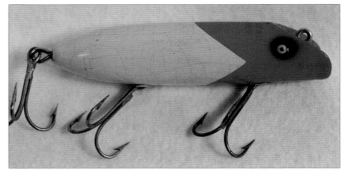

SB Bass-Oreno is the lure that supported the company for years. This one, Model 973, is wood, has a three treble hook, tack eyes, cup rig and is red head with white arrow pattern; 3-3/4", 5/8 oz; **$10-$15** for most, if truly mint; and maybe **$30-$40** if boxed. Early no-eye versions will bring far more and some over **$100.** It also came in the standard red head with white body without the pattern. Both red and white lures are common colors for the Bass-Oreno and Babe-Oreno lures. The cup rig tells us it is a bit earlier but the glass eyes with cup precede it and the cup rig with no eyes at all is the earliest version. Later versions have carved or painted eyes.

Here are some very collectible Model 953 South Bend baits called the Fish-Oreno, a Bass-Oreno type lure with a heavy metal head cup and piano wire line tie. Also shown is the original box and papers that "guaranteed" the lure to work or your money back. The photo shows some typical South Bend colors starting with rainbow in top left and going counter-clockwise to pike scale, orange with black spots, red/white, copper, copper scale with black spots and ending with a newer Gantron color. The first six are all glass eyed and the Gantron was not made until South Bend started producing carved or pressed eye lures in the early 1950s. The lure is highly sought. Many sales of **$400-$600** have been made for a complete set of lures, introductory box, papers and hang tag. The lures alone sell for **$75-$200**, depending on color. Newer pressed-eye versions would sell for **$50-$100**. I recently sold a couple in fairly rough shape for more than **$40** each.

Three nice combinations for a South Bend collector include two Sun Spot Spoons and a box, a Flash-Oreno and its box and an early Bass-Oreno box and a Model 973 white with red head glass eyed Bass-Oreno. As with most metal baits, the metal South Bend lures do not bring as much overall as the wooden ones but Sun Spot Spoons and Flash-Oreno lures are both hard to find; **$75-$125** each for boxed lures.

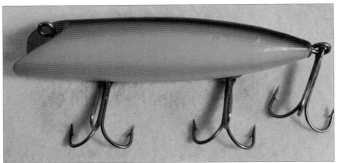

SB Bass-Oreno Model 973, earliest version of a Bass-Oreno, no eyes, wood, cup rig, rainbow color, 3-3/4" long, **$100+.**

SB Pike-Oreno, wood, marked on back, cup hardware, tack eyes, pike scale, 4-1/4", **$30-$50.** The diving plane also has leader attached for the line tie.

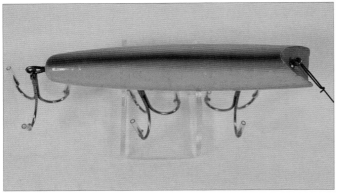

SB Troll-Oreno Model 978, wood, early no-eye version in rainbow, cup hardware, piano wire line tie, 6-1/4", **$200+.** This is one gorgeous lure and is very hard to come across in decent shape. It is catalogued as new in 1921 at 6-1/2" long.

SB Early Surf-Oreno, Model 963. A recent field find with the Bass-A-Lure shown in the Shakespeare section and one of the 150s shown in Heddon was this beautiful and early wooden 3-3/4" Surf-Oreno in "fancy green crackleback" paint. This is one of the earliest of the Surf-Oreno lures with no markings on props or the lure. It has reinforced front and rear spinner hardware, glass eyes and cup holders for the two belly trebles. The tail treble is part of the spinner mechanism, **$250+** for standard colors on these early ones with reinforced hardware and glass eyes, even more for blue head models.

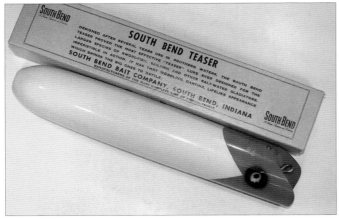

SB Teaser and box, Model 981 RW, wood, 11-1/2" long, **$200+** boxed. This is the largest of the Bass-Oreno types and was used as a "Teaser" lure in trolling for saltwater fishing for such giant prey as swordfish and sailfish.

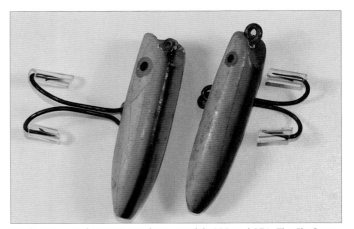

SB Fly-Oreno and Trout-Oreno lures, Models 970 and 971. The Fly-Oreno is the smallest of the Bass-Oreno wood lure line at 1", with a belly-mounted double hook; the Trout-Oreno is a bit larger at 1-3/4" length in wood and also came with a double hook. Fly rod lures have high values but not many collectors, so pricing is harder to determine as it varies so much. But the rare colors are the ones that bring the higher dollars for certain; **$20-$50** for most in excellent condition.

SB Midget (or Baby) Surf-Oreno lure and box, Model 962, tack eye, cup hardware, new in a two-piece standard orange/red box, 2-3/4" long, **$100-$150.** This is an unusual find showing the smaller size of Surf-Oreno. What makes it unusual is the "Obsolete" stamping on the lure belly. South Bend often stamped this on lures once the eye style or other designs had been changed in a lure or if it was being discontinued from the line. This likely dates from the early 1950s when carved (pressed) eyes replaced the tack eyes and surface rig replaced the cup hardware. Red/white is a common color but this is an unusual lure and is new in the box making it more valuable than most Model 962 lures.

SB Dive-Oreno and box, early 1950s color Gantron paint, carved eyes, back markings, **$75-$125** new in box, less for common colors. This is one of my favorite lure colors of all and is very attractive in my opinion. It was only made for a short time period by South Bend and on limited lures.

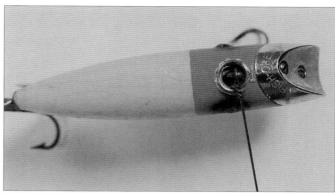

SB Babe-Oreno, Model 972, pike scale, marked back, cup hardware, earlier glass-eyed version of the 2-3/4" wooden lure, **$25-$75.**

SB Fish-Oreno Model 953, red/white, glass eyes, wood with line tie showing details, made from the 1920s into the early 1950s, 3-1/2", 5/8 oz, **$75+** for this color.

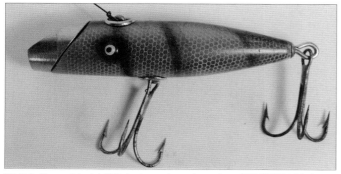

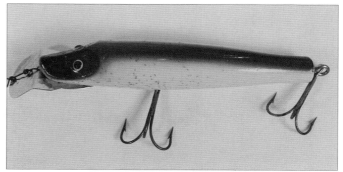

SB Fish-Oreno Model 953, tack-eyed perch version, **$75-$125.** This is newer than the red/white with glass eyes but older than the Gantron with carved eyes shown on Page 159. It likely dates from the 1940s.

SB Pike-Oreno, tack eyes, cup rig, wood, 4-1/4", **$30-$50.** This is a nice example of South Bend's version of silver flash or silver flitter paint. The green back with silver flitter is a common color for South Bend, as are perch and red/white.

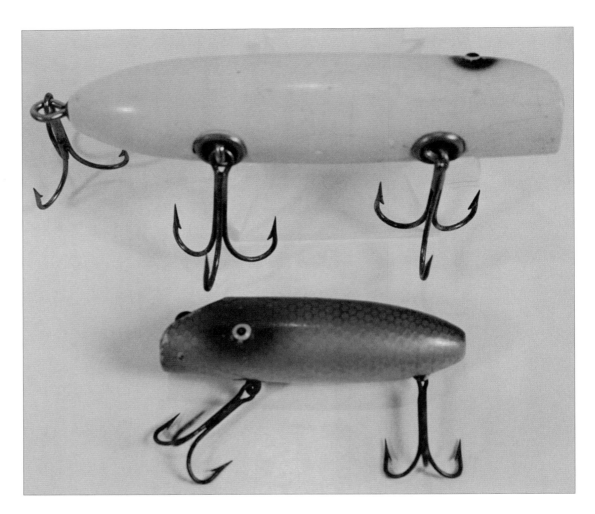

This shows a nice luminous Bass-Oreno in cup hardware at 3-3/4", compared to an early cup hardware Midge-Oreno at 2-1/4", also in wood with tack eyes; **$75+** for luminous Model 973 Bass-Oreno; **$20-$40** for Model 968 Midge-Oreno. The Midge-Oreno was new in 1932 and this example of a green scale finish in early cup rig must be an early one. The luminous is a highly desired color by collectors and worth more than most Bass-Oreno lures.

A 1950s South Bend Spin-I-Diddee lure, which Luhr-Jensen is still producing, **$20-$40.** This dates from circa 1952 onward and is one of the smaller versions of the Nip-I-Diddee designed specifically for spinning. The color is aluminum with dots and other colors added, a unique South Bend color offering. The lures had pressed eyes originally and later painted versions. It came with two props and two double hooks originally mounted with surface hardware. The Nip-I-Diddee and the Spin-I-Diddee were true South Bend success stories similar to the Bass-Oreno in sales figures for the time period of the 1950s.

SB Nip-I-Diddee Model 910 (floater), 1950s version, carved eyes, surface hardware, marked on back, in silver flitter color, wood, two double hooks, 3" long, **$20-$40** for common colors.

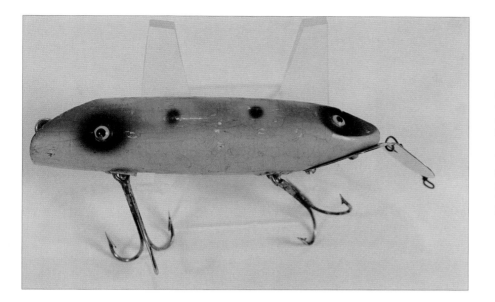

SB Two-Oreno Model 975, wood, four eyes, two line ties—one at each end designed for either diving or wobbling actions, 3-3/4", **$50-$75**. This neat plug was introduced in the 1930s and became the Two-Obite made of Tenite in 1938 and was discontinued in wood shortly thereafter. It is basically a Bass-Oreno merged with a Pike-Oreno (or Dive-Oreno) type lip and head. This one is tack eyed and has cup hardware in frog pattern.

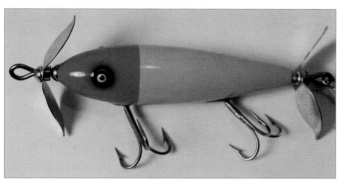

Nappanee "Ypsi" Bait, similar to an SB Nip-I-Diddee, Model 910. This earlier cup hardware version is as pretty a lure as I have seen, has tack eyes, two unmarked props, 3", **$75+**.

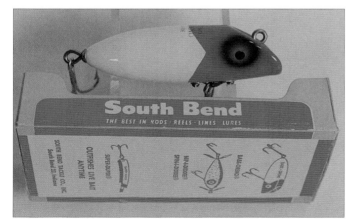

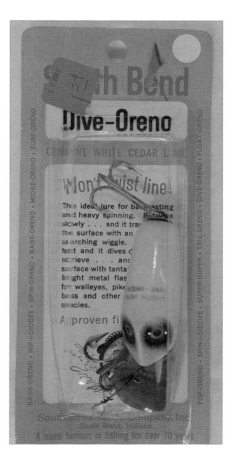

SB Dive-Oreno blister pack. This small Dive-Oreno with carved eyes was packaged in the late 1950s or early 1960s prior to being sold to Gladding in 1965, **$30+** on card. Note that the package indicated the lure was "Genuine White Cedar" and the location was still South Bend and pre-zip code. Also, the lure was simply marked "South Bend Dive-Oreno." These all help date the lure to the early 1960s period. I have found a few lures marked "White Cedar" on the bottom from the same time period.

SB Babe-Oreno Model 972 and modern box. This is the classic Babe-Oreno in wood, painted eyes, green/black blush in surface rig, 2-3/4", **$20-$40** boxed. Note that the back markings now adds "Wood Lure" to the name. This is a pre-zip code late 1950s, early 1960s box and is cardboard with a plastic top. This is the common r/w arrow pattern.

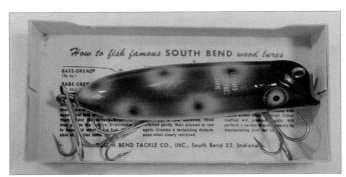

SB Babe-Oreno Model 972 RW and an earlier box, **$30-$50.** This Babe-Oreno has carved or pressed eyes and surface rig but comes in the earlier box with a plastic top; the box is full, e.g. no cut out on side. The lure also simply says "South Bend Bass-Oreno" on its back, making it earlier than the one shown on Page 163.

SB Bass-Oreno Model 973 FF, frog, lightly carved eyes (not as deep as most), surface hardware, in wood and has "Wood Lure" added to its back, 3-3/4" long, **$30-$50** boxed. This one is a transitional model with the added phrase on its back but still has lightly pressed eyes and not painted eyes. It likely dates from the late 1950s or early 1960s.

South Bend rarities, clockwise from top: Minnow 999 with glass eyes in mint condition in perch, **$200-$300** for this one; Plug-Oreno in white body with red head and glass eyes, **$350-$450**; Vacuum Bait in frog, cup rig, **$400-$750**; and an Underwater Minnow, **$300-$500**. *Photo courtesy of Tony Zazweta*

SB Nip-I-Diddee with nice two-piece box, perch scale, pressed eyes, **$40-$70.**

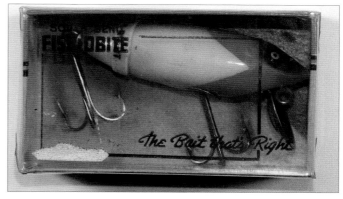

SB Pike-Oreno, silver flitter, pressed eyes, surface rig, **$30-$50.**

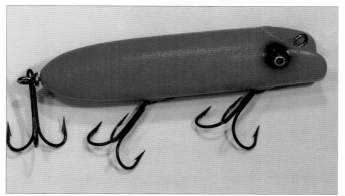

SB Gantron Bass-Oreno, tack eyes, cup hardware, early 1950s, wood, 3-3/4", **$75+** in this condition for this rare color.

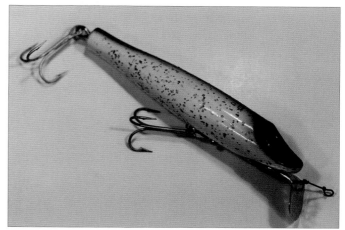

SB Fish-Obite/box. This successful Tenite lure was "insured" to catch fish similar to the Fish-Oreno. It is an early competitor of the River Runt and according to anglers using the lure it really worked! The little protruding ring on the body said "The Bait that's Right," the same as the box top. It came in a number of colors and had two hook types. They are all molded eyes and some of the early ones are Tenite 1 and disintegrate. Most are Tenite 2 and are fine. Some of the colors are hard to find and the lure is heavily collected; **$20-$40** for most colors new in the box, more for some, similar to Heddon River Runt pricing.

Rare Whirl-Oreno in RW, **$225+.**

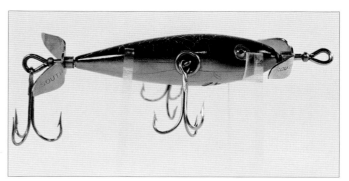

Three-hook Underwater Minnow, green crackleback, one belly weight, marked props, **$300-$500.**

Chapter 4

Fishing Rods and Reels

Reels are the second most collected fishing item and closely followed by rods, especially high-end bamboo rods. There has been relatively little written on collecting rods and reels with very few books on the market dealing with both, most covering only one type of rod or reel. My book, *Fishing Collectibles: Rods, Reels and Creels*, Krause Publications, 2005, fills this void to a large extent and you are referred to it for the most detailed book available on reels from the 1800s to the 1960s, and rods of both vintage and classic varieties. The book also covers creels, minnow buckets and other miscellaneous fishing items, some of which are also covered in this book in Chapter 5.

Due to space constraints, only a few rods and reels are shown here, in addition to the ones already shown in Chapter 3. Please refer to my other book on the subject for 2,000 color photos detailing rods, reels and other items in great detail, from the very earliest to modern items.

A shot showing some of the author's reels in his Hendryx collection remaining after the Lang's sale. Some are common (pressed steel) and the multipliers are fairly rare even for Hendryx reels. The reels are valued at **$20-$100+** for the better ones. Also shown is an early Cream City tackle box, **$20**; a large Mark Brunning trout decoy, **$175-$200**; a Bud Stewart fish decoy, **$150**; and part of the early Triner Scales from the Weber archives, **$75+**.

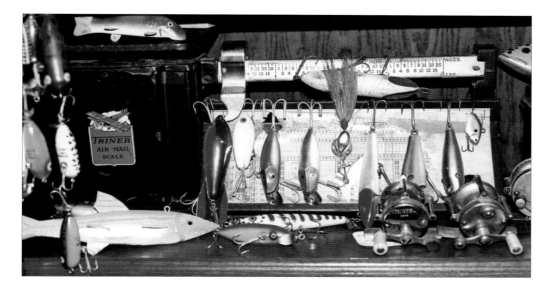

Another general shot of the author's collection of lures and reels and a better shot of the Triner Scales. The decoy on the left is a Sherman Dewey and is shown in Chapter 5 in detail. The little Rainbow lure is a rare Paw Paw 3-hooker from the 1930s, **$150+**; and the lure hanging from the balance beam is a 1908 Heddon prototype similar to Hastings lures never in production, **$500+**. A Larry Bethel lure is on scale platform and also shown later. Other lures are fairly common Heddon, CCBC, Bomber, L&S and Eger; **$20-$75+** for rainbow and Pikie.

Details of a beautiful and mint Pflueger Templar salt water reel for heavy gamefish, Model 1419 3/4 and the top of the Pflueger Protecto Reel Case it is stored in today. This is one of a few hundred reels recently purchased in a major Pflueger lure and reel collection, **$300+.**

A few reels, boxes of lures, reel parts, reels in boxes, and miscellaneous Pflueger items purchased in December 2006 from Wayne Neal who had been collecting only Pflueger items for a number of years. My thanks to Wayne for allowing me the chance to purchase his collection. The items are now all cataloged, valued and stored in containers for safe-keeping and the family can once again have dinner at the table! Most reels start at **$5-$10** each and go to **$30-$40** for the average Pflueger reels. There were a couple of early German Silver examples and some nice Supremes worth more than **$100** each.

Fishing rods

Fishing rods have become very collectible over the past 10 years with interest in them growing yearly. Bamboo rods have long been admired by collectors and bring hundreds to even thousands of dollars each, depending of course on condition, maker, age, rarity and the other factors determining value of any collectible. There are many fine texts dealing with bamboo rods and that will not be the primary focus here but the coverage will include some bamboo, steel, pack and fiberglass rods. One of the most rapidly growing areas of interest in tackle collecting is in the field of collecting glass rods from the 1940s and 1950s and many of these rods are shown.

Rods are very difficult to illustrate in their entirety and I have done my best to show close ups of the details instead of concentrating on photos of the entire rods. Remember that rods are also given a special nomenclature regarding tips and blanks, e.g. a rod with three sections and two tips (one spare or one for wet and one for dry flies) would be shown as a 3/2. Details that become important to collectors are primarily in the following areas:

Wrappings: Collectors do not want rods that have been re-wrapped as a general rule. Sometime you find one guide re-wrapped and this alone will diminish the value of the rod; however, a rod with all new wraps is not generally desired by collectors.

Guides: Again, along with re-wrapped guides, replaced guides greatly decrease the value of a rod. Of course, replaced tips are the most common ailment of a fine rod and it will decrease its value. In bamboo rods, broken tips are even more common and will hurt the resale of a rod. If the bamboo rod is a rod that originally came with two tips, the presence of at least one perfect tip is nearly mandatory for most collectors. The absence of two perfect tips will decrease the value greatly.

Ferrules: The items that hold rod blanks together are called ferrules and consist of female and male versions. These ferrules must be original and the rod blanks must fit easily into one another. The best fit creates a small "pop" when you withdraw the male ferrule from the female ferrule on a metal ferruled rod. Any rust, bending of the metal, or replacement of ferrules diminishes the rods value.

Markings: The original markings on the rod need to be clear, crisp and clean for a rod to maintain its highest collector value. Many rods were signed and numbered by their makers (bamboo and some high-end fiberglass) and most commercial rods were labeled with decals. A torn or worn decal or a stamping on the rod blank that is worn will decrease the rod's value. Mint labels will increase the value.

Handles: Rod handles are comprised of a number of signifi-

cant parts, all of which have an impact on rod value. On the butt end one may find a cap or protector that needs to be in place and unharmed. The reel seat needs to be intact and not marred. Any markings on the reel seat or the handle need to be crisp and clean. If the handle is wood or cork it must be in fine condition without mouse gnawing or other damage inflicted by the angler, such as hook scarring. Sometimes the cork has been over-varnished and this will take away from the originality of the item. The reel seat must be in perfect functional condition as well for the rod to maintain its highest value.

Blanks: All fishing rods are comprised also of "blanks" (the rod itself) upon which the above are built. Blanks must be original and original length to be of greatest value. The shortening of blanks is a common problem with bamboo rods that the average collector fails to note. Any shortening of the blanks will take away from the originality of the rod. Normally, all rod blanks are the same length on the older bamboo rods and many steel and glass rods as well. So, if you simply check this while examining a rod to purchase, it is a quick test to see if the rod is original as to length. Also, the blanks need to be in good condition without major chips, dings, dents or scars.

General conditions: This includes the fact of whether a bamboo rod has been re-varnished, over-varnished (too much varnish when re-varnished), has a "set" in the rod tip (bent tip), any "setting" in the blanks (bent blanks), if the wrappings were the correct color if re-wrapped, and a myriad of other little things. The same issues can apply to steel or glass rods and will determine the value along with age and rarity. Finally, rods were often packaged in "socks" that should be original and in fine condition (no holes, snags, tears, rot, etc.) and then the sock was inside of a tube that also needs to be in good shape. Tubes were metal, hard cardboard or even bamboo themselves in some instances. Marked tubes correct for the rod are more valuable than an unmarked tube. However, collectors should keep in mind that any new tube costs $25 or better to protect the rod so any tube should be valued.

Age/maker: The age of a rod is not nearly as important as its maker for the most part, especially high end bamboo or glass rods. However, some of the first metal rods are more valuable than the later varieties if in clean condition with company markings. For the most part, I would concentrate on the maker more than age in determining rod values.

As with lures, condition, condition, condition is important! The older or rarer an item, the less important is condition but it is still important to determine value.

Rods are not collected by as many folks as are lures and reels. However, many are interested in adding at least a few rods to their vintage lure. The best way to tell rods apart is by examining the grips, ferrule wrapping and brand data or names on the shafts. Bamboo rod experts are also able to easily tell makers by examining the wraps and/or ferrules. Also, reel seats often identify a rod maker even without other markings.

Collectible rods include both bamboo and fiberglass. There are even some metal rods of interest to collectors but as a general rule bamboo and fiberglass rods bring more money and have a greater collector following. The early Gep, Richardson, Union Hardware, Bristol and Action Rods are just a few examples of collectible metal rods. Early Shakespeare, Tru-Temper and Philipson fiberglass rods are all excellent additions to any collection. Bamboo rods are a true specialty in collecting and I would advise the buyer to beware, caveat emptor, in any dealings with others when buying bamboo rods. The value of a bamboo rod is rapidly diminished if it has been altered in any way, over-varnished, re-varnished, re-wrapped, or it has had broken tips replaced with others. I would suggest reading all of the many books available on bamboo rods prior to spending any significant funds on an addition to your collection of a fine bamboo rod. Of course, if lucky enough to find any Heddon bamboo rod or Shakespeare bamboo rod in the field for a few dollars, buy it! But be careful before spending hundreds of dollars on a bamboo addition.

Rods featured are shown based upon valuation of known recent sales or other solid data based upon my selling and buying experience and research. I have bought and sold hundreds of rods in all categories over the past 10 years and the valuation is based upon this experience. The fishing collectible market has been quite volatile the past few months and rods have been no exception to this rule with prices widely fluctuating and in general being a bit depressed. However, the better rods still command a premium and will have a following of hundreds of potential buyers online for a good rod such as a Heddon Expert, as one example (a recent auction had nearly 200 lookers). But beginning collectors need to realize that the rod market is much more specialized, and to a degree limited, compared to the market for reels, lures and miscellaneous items.

One reason for less demand for rods is lack of information on them and hopefully my earlier book and this one will at least partly remedy that problem. However, storage and display are a real challenge with rods as they should be stored vertically and that limits rod length to 7-1/2 feet for most of our modern homes. I have a nice old farm home with nearly 10-foot ceilings allowing vertical display of longer rods; however, most people cannot display an 8-foot rod properly. If you do not store a rod vertically it might set, especially bamboo rods. I have examined dozens of fine old bamboo rods found in the rafters of a ceiling or the floor joists of a home only to determine set to the tip or mid-section due to being stored flat.

Finally, please remember that rods were meant to be used and you should not be afraid to enjoy the beauty of an old rod from time to time. I doubt I would fish with a $1,000 plus Leonard or Payne but some do. However, I personally enjoy many of my glass rods and actually use a variety of them each summer to test the differences and "feel" the evolution of our glass rod history. One of my favorites is an original Tru-Temper Uni-Spin, later made by Johnson. It is fun to still catch a bass or panfish on a rod built more than 50 years ago and realize that collecting has both form and functional aspects. Actually, this is one reason 7-foot bamboo rods bring more money here in Michigan: you can still use them in the brushy stream-sides common in pursuit of our brook trout.

They also are able to be properly stored adding to collector interest. Of course, out West the 9-foot and even 10-foot rods are often used on the big waters of western rivers so the longer rods are appropriately valued more in the that region. Regardless of your reason for collecting old rods, I hope this information assists all collectors in their goals.

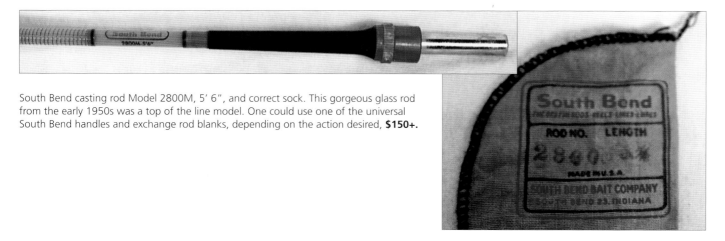

South Bend casting rod Model 2800M, 5' 6", and correct sock. This gorgeous glass rod from the early 1950s was a top of the line model. One could use one of the universal South Bend handles and exchange rod blanks, depending on the action desired, **$150+.**

Four Fenwick Examples: Fenwick Feralite glass rod, Model FF 807, 8' 2-piece rod, 3-3/4 ounce for AFTMA #7 line; Fenwick Feralite FF 755, 7-1/2' 2-piece rod, 2-1/2 ounce, AFTMA #5 line; Fenwick Feralite FL-90, Special; and, a Fenwick Woodstream (after Woodstream purchased Fenwick) with a custom wrap and a foam handle (details shown of the FF 755, FL-90 center section and the Woodstream model). Many rod makers and designers later copied the fiberglass ferules. Fenwick glass fly and spinning rods often sell for **$75-$125.** Some of these rods sold at the Lang's Discovery auction in November 2006 and averaged **$55** each.

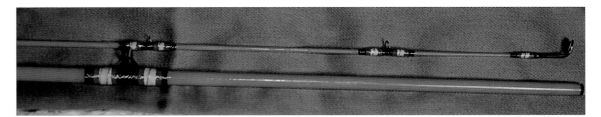

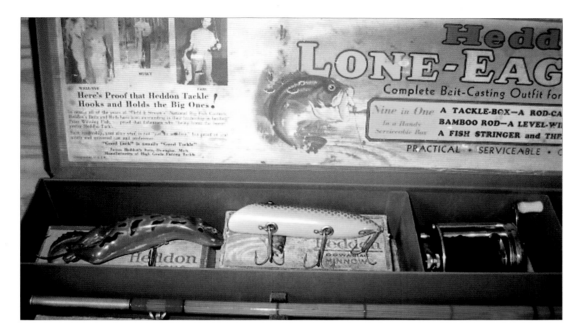

Heddon Lone-Eagle Kit. This kit was recently purchased by a friend and it included a Heddon Lone Eagle bamboo casting rod, Heddon Lone Eagle reel, a Heddon Pal-On line spool, three "choice" Heddon baits in boxes (two were older downward bass boxes) and a Heddon stringer. You simply do not find an item like this very often and it came from a very "high-end" collection, **$1,000-$1,200.**

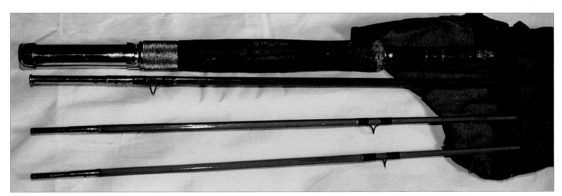

Montague Sunbeam bamboo rod in correct sock, 8-1/2' 3/2 rod, fairly common for bamboo. Montague is on the lower end of bamboo collecting for the most part. Condition is very important on these rods due to the plentiful nature of them compared to Heddon and other makers; **$250-$300.**

Orvis Bamboo Kit Rod, #6 weight, 8-1/2' 3/1 rod, called the Manistee River Rod and made in 1979 by a rod maker in Traverse City, Michigan. The tip is slightly set, very good plus condition overall and extremely tight and beautiful "popping" ferrules. It sold on Oct. 27, 2004 for **$355** online after an active 17-bid auction.

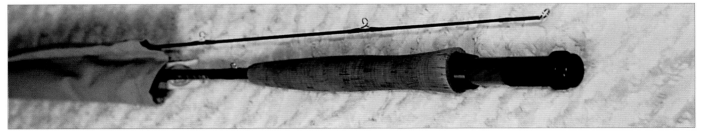

Orvis Silver Label Graphite rod, 9', #5 weight TL Mid-Flex 6.5, excellent in green Orvis carrying case/tube combination, **$75.** Sold at Lang's Discovery Auction, November 2006.

Wards Thorobred bamboo rod, correct sock and case. This nice 3/2 bamboo rod in 9-1/4' length was made by Heddon for Wards. It is unusual not in its rarity as much as being original, as often the cases and socks are gone for these rods, **$350+.**

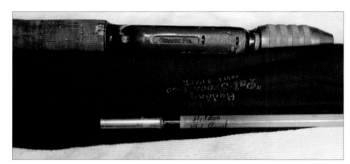

Heddon Pal Spook, #4451, 5-1/2' glass casting rod in original case, all matching a serial number, **$175+.**

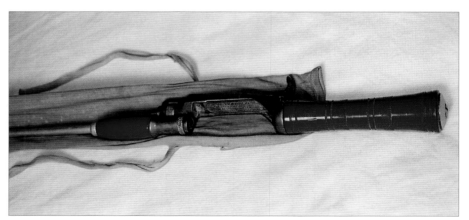

Action Rod Model 47, "Solid Steel with Bamboo Feel." The metal Action Rods by Orchard Industries were great rods and set the stage for the company's manufacturing of fine glass rods also. I purchased this example in a private sale. Some of the rods are selling for more than **$200** if pristine such as this one and collector interest for Action Rods is rapidly increasing. Sears and other stores also marketed these rods; **$150+.**

Fishing reels

Reels have been collected nearly as long, or maybe even longer, than lures by many individuals. During the fall of 2003, a major reel collection was dispersed in Kalamazoo, Mich., with many reels bringing hundreds of dollars each and some topping the four-figure number as well. The collection also contained some lures but they were only lures "picked up while buying reels." Thus, not all collectors focus on lures but many would rather collect the more substantial and mechanically operating reels.

It is no surprise to anyone that has ever held a Vom Hofe, Meek, Milam or early New York type reel in their hands. These are truly works of the jeweler's art and to operate a reel more than 100 years old that is still smooth as silk is a real joy. Another reason collectors are now turning toward reels in greater numbers is due to their availability and oftentimes lower cost than comparable lures. When I first really started to grow my collection about a decade ago, most ignored any reel unless at least 75 years old or more. You could easily buy all the 1940s-'60s reels wanted for $5 each or less. This is no longer true as collectors have learned the true value of reels and they often trade now for four to six times that price for even the common Shakespeare, Pflueger or similar models. Another new area of interest is in spinning reels, as with lures the spinning era of reels has only been discovered by most collectors since the publication of my first book in 2002. My book did not cause the interest; it was simply a reflection of a growing interest in reel collecting.

Both its appearance and working condition determine the value of a reel. This is up to each collector to judge; however, I certainly think that reels in great working order should be valued higher than those that are perfect in appearance but do not work. Missing parts lower the value of a reel, replaced cranks and screws lower the value, damaged screws lower the value, soldered foots lower the value, etc. Of course, how a reel has been cared for will determine its value as well. Collectors are far more interested in an old Meek with original patina than one cleaned inappropriately by someone. The addition of boxes, wrenches, papers, parts lists and oilers will also increase the value of a reel.

Most collectors actually prefer that you not clean a reel if it is going to be offered for sale, as the patina is often harmed by harsh chemicals or polishing. Of course, you should clean reels for your own collection in any fashion desired. However, if you find a Meek with beautiful patina it would be my personal recommendation to leave it alone. These are areas to watch for in a reel:

1. Mechanical condition: reel collectors usually use a 1-10 scale on working condition and if rated a 10, the reel should work perfectly.
2. Appearance: reel collectors also use a separate 1-10 scale to grade a reel on its appearance. A rating of 10 indicates the reel is in mint/new condition.
3. Parts: all reels are devalued if any of the parts are missing or have been replaced, this includes screws, the reel foot, line guides, jewels, end caps, level wind mechanisms, etc.
4. Wear: many reels have "boat rash" on the rims caused by bumping and rubbing in the boat or while in storage. This is part of the grading on appearance above but should always be noted when selling or buying a reel.
5. Marring: collectors greatly downgrade the condition of a reel if any of the screws have been bent, scratched or marred by attempts to remove them or during repairs. This is also true if other items on the reel are marred.
6. End-caps: end-caps, including any jewels, need to be present and original. This includes original star washers on Vom Hofe reels and similar drag accessories.
7. Reel foot: all reels have a "foot" that fits into the "seat" of a rod. Many very old reels have had the foot soldered and/or altered in some way. Many times the foot has been shortened to fit a particular real seat and this would harm the value. Also, many old small Hendryx type reels have had two small holes drilled into the reel foot to allow them to be screwed onto ice fishing rods here in the north. As a collector of early Hendryx, Vom Hofe and Montague reels, I have often been disappointed when finding a premier reel with two holes in the seat. Any soldering or alteration greatly depreciates the value of the reel.
8. Patina: this is of course not an original element of the reel and is a natural aging function of the reel interacting with the air. Original glowing patina on a 100-plus-year-old reel is beautiful and should be left alone. A nice patina will only add value to the reel. Buffed, polished and scratched reels will lose value in the eyes of most collectors.
9. Click: most reels have a "click" mechanism that functions to slow the reel down and is a replacement for a drag on some reels. Collectors normally grade a reel's click mechanism in two ways: strength of click mechanism internally while the reel is being used and ease of how the clicker itself works.
10. Rarity: of course the greatest value condition is the rarity of the reel itself and only collecting for some time will show this importance. An early Vom Hofe, Meek, Milam, Conroy and others has no comparison in value to most reels by the major lure companies of the 1900s. However, some early Shakespeare reels indeed are worth thousands of dollars and the high of sale in the 2003 Kalamazoo reel auction was actually a rare and early Shakespeare.

Reels are also usually sorted as to type of reel. Many of the early reels were little more than line retrievers that would later be emptied again onto a line Dryer (see examples later in the book) to

keep the silk line from rotting. However, eventually reels were manufactured for a specific type of fishing: trolling, casting, fly-fishing, spinning, larger salt-water versions and some interesting combination reels. Many collectors concentrate on only one type while others will collect any reel of interest. Most collectors ignored spinning reels until the past few years but the interest in them is now keen indeed. There are also rod/reel combinations that are very collectible such as the Chicago and Hurd rods.

Reels in my *Fishing Collectibles* book are shown in great detail to assist the collector in identification of unknown reels and to show the importance of small differences in even the more common company reels. Reels in this book are shown with fewer photos due to space limitations. Identification of reels is one of the greatest challenges to the collector as there has been little reliable data generally available until the recent advent of a few Internet sites that truly are invaluable to the collector. Many of the early collector books had major errors as to company information and it becomes further confusing because many companies were bought and sold a number of times, often with only minor changes in the reels being made and distributed, e.g. Hendryx to Winchester, Meek to Horton, Meisselbach to Bristol, etc.

One of the most common errors regarding the name "Pennell" with many authors is thinking it was a company while it was merely a trademark of the Edw. K. Tryon Company of Philadelphia, Pennsylvania, an early and major distributor of rods, reels, tackle and lures. The Tryon Company had many trademarks for its lures, lines and other items that were made for them by major companies. Pennell is found on reels made by many companies, including Montague and Vom Hofe.

In addition, many of the major manufacturers of early reels, such as Edward Vom Hofe, would also sell reels made by other companies and stamp their names on some reel part, such as the crank. A reel is later shown that appears to be a Montague that is marked Edward Vom Hofe. So, the company one would believe at "first blush" is the manufacturer when examining the reel is not always the maker of the reel. Many unscrupulous sellers are taking advantage of this fact online by claiming reels to be something they are not, so beware.

There are at least three related Internet sites that are indispensable to the reel collector, the best being the one owned and maintained by fellow author and reel collector Phil White at www.oldreels.com. This site is unbelievable as to the details offered the collector of reels. His sections on manufacturers, identification and common reel names are wonderful and should be examined in detail by anyone serious about fishing reel collecting. His section on identification by reel foot style is superb and will quickly help one learn a Pflueger from a Hendryx for example. Another great site is also owned and maintained by Phil White at www.oldfishingstuff.

com. This site has collectible tackle of all types giving reel history, company identification and most importantly links to other sites with reel sales data. Finally, the growth in the interest in spinning reels will only increase partly due to the wonderful site now available to all at http://www.oldfishingstuff.com/spinreel_report.htm. This is part of Phil White's site but is furnished generously by collector Ben Wright, an early and major collector of spinning reels. He has compiled sales data from online sales that is very detailed and complete for spinning reels, and some others as well.

Phil has also included major links to other sites of interest including the club known as Old Reel Collectors Association, ORCA for short. ORCA is the one club dedicated to the furtherance of knowledge and collecting of reels and should be joined if interested in maintaining current information about the field of reel collecting in America. Of course, the NFLCC (National Fishing Lure Collectors Club) also has a site and is dedicated to reel collecting as a part of its interest in lure collecting and history. There are also sites dedicated to European reels and collectors, early spinning reels, particular brand names and more. A simple "virtual trip" to www.oldreels.com will keep you busy for days reading and sampling reel collecting around the world. Phil was one of the first serious reel collectors that I was lucky enough to meet early in my reel collecting and I cannot thank him enough for his willingness to share information at shows and now online. This resource is just too good to miss!

Not all reels are identifiable at this time. Many of the earliest brass reels are very similar and some may be English and not American. Early ones with horn, bone and ivory crank knobs are beautiful and likely date from the mid-1800s. However, it is not always possible to identify them with precision. Two early types were the Terry reels and the Kopf patented foot reels (see Lang's sales photos in Chapter 3). But, we are still learning about this period and I am sure more information will come forward to help us better identify these beautiful little reels. The fact of not knowing the exact maker does not detract from the value of these early reels.

One of the first major reel makers in America was the Hendryx company, which also made early metal lures that make a fine addition to the reel collection. Hendryx made bird cages and other metal objects as well in the later half of the 1800s and started producing reels after receiving an 1886 patent. An advertisement appearing in 1900 claimed that the company had already sold 2,000,000 reels in 18 years. This would indicate that major production began in 1887 or 1888. Most of the early Hendryx reels were "line gatherers" and not reels as we would think of them today. However, they also produced early fly reels and multipliers. The stamped metal reels without a click are very common but the multipliers and any of the hard rubber reels are scarce. It is not unusual for the first raised pillar reel in any collection to be a Hendryx made reel.

Montague is also a common reel and one often found. However, as with the Hendryx reels, the better Montague reels are far scarcer and have truly skyrocketed in value recently. The hard rubber/German silver fly reels are as beautiful as any and no longer sell for $30 to $50 as was common five years ago. Montague also jobbed reels through many sources and many are marked Pennell that were sold by Tryon. They also furnished reels to many other jobbers and wholesalers and also some major reel makers.

Pflueger, The Enterprise Manufacturing Company, was the major player in reel production from the early 1900s until being merged with Shakespeare in 1960. Shakespeare was Pflueger's major competitor in the 1920s-1950s and the merger of the two companies brought one era to an end. Many early Pflueger reels are not marked except as to yardage on the foot. Pflueger also used the trade name of "Portage" on many of its early raised pillar reels. They also used the name "Four Brothers" on early reels.

The invention of the Pflueger Supreme was a landmark in reel making history and the reel made the company both famous and financially sound for many years. There are many evolutionary stages to the Supreme and you will find numerous variations in the field.

The early Supremes were selling for over $25 in the 1930s making them rather expensive then and harder to find today. Pflueger produced many reel types and models with the Summit, Nobby, and Akron being just a few. The Summit is actually one of the prettiest of all baitcasting reels with its decorative stamping on the plates.

Other significant contributors to reel history include the

famed Kentucky Reel Types made by Meek, Milam, Horton and others and the early New York style reels with ball handles by Conroy and others. Carlton was in business only a few years but made beautiful reels also in New York. The Meisselbach company history has been thoroughly researched and documented by Phil White in his book on the company and the reels are in great demand today.

Spinning reels became important beginning in the 1940s as I have documented in *Modern Fishing Lure Collectibles*, Volume 1, and elsewhere. Returning service personnel brought home early spinning reels and rods and lures from the European Campaign and the rest is history. Airex was our first major producer of spinning reels with the Bache-Brown reels that were soon thereafter purchased by Lionel, the toy train giant. Garcia Mitchell reels were one of the first major European invasions and eventually won the contest for gaining ground with American anglers with the Model 300 becoming one of the most popular reels in history. Other significant European reels included the Swiss contribution of the Record and the Abu Cardinal of later years.

The post-war era of the 1950s saw the eventual introduction of many Japanese baitcasting, fly and spinning reels. The other significant historical event of the 1950s was the popularity of the Abu Ambassadeur reels when introduced to America. These reels are beautiful, superbly made, easy to use, and still in demand for fishing as well as collecting. The Model 5000 set the stage for many others to come and this author still recalls studying catalogs in the 1950s dreaming of one day owning an Abu Ambassadeur 5000!

This nostalgia contributes to all collecting interests and it, along with the quality of these reels, has driven the prices to unheard of levels in recent years. Many Ambassadeur reels command $200 plus and the presentation models in the wooden boxes sell for thousands of dollars. Hi Speed models also usually command a premium, as do models with unusual crank configurations or other special features.

The foregoing is not a "history" of reels as much as a highlight of a few of the big "players" in reel manufacturing. As to history, many sources are available but still one of the best is a simple book on antique fishing tackle advertising called *Great Tackle Advertisements: 1874-1955* compiled by and copyrighted by Larry M. Smith in 1990. In this one source collectors are able to find early advertisements for Hendryx, Meisselbach, Carlton, Cozzone, Yawman & Erbe, Heddon, South Bend, Pflueger, Shakespeare, Montague and many other classic reel makers.

Disappointedly, the book ends in 1955 as it was written before many collectors were concentrating on the 1940-1985 era as is now the case. However, it is an excellent source of historical data nicely compiled in one volume.

Pflueger Medalist Model 1495 fly reel, **$42.**

In general, the earliest reels were the solid brass reels as shown under Kopf followed by the raised pillar style made popular by Hendryx, Pflueger and others. The hard rubber side plates are from the later 1800s and early 1900s. The Kentucky-style reels date to the mid-1800s as do the New York-style ball handled reels. However, most of these reels are really from Horton and Montague and other companies after the 1920s. The modern level-wind was a concept dating back to the early 1900s with the South Bend type being one of the first and the Pflueger Supreme also being very early. Most of the reels found in collections of the more modern baitcasting type date from the 1930s-1950s for the most part. Spinning and Spin-Cast reels date from 1947 and about 1950 respectfully. Zebco was actually a very early manufacturer of closed face spinning reels (Spin-Cast), as was Shakespeare. The European reels such as the Mitchell and Record started showing up in large numbers in the early 1950s. The Ambassadeurs became major competitors with Pflueger and Shakespeare baitcasting reels in the mid-1950s and beyond. Japanese reels started appearing in the early 1950s in America and became very common by the late 1950s and during the 1960s. This should give you a little sense of reel evolution.

As with lures, reels in their original boxes increase the value of the item. Most reels were packed into a two-piece cardboard box with a cloth bag or sock, a tube of reel oil, some paperwork explaining the reel, often a separate paper "parts list," sometimes a list of repair stations, maybe an extra pawl or crank or line guide, and often a screwdriver designed to repair the reel. The presence of any or all of these items increases the collectibility (and value) of the reel. The two-piece boxes became one-piece fold over boxes in the 1960s for many reels but the presence of the box is still important.

One nice aspect of reel collecting is the ease of displaying reels. The older boxes are often used as stands for the reels and many reels can be displayed in a small area. Also, they are ideal for shadow box displays.

Regardless of your interest in reel collecting at least a few truly add to the beauty of a lure collection and a collection of just reels is stunning, indeed. I enjoy all of my reels as they are fun to examine periodically and I enjoy seeing them function. Also, they have a far less chance of deteriorating than a wooden lure with fragile paint from 90 to 100 years ago.

Recent reel sales data

In addition to the few sales shown below and all of the reels shown in Chapter 3, you should consult *Lawson's Price Guide To Old Fishing Reels*, 3rd edition, 2001, Monterey Bay Publishing, and Lang's auction sales records of recent reel sales, along with the other sources mentioned, to get a complete picture of the variety of pricing for reels. The reality is that most common baitcasters still only bring $5 to $10 each at shows and double that if boxed. Some will indeed bring $20, $30 to $40 if boxed. It takes a special baitcasting reel from one of the major companies to start pushing up values. Not always an early one as the Bronson Invader selling for $300 to $500 proves, but the early ones in general do a little better if in excellent condition.

Most of the raised pillar reels start at about $20 and level off around $60 unless special. The hard rubber/German silver or hard rubber/nickeled silver reels will command more than $100 and often up to $300 or more depending on type and maker. The Meeks will easily bring from $300 to $2,000 for many models and the Vom Hofe reels sell for $100 to four figures depending on the reels. The Heddon German silver models do as well as comparable Meeks. Areas to watch include the increasing prices of spinning reels as more collectors venture into this area of collecting and some of the sleepers as to values such as the automatic fly reels that actually date back to the 1800s in some instances. Also watch for any Bakelite reels in excellent shape as they are generally undervalued at this time. The sales data from Lang's in November 2006 confirmed these prices.

Champion Sports Equipment Co. "Fly-Champ" fly reel with ratchet retrieve handle, built in clicker, **$48.**

Lou Myer Flo-Line Reel new in box, very unusual reel from Wisconsin, **$75** new in box.

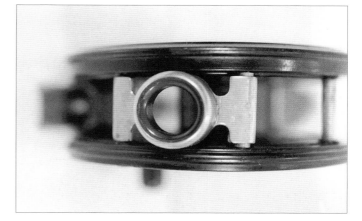

Meisselbach Symploreel Model 972 with agate guide, sold online for **$88.84.**

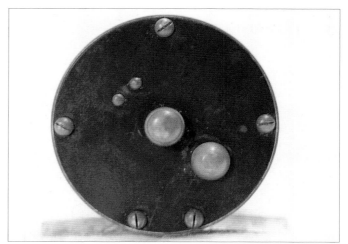

Early hard rubber side plates 40 yard Montague fly reel, double click mechanism, foot marked as to yards only, single counter-balanced crank, all screws perfect and no major problems with side plates, **$225+.**

Chapter 5

Miscellaneous Fishing Collectibles

The most common miscellaneous fishing collectible is likely the creel, closely followed by more and more interest being shown for minnow buckets and traps. Also of interest are such items as sinkers, bobbers, floats, line spools, line dryers, old tools and tackle boxes. Some of these items are worth hundreds of dollars while most of the more common items are worth only a few dollars. This chapter highlights some of the more common and collectible items you may find in the field while hunting for sporting collectibles.

Creels

Creels are another example of a crossover collectible, with many home decorators and basket collectors competing for fishing creels or baskets. Creels have been made of various materials but the two most common are rattan and willow, either split or whole. Here in Michigan we also encounter Native American fish baskets made of birch bark. There are specialty books on creels available and I would recommend anyone specializing in creels to purchase any and all available. Likely the best source for pricing creels is to follow the Lang's auctions and get the actual sales prices for creels sold at auction. Known brands such as Lawrence, Macmonies, Simeonov and Turtle often command $1,500 or more if in excellent condition. A Simeonov from 1930 sold for $3,050. Turtles hover around $500 and many Lawrence creels bring $1,500 plus, with recent sales exceeding $2,000 each.

Most fish baskets or creels were first designed for trout fishing, or at least for stream fishing. You could simply place the creel over your shoulder and then have an instant carrying device for the fish until they hit the frying pan. Thus, many creels will still have their "shoulder harness" on them and that should

increase the value overall. Nearly any creel will sell for over $50 and some of the great leather adorned brand name creels command easily over $1,500 and better in many sales. This is a huge variation so how do you tell? Well, most creels came to America from Japan or British Hong Kong. Some were imported from France. Many were leathered after coming to America. Artisans specializing in creel making in America handcrafted some. And, quite a few are American made by either local individuals or Native Americans. The name brand creels are the ones with the most value and these are normally marked in some way. Japanese creels are at the low end and most British Hong Kong creels are moderately priced due to the added leather. French weave creels are a little more. Native made creels vary widely in pricing. Most of the creels that I have owned and sold (50+) have sold for between $75 to $125, with a couple of exceptional versions bringing more than $200. I have never owned a "named" creel and have never sold a creel for over $200, but know many better creels easily reach the four-figure mark.

Some general things to note are that when the hole (through which to drop the trout) is in the center of the lid, it is normally an older creel. Creels came in a number of shapes and sizes and some were even made for children. Repairs made to the creel will harm its value, whether it is repaired caning or new leather hinges. Many fraudulent creels exist on the market, so beware! This is one area where caveat emptor is extra important. It takes little to "age" a creel and many unscrupulous sellers have done just that so be careful and buy only from a reputable dealer. Many creels made in the 1960s are indeed collectible but you need to understand that creels were still available in the 1970s from Cabela's and other wholesalers that were not much different from earlier versions of creels.

As to value, I think they should start at $50 and go up from there. I sell most of the Hong Kong creels with leather trim and a harness for $150+; $125+ without the harness. Creels have not gone up much in the last 10 years because they were already fairly high priced often bringing $100+ at a farm auction as early as 1995. I sold two Japanese creels at auction last year and they each sold for $125+.

Large whole reed creel with carved wooden peg lid latch, center hole and leather hinges, heavy weaving on the bottom, harness with it is not original. This is in excellent condition and fairly unique. I paid **$200** for this in 1997.

British Hong Kong whole willow and leather trimmed creel, 9" across the top, back of the leather has ruled markings for measuring the trout; tooled harness is not original with creel; **$225+.**

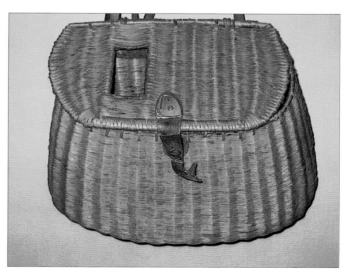

Small British Hong Kong whole willow and leather trimmed creel shown with some other fly fishing collectibles, 7", **$200+**; **$10-$50** for other items.

Nice Japanese split willow with fish latch in excellent condition, **$200+.**

Small British Hong Kong wicker construction with leather trim creel in excellent condition, 7", **$150+.**

My favorite Japanese-type creel with the fish-shaped leather hinge. Most of these hinges are found with the "tail" below the metal clasp broken off or torn. This is a wicker creel with hole on side and all leather is original with only minor edge wear on the side of the top, **$150+.**

A second wicker Japanese fish hinge creel, tail broken, harness may be original to creel, creel is actually a little nicer than the previous one shown, except for the tail being gone; **$150+.**

Wicker creel with leather latch strap, stamped metal base on strap, side hole variety, leather hinged, rough shape on lid, harness likely is not original to creel, origin most likely is Japanese, **$75-$125.**

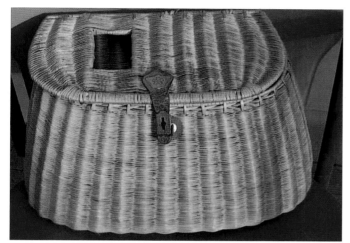

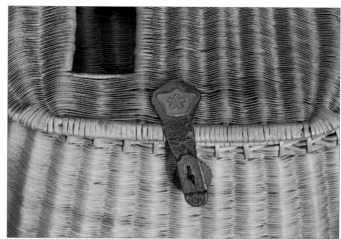

Split willow Japanese creel with same latch type as previous creel, dates from the 1940s or 1950s, excellent condition, **$150+.**

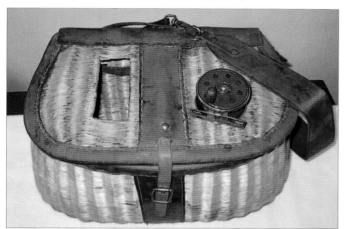

Split willow Japanese creel with nice tight weave split willow and leather trim, long type of side hole, simple latch, wide leather harness is not original to creel. Also shown is a rare little 2-1/2" fly reel made in 1884 in England out of Ebonite; reel, **$300+**; creel, **$250+.**

Another finely made Japanese split willow creel with older leather harness and a beautiful fish latch, has a small leather rosette under the fish hinge that surrounds the latch mechanism, **$225+.**

Green-tinted Japanese split willow creel with a simple latch, side hole, and nice leather trim—often this trim was added in America; **$300+.**

Lawrence-made creel dated 8-11-99 with a nice bird pattern, full leather top, front fly wallet pocket, and 12" rule sewn in at back of top; similar to the Hong Kong creels above, only this one is hand crafted and beautiful; **$1,500.**

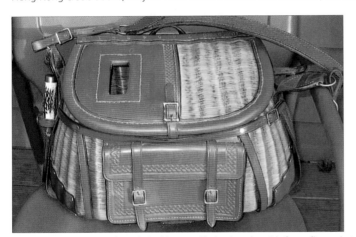 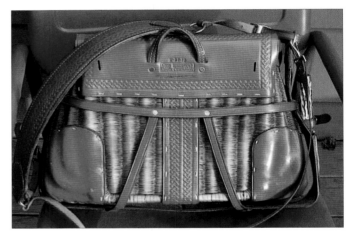

W. C. Lawrence III creel made in his grandfather's style with front fly pocket, side knife holder, half-leather top, stamping on harness, beautiful split willow weaving, **$1,500.**

W. C. Lawrence III creel made in grandfather's style in 1999. This one has a tooled leather top (about 60 percent), a side knife holder, an intricate narrow leather harness system and beautiful leather trimming all around, **$1,500.**

Creel made by great-grandson of George Lawrence using the original tooling and techniques developed by his grandfather, **$1,500.** Original Lawrence's are selling for **$1,500-$2,200** at this time.

Simple wicker creel with peg and leather latch system, braided hinges, wooden framed top, nicely made, **$150+.**

Beautiful splint creel with reed interweave design on top, bottom and middle, interesting shape with concave back, half-round front, **$400-$600.**

Huge whole reed creel atop of a center-hole boat/canoe creel with legs. The creel has an intricate weave pattern front/center and a hanging loop on the rear. The bottom of the creel is reinforced with a double reed weave pattern and the top has a decorative weave pattern as well. The latch is a wooden peg into a braided reed. The leather boat strap is similar to one that just appeared in Lang's auction as well and may be original to these creels. Creel, **$400+**; boat/canoe creel, **$200+**.

Contemporary Native American child's creel, **$100+.**

Whole reed child's creel with intricate woven front and handle, **$200+.**

Buckets, traps and boxes

This section covers the growing area of collecting minnow buckets, minnow traps, bait boxes and tackle boxes. Most of these items in the past were seen as $5 to $10 items at auctions and garage sales. Actually, many of the tackle boxes found are not even worth that due to weight and difficulty of shipping. However, many early boxes are collectible and the field of minnow bucket collecting is rapidly coming of age as well. Minnow traps have been long valued and I cannot remember an Orvis selling for less than $100 in the past ten years. Traps by Shakespeare and others will command hundreds of dollars. Other interesting containers include cricket cages and many other types of bait containers now being collected.

There is no "standard reference" at this time to these items and maybe this chapter will serve as a benchmark for collectors interested in these more functional aspects of fishing. One thing is certain: the days of the $5 minnow bucket or cricket cage are rapidly dwindling as folks recognize the value of these items. But keep in mind that not all tackle boxes are worth collecting and sometimes the best value is found in keeping them for storage and not posterity. Yet, a good UMCO, Kennedy, Heddon, Outing, Falls City, Union or Shakespeare box is certainly something with intrinsic value worth collecting.

Minnow buckets, traps and bait containers

Not all anglers use lures and baits; many use live minnows for their prey. Numerous inventions have come along over the years to trap minnows and then to keep them alive after being trapped. This is a growing area of interest to collectors and little has been written on the subject. It is with great thanks to Terry McBurney of Ada, Michigan, for his generous contribution of photos for many of the buckets shown.

In addition to minnow traps and buckets, live bait was also contained in any number of interesting bait boxes and contraptions and a few of those are also shown. Again, little has been written on these items and they all used to trade for $5 to $10 each, but as we learn more, the older and more unusual ones are commanding the value they deserve.

Clipper heated minnow bucket, made by E. L. Walstedt & Co., Minneapolis, Minn., **$100+.**

River model bait box details, **$25-$35.**

Grouping of minnow buckets showing The Clipper and a Lucky Floater, Green River, Stay Alive, Flambeau and Falls City. Also shown is a small river model minnow bucket and three common bait boxes; buckets, **$30-$150** each; boxes, **$10+** each.

Frabills "Long-Life" with star air hole design and unmarked galvanized bucket with minnow air hole mechanism installed, **$20+** each.

Small unmarked river model minnow bucket, **$25+.**

Very old and rare William Shinners minnow keeper and newer Frabills minnow bucket. The "Hartford Minnow Float" is not often traded, but when it is, it brings **$800-$900** if it has the original plated-brass nameplate with the Wm. Shinners name and the Dec. 19, 1905 patent date. Frabills is **$20.**

Common Orvis minnow trap, about 13" long; I sold one at a farm auction in 2002 for **$125,** and the usual range is **$100-$150**.

Interesting shaped small minnow trap, **$200+.**

Air-Fed Floating Minnow Bucket, Air-Fed Mfg. and Stamping Co., Quincy, IL, **$50-$100.** The angler would pump up the air chamber with the attached brass pump that would then automatically feed a bubbling supply of air into the water, keeping the minnows fresh and lively. It was offered in two sizes, 8-quart and 10-quart, and was available during the 1920s through the 1930s. *Ken Irwin Collection; Terry McBurney photo*

"Jones" 12-quart Aquarium minnow pail, **$175.** Deschler's "Jones" Aquarium minnow pails came in two sizes: 8-quart and 12-quart. The main difference between the two was that the 12-quart version had a recessed outside lid that you could put ice on to keep the water cool. *Terry McBurney photo*

McConnell Minni-Sacs, McConnell Mfg. Co., Cambridge, Ohio, **$50** each. These were collapsible bait containers that came in three sizes: 1-1/2-quart, 3-quart and 8-quart. The lower half was made of canvas material and the upper half was mesh netting with a "duffel-style" drawstring. They were made during the 1940s. *Terry McBurney photo*

Allred "10-quart Special" oval minnow bucket, Indianapolis, Ind., **$50-$100.** This is an early heavy-duty galvanized non-floating minnow bucket with a simple black stencil and a brazed-on oval company logo. It was probably made in the 1910s or early 1920s. *Terry McBurney photo*

Shakespeare #7785 5-gallon "Stay Alive" minnow bucket, Kalamazoo, Mich., **$100-$150.** The 5-gallon size of the Stay Alive minnow bucket (7-1/2" h x 17" in diameter and 12 pounds) was introduced in the mid-1930s primarily to transport small fish.
Bob Rogers Collection; Terry McBurney photo

Falls City #608 "Submarine" 8-quart Round Floating Minnow Bucket, Louisville, Ky., **$75-$100.** This unique style was a one-piece galvanized floater. The dome-shaped perforated top had an air chamber attached to the bottom side of the lid. The float allowed the bucket to ride just submerged under the water's surface and water would circulate through the perforated holes. This rare style was made in two sizes, 8-quart and 10-quart. It was relatively short-lived, being made for about five years in the early 1930s. Value is based on the condition of the bucket and the condition of the green and gold Falls City "fish" transfer.
Blane Bollaert Collection; Terry McBurney photo

Nicely embossed Old Pal bait box, **$20+.**

Lucky Floater Minnow Bucket by the Lucky Floater Company, Chicago, Ill., **$70+.** This bright green 10-1/2" h bucket has an unusual shape, with a narrow 7" diameter base section and a wider 9" diameter top section, which floated the bucket.
Jane Fladung Collection

Very old bait box, Old Pal with a Hendryx raised pillar reel; box, **$35+;** reel, **$75+.**

Tackle boxes

Most tackle boxes are not collectible but many are of some value and a few are collectible indeed. UMCO boxes are a superior product and have gained a great collector following. Many of the early metal boxes made by Heddon, Shakespeare, Falls City, Kennedy and others also have value. Early boxes by Vom Hofe are very valuable. However, most of the tackle boxes from the 1960s and newer are merely anchors to the average collector, e.g. weighing them down. One real problem with tackle box collecting is the shipping; due to weight it is very costly to ship a box. Another issue is to display them: they are large and demand a lot of space. Of course, the ideal situation is to collect lures and reels and fill the tackle boxes with the collection!

They simply do not come much nicer than this Tronick Tackler wooden tackle box. Note the reinforced corners and beautiful brass hardware everywhere. The box is full of Wisconsin lures including some Worth and a couple of Musky Lunch lures, among many others; **$250+**, with one recent sale exceeding **$500**.

Beautiful Musky fishing box made by Ron Kommer. Ron sold me this and all of the drawers are divided with a light brass material and it's even large enough to sit upon while fishing, if needed; **$200+.**

Early Shakespeare tackle box with japanned interior. **$50+.** This was my find of finds for tackle boxes due to its contents that included a Rhode's Frog, new in cardboard box, that sold at Lang's a few years back for **$4,000**, and a few other pretty good baits.

Early Climax tackle box by Horrocks-Ibbotson, outside is repainted but inside is original and it still has the nice decal, **$50+.**

Union Hardware tackle box, all original with key, **$75+.**

Non-descript "Pocket Tackle Box," not real valuable but a cute little multi-compartment box ideal for fly-fishing with poppers, **$5.**

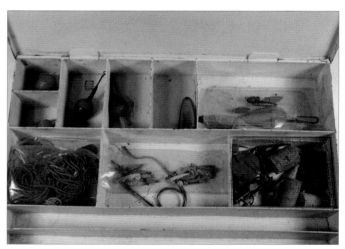

A very early Japanned tackle box with multiple layers, believed to be a Vom Hofe or Mills, japanned black exterior with gold trim and letters of angler on box, some of the contents shown. This is the box in which I found one Julius Vom Hofe reel and another unmarked hard rubber fly reel. This also had many early Archer baits and other items from the late 1800s and early 1900s. Box, **$200+**; contents vary widely from a few dollars to maybe **$50** for the "priest."

Heddon cantilever box, two trays, **$50+.**

Saltwater box made on the Pacific Coast circa 1950s, **$75-$100.**

Nicely made unmarked large wooden tackle box with lure tray and nice brass hardware, **$150-$200.**

Small wooden tackle box with brass corners and hardware, 9" long, 5" wide and 3" h, **$75-$125.**

Chetek Tackle Box from Chetek, Wis. These are very collectible boxes as this boat and tackle company made them and the wood has such a mellow tone from rubbing it with cranberry oils, **$250-$350.**

Shallow aluminum bi-color box, has plastic lure insert, unmarked, about 4" deep, **$10-$20.**

Ted Williams Model 34454 3-tray tackle box with brass hardware, top tray has polyurethane foam for placing small lures and flies, made only for Sears, 14" x 7" x 7-1/2", **$75+.**

Meadow Brook old metal tackle box likely made by Union Hardware for Sears Roebuck & Co., **$50-$75.**

Kennedy tackle box I use yet, **$10+** due to its rough shape.

Earlier Kennedy with the signature scrollwork on top, leather handle, nice large compartments for large lures, **$20-$30.** One reason I like the Kennedy "Kits" is because you can store lures in them so well. Many of the boxes from the 1950s-70s were designed only for spinning or smaller casting lures; this is one problem with many UMCO boxes, but the Kennedy boxes are from an era of large lures we all love to collect.

Hip roof aluminum Kennedy box with nice large compartments, very nice and makes a great storage spot for those collectible lures and reels, **$75+.**

The king of all aluminum boxes is the UMCO line of boxes. This is a 1000A and they sell very well to collectors, **$75-$100.**

Model 3500 U tackle box by UMCO. This is the line they called Umcolite made out of a light plastic material that is very strong. These are wonderful boxes and this one is in excellent shape, **$250+.**

Model 173 A UMCO box in aluminum, note the reel holder in top, **$50-$75.**

Model 173 US box designed specifically for spinning in Umcolite material, also note reel holder, **$100+.**

Early Falls City (Louisville) tackle box with japanned interior showing one of the pull-out trays (there are three, one large and two small) and some related collectibles. The most unique item is the Weber Hoochy feather duster, one of a kind made by the factory and found in archives when purchased, **$75+.**

Box on the left is a 1950s Old Pal in metal and the one on the right is an early 1950s Plano box designed specifically for spinning in the Plano marbleized plastic style. I have found a few of the nice casting type boxes in this material but this is the one and only spinning box I ever found; **$25** for Old Pal; **$50+** for the neat early Plano.

Awards, badges, fobs, etc.

Many unusual collectibles exist that would fit into this miscellaneous category. Magazines such as *Field and Stream* gave awards for different fishing categories and one of the prizes was a nice metal award that has now become highly desired by collectors and normally sells for at least $75 each and up to $200 for some types. There are also many watch fobs of interest related to fishing tackle and fishing. Badges include items given away at conventions to the exhibitors, such as an Evinrude Motor badge shown in one of my other books. Many states used badges for conservation officers and also for licenses at times. In addition to these items, some fishing lure, rod and reel companies also distributed items such as lapel pins, tie clasps and other jewelry advertising their products. Any of these small items are collectible and many of them are rare and in high demand. Also, they often go unnoticed by collectors as they are often found in miscellaneous areas of antiques stores and malls and dealers do not always classify them as "fishing collectibles."

Wisconsin Guide License Collection from 1917-1942 for Mr. Melvin G. Long, Sr. Badges were issued each year except 1924, 1926 and 1928 when the previous year was still valid. The 1917 "shield badge" is worth **$200**; the other early 1918-1919 police-type badges trade for **$150**. The round tin-type badges trade for **$50-$75** each.

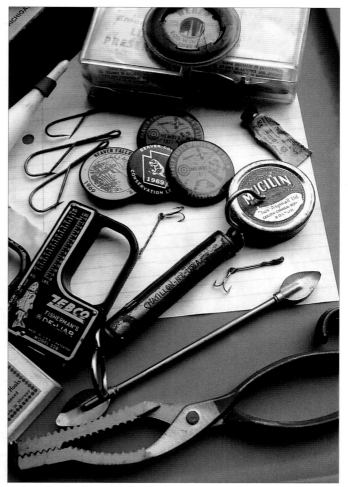

Variety of collectibles with four badges top center from Beaver Falls Sportsman's Club (1969 and two 1977) and a Beaver County Conservation badge from 1969. Also shown are a variety of other collectibles including the tip of an 8" float, Zebco De-Liar, scale, Weber line, old disgorge, Mustad hook box, Mucilin dressing and the pliers at the bottom were made by Detty in the 1950s; **$10+** each.

Wisconsin Guide badge from 1917 issued to Tim Kennedy at the age of 20, **$200.**

An assortment of pins from the biggest ice fishing festival in Michigan, Houghton Lake's Tip-Up-Town, U.S.A., a festival dating back to 1951 on Michigan's largest inland lake. The first three or so pins were made of wood and are valued at **$100** plus, the pins shown would average **$5-10** each.

Fishing licenses

Fishing licenses have been a necessity for many decades in nearly every state and country where sport fishing is popular. The licenses themselves have taken on many forms and now are computer generated ugly paper items in many states. However, historically many states prided themselves on the artwork involved with the licenses and those are indeed collectible. Here in Michigan we were fortunate to have "fishing buttons" that also contained a paper license insert on the rear of the button (badge) for a few years in the late 1920s and early 1930s. Pennsylvania used this type of license for years, as did many other states.

However, all fishing licenses have collector appeal and many seek out licenses from their birth year, their parent's birth years, some special year to them, or a series of years. The licenses themselves are also interesting historical references and you can find quite a bit of information on some. Along with the license, each state issued some regulations for fishing and these, too, are collectible, sometimes of greater value than the licenses themselves. In addition to licenses and fishing regulations, some states also issued "shipping permits" that needed to be included if any fish were shipped home from the out-of-state angler's catch. Finally, this is the other point of interest to collectors: "in-state"

versus "out-of-state" licenses, with the out-of-state generally being harder to find and more valuable due to scarcity.

In addition to the licenses already discussed, many states have also issued special "stamps" for trout or some other species. Again, Internet license sales have ruined the Trout Stamp collecting here in Michigan but for generations, the Trout Stamp was the most beautiful aspect of one's license. As with duck stamps, the stamps produced by states for particular species are crossover collectibles with both anglers and stamp collectors competing for the same resource. Stamps are usually graded as to both condition and if signed or not. Unsigned mint stamps are worth the most unless you find a stamp signed by a famous person, such as President Hoover. A few states also issued original and limited artwork related to the species stamps and it, too, is collectible and valued highly. A number of companies also produced general conservation stamps with fishing themes and the United States Postal Service also issued many commemorative stamps related to fishing. Any of these stamps or First Day Covers by the USPS would be nice additions to a fishing tackle collection.

Michigan 1930 Resident Trout Badge, front and back. Note the back had a place for the paper license to be folded and inserted. The presence of the paper license increases the value. Also note the crack in the celluloid covering which detracts some from the value. Most of the Michigan hunting or fishing licenses from 1929-1933 sell for a minimum of **$100** to more than **$300** each.

October 31, 1985 Special Muskellunge License from New York in top left and a variety of metal and plastic New York State Muskellunge tags. Note that the license (pink paper) has fish spelled Muskellunge; the tags are either Muskie or Muskalonge; **$10-$20** each.

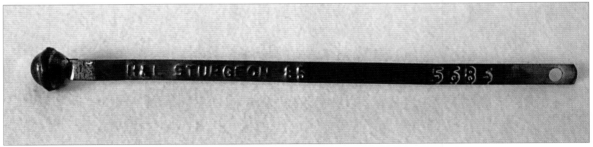

1985 Wisconsin Hook & Line Sturgeon tag, unused, **$10+.**

1996 Wisconsin Hook & Line Sturgeon tag, unused, **$10+.**

Miscellaneous paper items

Many paper items of interest exist related to fishing collectibles in addition to the ones already mentioned. The first to come to mind is the highly valued and collectible area of catalogs. My book on Heddon Catalogs covers that company's catalogs in detail and documents the value often reaching three and four figures for early ones. The earliest catalogs would command five figures. This is true of many early (1900-1910) catalogs and all of them are highly desired by collectors both for reference and the intrinsic value of the catalog itself. The most valued catalogs seem to be from the major lure and rod and reel makers; however, any manufacturer's catalogs are valuable.

In addition to the company catalogs, general wholesale house catalogs are also valued. These usually do not command the high dollar amounts of a specific catalog, such as a Heddon 1936, but are nonetheless invaluable as references and often contain the only available color chart for some companies from a specific period of time.

Companies also produced fliers and special brochures to send to dealers to commemorate the release of a new lure, rod, or reel. These little fliers are starting to gain collector interest and bring a few dollars each and some very early ones will bring over three figures. Posters and larger advertising items from any of the fishing tackle companies bring hundreds of dollars each if original and in good condition. Many companies supplied large cardboard cutouts for store display and these are high demand items if you are ever lucky enough to locate any. A more common, but still highly valued, find is the dealer display of lures.

Although mentioned earlier, parts lists, repair directions, use directions and other items supplied by manufacturers are also collectible. This would include such items as directions for using a collectible boat, motor, rod, reel or whatever is related to fishing.

Another category of collectible is the area of fishing magazines and fishing annuals. Garcia published a wonderful annual, as did Sports Afield, and either of these items are valued. Any of the early magazines are also collectible and the value simply increases as they get older. One caution is that they have to be in fine condition with no mildew or other odors as this makes them about worthless.

Books on fishing are also collectible and autographed books are always more valued and a special autograph will greatly increase a book's value.

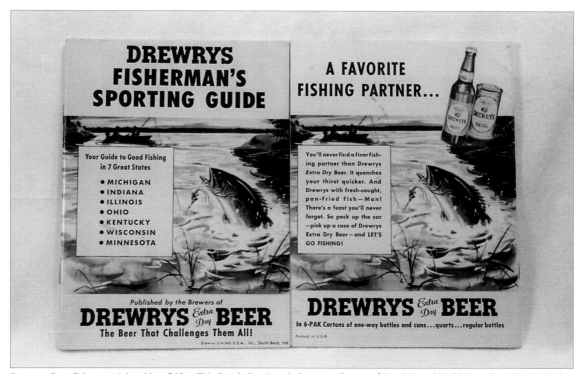

Drewrys Beer fisherman's booklet, **$10+.** This South Bend, Ind., brewery (home of South Bend Tackle) produced a nice little "give-away" booklet on fishing during the 1950s that is collectible and primarily a lake guide with a little information on tackle.

A colorful little booklet from 1946 advertising the lines of Powerline Tackle Company of Grand Rapids, Mich., **$20+.** An unusual find in mint condition from a very small company. The booklet gives instructions for using the products and shows them.

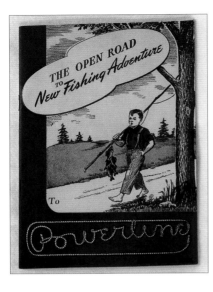

Little Suzy display board of lures from the mid-1950s from Charles M. Six Tackle Co. of Carthage, Mo. Hildebrandt of Indiana later offered very similar lures as did Cotton Cordell lures. This board went back to Carthage to a collector that remembered the lures as a child; sold for **$46** online in early 2004.

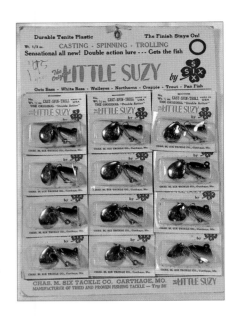

1929 Catalog from Guy H. Dixon & Son Co., Racine, Wis., **$75-$100.** This wonderful catalog not only has fishing and camping items but also lists all fishing laws in America for 1929.

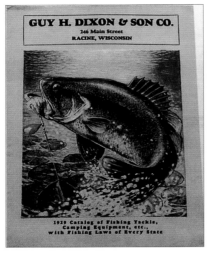

Reminiscent Tales of a Humble Angler, a one-of-a-kind book by Frank M. Johnson, signed and dated as a gift to O. L. Weber, founder of Weber of Stevens Point in 1923, **$500+;** an archival piece from Weber archives when purchased.

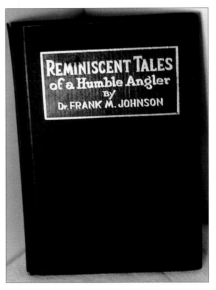

P & K 1947 catalog and insert introducing the new Re-Treev-It fly reel by P & K, **$75+.**

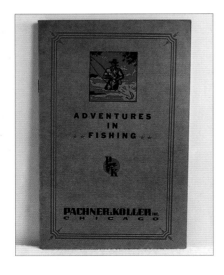

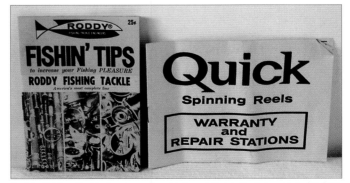

Roddy Fishing Tackle Engineers booklet and Quick Reels booklet, **$5-$10** each.

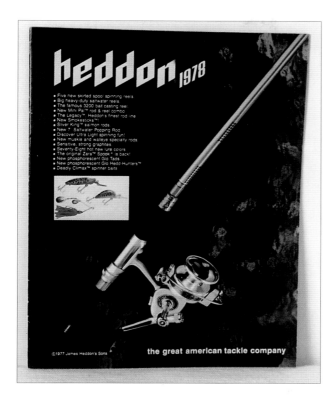

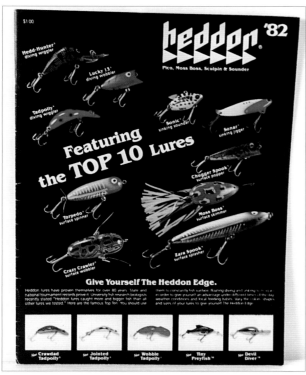

Heddon catalogs from 1978, 1981, 1982 and 1984. The 1984 is the last one ever made as the company designed it and printed it before selling to EBSCO, Inc. in 1983. All Heddon catalogs are valuable and some recent ones (e.g. the 1984) are very hard to find, **$50-$100** each if mint.

Advertising items are quite valuable and this 1938 Shakespeare Catalog is no exception. Due to its early date and mint condition in its mailing envelope, this is worth about **$300.** Also shown is a color chart for the famous Shakespeare mouse lure as an example of one lure to collect.
Lewis Collection.

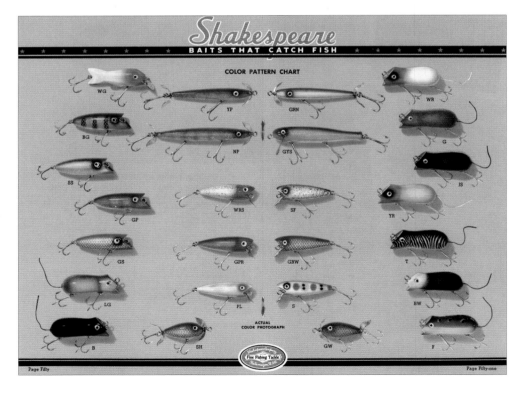

Nets, gaffs, blunts and spears

As an attorney teaching police officers in Michigan, I always have fun on the legality/illegality of blunts, or "priests" in our state. It is illegal to carry a club with which to kill fish unless fishing, or if it is part of a collection being transported. It is easy to see why when you realize how easily it will kill a pike or muskie! I do not find many of these tools in collecting but once in while an interesting blunt will come to fore that should be kept. I really do not think they have a lot of trade value yet, as most people do not even know they exist. However, some even have brand names on them and those would be valuable for certain.

Gaffs, on the other hand, are well known to collectors and many bring over $100 each, especially the early Marbles and/or Nordlund brand gaffs. Gaffs were made with spring action, gripping action, snagging action, some folded, some extended, some were made by a local blacksmith. Again, there is not a "standardized" value on gaffs but I think most are worth at least $10 and many are worth three figures or better.

Nets have been collected by some, especially the wooden framed trout nets. Ed Cummings from Flint, Mich., distributed a beautiful wooden framed net marked with his trademarked design that normally sells for $75 to collectors. There are other collectible nets available and all nets have interesting display functions for a lure collection as well.

Spears are an excellent fishing collectible to add to any collection, as they go nicely with fish decoys here in the north and were also used for stream spearing in most of the country. Spears include both fish and frog spears and major companies such as Pflueger made both, as did many local companies. Some collectors are only interested in collecting the "head" with the tines due to space constraints and others want the entire spear, handle and all. These are probably the most underrated of all fishing items at farm and estate auctions, often selling for $2 to $5 each. A Pflueger spearhead alone is worth $50+, so you can see many bargains can be found in the field.

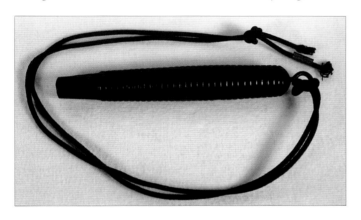

Hard rubber blunt found in the old japanned tackle box believed to be a Vom Hofe or Mills, **$25-$50.**

Very unusual heavy bamboo blunt, **$25-$50.**

Grizzly brand gaff, new from shipping carton, pre-zip code era, made by Maxwell Manufacturing, Vancouver, Wa., **$20+.**

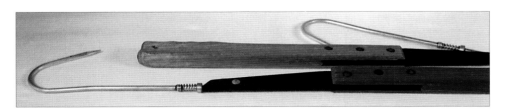

Unmarked folding gaffs, new, 1960s era, **$20+** each.

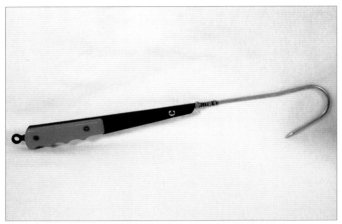

Unmarked folding gaff, **$20.**

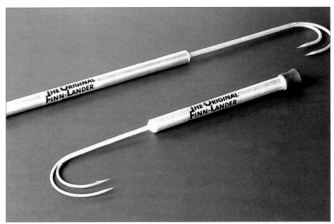

Two examples of the rare Finn-Lander gaff made by Katchmore Bait Co. of Wisconsin, **$50+** each.

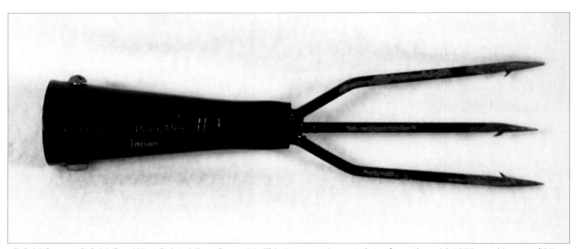

B & M Spears, B & M Co., West Point, Miss., Spear #1. This Japanese import dates from the mid-1950s and is new, **$25+.**

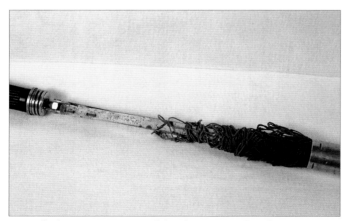

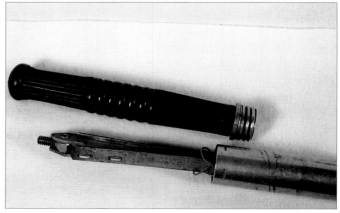

Unusual tube containing net and then becomes net handle, also has a screw thread in the end to allow another extension piece to be attached. This net was advertised in 1926 as the Chummy Getum Landing Net and sold new for $3.50; **$50+.**

Interesting net with vise handle for side of boat or dock, **$20.**

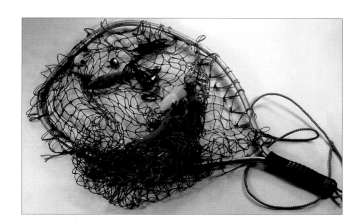

Common 1950s-1960s aluminum nets that replaced the classic
Cummings-style wooden nets, **$5** each.

Bobbers and floats

Lang's spring 2004 auction featured a collection of floats from Pequea Tackle of Pennsylvania that were projected to sell for thousands of dollars for a salesman's sample case of 58 different floats. It did. Many of the floats seen in my collection shown below are Pequea. Some are Ideal. Many are unknown with any certainty, as many companies jobbed floats and bobbers. It is unusual to even find newer (e.g. 1950s-1960s) bobbers new with packaging as they were normally sold loose in tackle shops by then. A recent find was a Montague float from the classic era in its package and I did not hesitate to spend $150 for it. Recent bobbers only command a fraction of that unless they light, sing, reel in your fish, or any number of ideas newer floats have shown. However, any float with identification is a plus as we are really lacking in good data on this colorful and interesting fishing collectible.

Early floats are hard to date as the painting style changed little on them over the years until modern times. However, some of the earliest have brass hardware on each end of the float as one indication. Another way to tell is the paint, early ones all had lead-based paint and it is far more vivid than paints of the 1950s-1960s. Bobbers have come in a number of styles for years including cylindrical, oval, egg shape, round, tapered round, quill style, and long cylindrical with a round bobber added at the top.

Many companies (Pequea and Ideal included) offered a simple bobber/float combined with a hand line wrapped around a little wooden frame (later plastic) that could then be transferred to the trusty cane pole or used as is for fishing. This was my standard fare as a small child when I went to the bait shop: new line and bobber on a winder for my pole. I sold a dealer dozen of these in 2002 for more than $200 at a farm auction we had. I also sold an earlier version similar to the one shown in Lang's Spring 2004 catalog for $500 nearly 10 years ago. My floats and bobbers sold at the 2006 Lang's Fall auction did well as well, bringing hundreds of dollars sold in small and large groupings, as shown in Chapter 3.

One of the impossible things about bobbers and floats is to ever identify the pure "cork" floats and bobbers without finding them in a display or package. They all are made of natural cork and thus look alike. It may be that we will come up with a technique to assist us in figuring this out but I cannot see it in the near future (DNA analysis of the cork source is a little pricey for a bobber). But the patina of an old cork float is obvious and something that adds nicely to a fishing collection. Is there a more obvious symbol of peace and tranquility related to old fishing memories than a cork float at the end of a cane pole?

Examples of old cork floats/bobbers, **$2-$5** each.

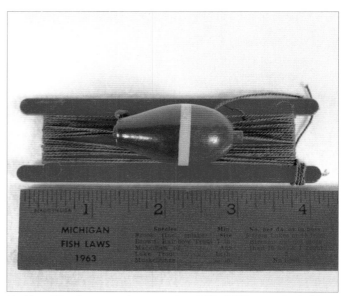

Ideal hand line for cane pole usage, circa 1950s/1960s, wooden bobber with braided line on plastic winder, **$20-$25.** This is similar to the set of 12 I sold for **$200+** in 2003.

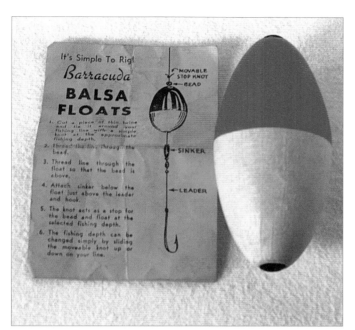

Barracuda brand (Florida Fishing Tackle) balsa float with paperwork, **$20-$25.** This 1950s float is very common as to design but rare to find with any paperwork identifying the source.

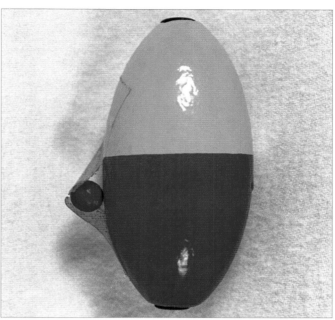

A similar float to the previous one shown, with a bead that goes between the float and the stop taped onto the float, **$10-$15.** This is not marked but is also from the 1950s and could be one of any number of company's floats.

Arnold Tackle Speed Slip float new on card, **$10-$20.** This is from the late 1950s and was an unusual tackle shop find made in the Upper Peninsula of Michigan just five years ago at the Lake Ruth Marina. It would be of little value by itself but at least on its card it gives us an idea of what this 1950s tackle manufacturer was selling.

Advertising bobber for Doodle Oil, **$5-$10.**

Line spools

Wooden line spools were a true work of art and advertising genius by early makers of line and tackle. The companies put a lot of effort into layout and design on the small circular labels glued onto the wooden line spools. There were a number of line makers but Cortland, Gladding, Hall, Newton, Sunset Line & Twine, and U.S. Line Co. all quickly come to mind as some of the big ones. Most of these companies furnished the lines for all of the big tackle makers as well.

Value on line spools is determined by two different factors, in addition to condition of course: colorfulness of the graphics and company affiliation. Wooden spools command more than most plastic ones but some rare plastic line spools such as the Wallsten (Cisco Kid) or some Heddon spools still are valuable indeed. The major factor really is the graphics but a "big six" line spool

will usually have "added value" for an item. Condition must be very clean and it is ideal if the little center hole has not been punched out in the spool center damaging the graphics. These are similar to floats/bobbers inasmuch as they are attractive even to those who do not collect fishing collectibles; this in turn drives the prices up a little due to competition for ownership with other collectors.

Most wooden line spools start at $10 if excellent and some quickly go up to $50. A Japanese Silk example sold for nearly $70 with its cardboard shipping box. However, many fine examples can be purchased at shows and online for $10 to $20 each and often even less. But two Winchester spools, both with center holes punched, sold for $100 to $300+ so there is value in some of them!

Blackstone Japan silk line on wooden spool in original shipping box; sold online for **$68+** in early 2004.

Newton's Finger Lakes spool for silk line, **$20+.**

Newton's Princess Pat spool for braided linen line, **$20+.**

U.S. Line Co. Black Knight brand early Nylon spool and line, **$30+.**

Sunset Marina Cuttyhunk spool and line for saltwater fishing, **$30+.**

Jone's Line Co. Kilrush Cuttyhunk wooden spool, **$30+** if excellent; **$10-$20** as is.

Newton's Dictator 20-lb. silk line on wooden spool with great rooster; **$50+** if excellent; **$20-$30** as is.

Cortland Cam-O-Flage Bait Casting line new on spool, **$10-$20.** This was a standard line in the late 1950s and early 1960s.

Cortland "333" Fly Line new in box with papers, **$75+.**

Horrocks-Ibbotson "Imperial Special" fly line box only, **$40+**; **$100+** if line is present.

Western Auto "Silver Anniversary Nylon" fly line new in box, in container and line wiping cloth, **$125+.** This is a rare find from Western Auto and is in excellent shape with only minor corner damage to the cardboard box; it was a recent find from a California 1950s estate.

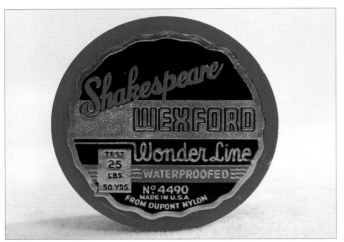

Shakespeare Wexford Wonder Line, **$10-$20** each without cardboard box, much more if boxed.

Heddon Monofilament Spinning Line new on spool, **$10-$20.**

South Bend Strong-Oreno casting line, **$30+.**

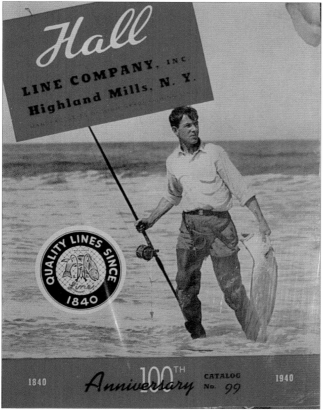

Hall's 1940 lines in salesman's kit and mint 1940 catalog. This was the 100th Anniversary of the Hall Line Corporation. Note the many different companies and brands used by Hall: "Badger" for Diamond Mfg. Co. of St. Louis; "Oh Boy" for Cohantic Line Co., Philadelphia; "Belknap" for the famous supplier of hardware and tackle from Louisville and many others. This display has 23 wooden spools, 5 carded lines and 5 rolled lines. Some of these displays have been listed online but not sold, as the reserve was higher than the highest bid of $200, **$200+**.

Fish decoys and ice fishing items

One of the fastest growing areas of sporting collectibles the past 20 years has been the hobby of collecting fish decoys and related items. Fish decoys are as old as early Native American societies and many beautiful ivory decoys are still in use in Inuit lands in Alaska, Canada and Greenland. Some fish decoy prices now rival good duck decoy prices, with decoys by the great Cadillac, Mich., fish carver Oscar Peterson often breaking into four figures or more. But all fish decoys are collectible and many rare ones exist as well as many carvers that were prolific, making examples easy to find such as the Bethels of Minnesota. As with duck decoys, there were also factory fish decoys made by Heddon, South Bend, Pflueger, Paw Paw, Creek Chub Bait Company and others. Some of these factory decoys are very desirable due to

rarity and also because of the crossover function of having lure collectors want one in their collection as well.

In addition to the obvious decoys, there are also collectible spears, ice rods, jigging sticks, ice fishing sleds and other miscellaneous items used by the ice angler in pursuit of game fish. There are a few books out on decoys and some include a good selection of spears and other items that I refer the reader to for more detail. However, keep in mind this growing field of collecting when you run into a good deal on a spear or decoy at a farm auction. Spears quite often sell for a low amount at auction but can bring a premium to a collector, especially if marked with the maker's name, such as an early Pflueger spear.

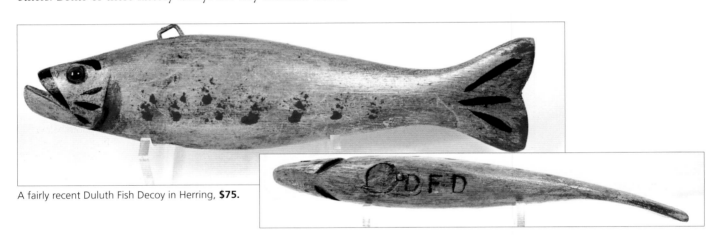

A fairly recent Duluth Fish Decoy in Herring, **$75.**

D. Bergland fish decoy, **$75.**

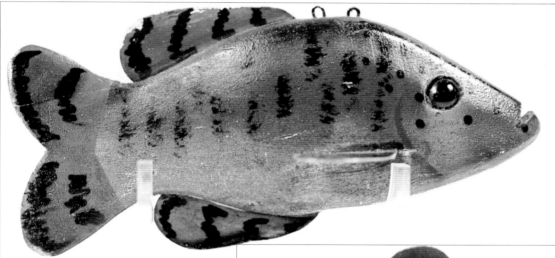

Two examples by Larry Bethel of Minnesota, trout and crappie, **$80+** each.

The photo below shows the mark of "B" on Bethel decoys.

Rare Chub spearing decoy from Grosse Isle, Michigan, circa 1940s, used to spear perch and walleye, 4-3/4" long, **$95-$125.**

Unknown but nicely done Sunfish example, Upper Michigan, **$150+.**

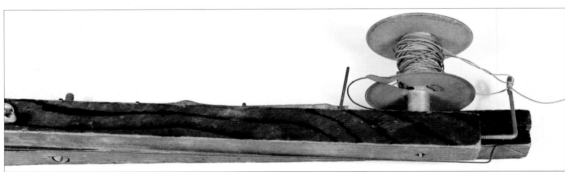

Collectible wooden tip-up and ice fishing rod, **$20+** each.

A 3-3/4" Larry Bethel sucker, **$60+.**

At the top is a Jerry Matson trout decoy, Minnesota, 8-3/4" long, marked on weight, modern "known" carver, **$300+.** In the center is my favorite Sherman Dewey, Manistique, Mich., decoy in Rainbow, 7" long with S and D stamped into front fins, **$75+.** Sherm is deceased but made a lot of decoys for use in the clear waters of the Upper Peninsula. Bottom is the Larry Bethel 3-3/4" sucker, **$60+.**

Unknown pike-shaped decoy with wooden tail found in Michigan's Upper Peninsula, very folksy, 10", **$75+.**

Scarce Jimmy Wayman, Wisconsin, rainbow trout decoy, 6-1/2" with tack eyes, **$150+.** This decoy is also shown on the front cover of this book.

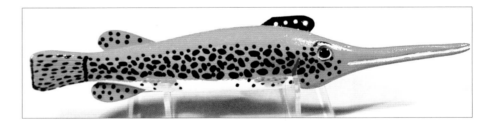

Three examples of Jim Nelson decoys. Being from Cadillac, Mich., Jim learned to carve fish by watching Oscar Petersen, a good friend of his father's. Jim has made over 6,000 decoys to date and still makes about 100 a year. Any of Jim's new decoys go for **$100+** and the older ones average **$300** to **$800** each. Jim has been carving since the late 1930s and in recent years his wife Mary has also carved some beautiful little fish.

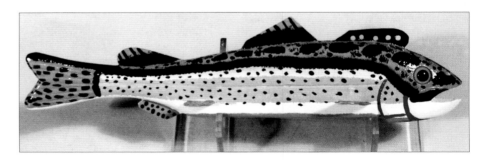

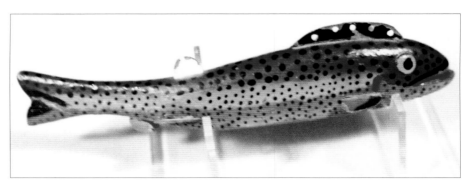

An example of an A. J. Downey decoy. A. J. has been carving fish since 1981 in the Upper Peninsula of Michigan near Newberry. He has made to date about 700 to 750 decoys and they sell for **$300** for the smaller ones to **$600+** for any larger decoys.

Carl Christiansen is one of the Upper Peninsula of Michigan's treasures who has a national following for his fish carvings, and also his folk art carvings. His decoys have sold for **$50** to **$3,000** and his bowls, vases and related items sell for **$400** to **$800** with regularity. He started carving in the late 1970s and any of his early works demand a premium. Some of the Christiansen decoys sold at Lang's are in Chapter 3, showing prices commanding **$150+** each for even his newer items.

Other miscellaneous items

In addition to the items already mentioned, I have noticed many other items people collect related to fishing tackle including sinker boxes, hooks, hook displays, terminal tackle, salesman's samples, fish rulers, fish cleaners/scaling devices, knives, thermometers, oil cans, oilers, reel oil tubes/jars/bottles, mosquito repellents, catfish food tins, sardine tins, printer's blocks for advertising fishing items and much more.

A beautifully restored Super Elto outboard motor used in early days of fishing. Restored motors sell for hundreds to thousands of dollars depending on make, rarity, condition, etc. and this one is worth at least **$500.**

Part of the author's collection showing collectible bottles, **$5-$20** each; three Fin-Dingo lures, **$50+** each; a Terry Patent reel, **$100+**; a 1929 Michigan Small Game button, **$50+**; a Marlin match book, **$5**; four Montague reels, **$100+** each; a nice creel with leather trim, **$125+**; a fairly old bait box by Old Pal in green, **$25**; a Bristol pack rod in case, **$25-$40**; and part of a beautiful display unit by Montague for line wrapping threads and rod ferrules, **$250+.**

More of the author's collection showing the early 1950s Weber display stand, **$75+**; a Bluegrass 33 reel, **$75**; a Winchester reel, **$150+**; the very early 1950s Zero Bomb spinning reel, e.g. Zebco, **$50-$75**; a Zee Bee box/reel, **$30**; a South Bend 450/Box, **$40+**; and to the left of the stand you can see part of a Precisionbilt Marquette baitcaster with the beautiful translucent deep red end plates, **$75+**; and a Ruby baitcaster, **$100+**. The stand has collectible "Modern" lures such as the four Flutter-Fin seen in front, **$75-$100** each; some Fin-Dingos, **$50-$75** each; Punkinseeds, **$50-$100** each; and a very old Artistic Minnow by Heddon, **$100+.**

Another general overview of the author's collection showing a rare Ranger Reels display case from early 1950, Rockford, Mich., **$200+.** It is full of Heddon Punkinseed lures ranging from **$50-$150** each. A Ranger reel is to the far left on the same shelf as the display unit, **$30**; next to a rare brass Julius Vom Hofe, **$300+**; the fly reel in the rear is a Weber, **$50+**; and the other items were described previously in the book.

An Art Best's Fishing Lures display board and one of the duck decoys also attributed to him. Many anglers and lure makers also hunted ducks and even made decoys; display board, **$50;** decoy, **$300+.**

A compass from the 1960s, **$15-$20.**

Two versions of Otab tablets to put in minnow buckets to help the minnows get more oxygen, **$5-$10** each.

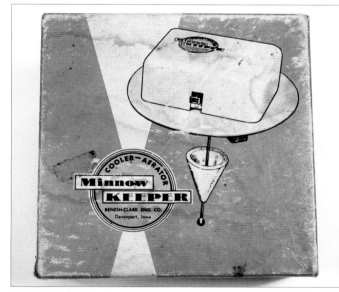

A pre-zip code Minnow Keeper contraption new in rough box to aerate the minnow buckets shown earlier in this chapter, **$15-$20.**

Nice dealer display of Tied-Rite Flies from Wisconsin, circa 1950s, **$75+.**

Old Town Canoe Co. Repair Kit new in pre-zip cardboard tube, **$50+.**

Fish Lo-K-Tor fish finder, one of the earliest of the fish finding machines and very collectible, especially if mint as in this example, **$200+.** Above it are some of the collectible Rebel Naturalized minnows, **$15+** each.

Shakespeare Reel Oiler, similar to one also distributed by Orvis and others, this one has the famous reel company name on its front, **$20-$30.**

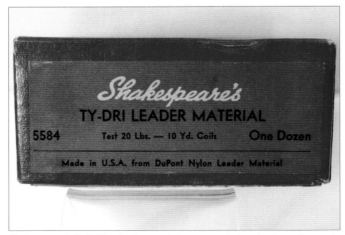

Shakespeare's Ty-Dri leader box and dozen new in box leaders, circa early 1950s, **$25+.**

Neat little change holder made of base metal/pewter material of a fish creel, tail of trout is broken sorry to say, **$5** in this shape; otherwise **$25+.**

Three examples of weights used to roll down a wire line to get the bait down deep in the Great Lakes or other deep water fishing spots. The fish would be the most valuable with the long unmarked one the least valued, **$20-$75+.**

Colorful Hump Tiger (Hump Lures, Texas) Key Chain fobs, **$50+** each at least. These lures were made in the early 1980s when the last owners of Bingo Lures also owned Hump. They are very rare and were loaned to me by the former company owners, Ray and Patty Zapalac.

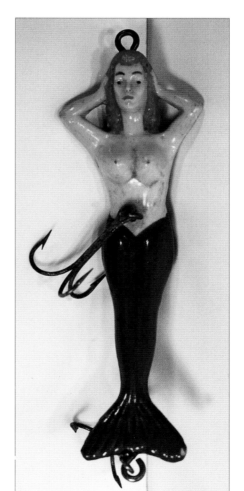

Mermaid fishing lure, **$50+.**

American Fork & Hoe Co. Pork Rind Jar, very unusual find, **$20+.** Al Foss lures depended on the addition of the pork rind for the wiggle and this early jar is not found often.

U-Fibb-R scale and measuring tape, **$50+** boxed. Many collectors know the De-Liar scale and tape but have not seen the U-Fibb-R model. This one also has a small first aid kit and serves as a match-safe, too. Note the little fish design under the name.

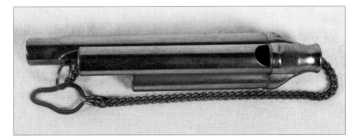

German made silver boat whistle, **$150+.**

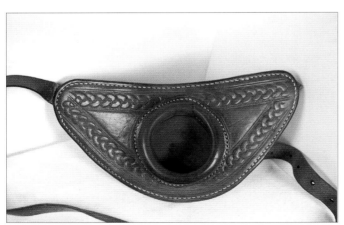

Tooled leather surf rod holder, California origin, **$25+.**

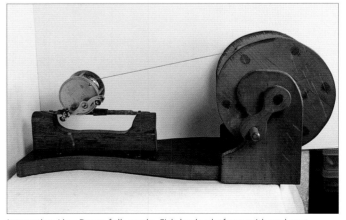

Interesting Line Dryer, folk made. Fish body platform with reel seat mounted on upright board and a large wooden spool to hold the line with wooden crank knob. Line is spooled off of a Portage (Pflueger brand) Medina reel. Dryer, **$100+**; reel, **$25-$40.**

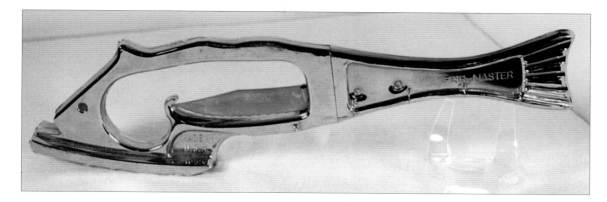

Fish-Master Stainless Steel knife/scaling combination, **$40+.**

Weber, L & C and Newton's line dressing tins and kits; tins, **$20** each; Weber in rare cobweb box, **$50-$75**.

Chapter 6

Miscellaneous Hunting Collectibles

This is a broad topic including shot shell boxes, shell boxes, shell crates, bows, quivers, knives, compasses, cleaning rods and tools, oilers and oil cans, match safes, shooting awards and other miscellaneous tools and equipment related to hunting that has now become collectible.

There are many books covering just knives and it is recommended that the specialist consult any one of these books for a good introduction to hunting knives. Major brands of knives collectors seek related to hunting include Remington, Marbles and Case among many others. One of the nice things about collecting fishing lures is that once in a while I find a nice collectible Marbles knife in a tackle box. Marbles is also a premier brand name for compasses, match safes, gun cleaning kits,

cleaning rods and a few other hunting items. This Gladstone, Mich., company is still in business today but most of the collectible items were made prior to the 1960s. Of course, many of the same items could be classified as both hunting and fishing collectibles, especially oilers, compasses, match safes and knives.

Cleaning rods also include fine old wooden rods, made of a single piece of wood or multiple parts screwed together. Some of these rods are quite fancy with intricate carving, while many others are simple lathe turned rods with minimal decoration. Rods are also found in brass and aluminum but most collectors focus on the wooden rods or rods with a known brand name such as Marbles.

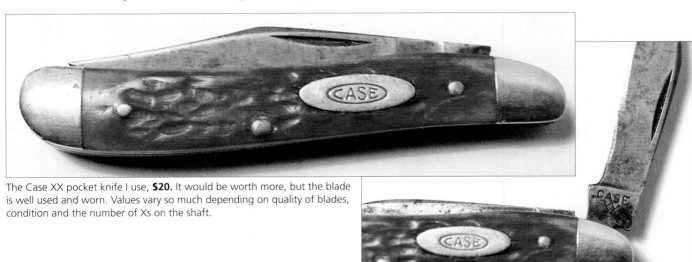

The Case XX pocket knife I use, **$20.** It would be worth more, but the blade is well used and worn. Values vary so much depending on quality of blades, condition and the number of Xs on the shaft.

A Marble's Arms knife found in a tackle box. It's not in the best shape but is still a nice find, **$25-$30** in this condition. Mint ones bring three figures plus.

Oilers and oil cans make for some of the best additions to a collection. Most people do not realize how rare the Winchester Utility can is and thus it is often found under priced. But collectors in the know fight for this rare can and drive prices up to $700 on occasion. The majority of Winchester cans and similar ones can be found for $25 to $75 most often. Hoppe's cans, boxes and tubes also add a colorful dimension to a collection, as do many other brand names, and can be purchased for even less money at sales. The nice thing about oilers and oil cans is that they can sometimes be found for a bargain price at a farm auction or even in an antiques store.

There are also many collectible tools related to hunting such as reloading equipment, powder measures, powder containers and specialized wrenches and screwdrivers used on weapons. As with most items, the known brand names such as Remington, Winchester, Marlin, Browning and others garner the highest prices but any old reloading equipment is collectible.

Items such as patches and pins related to skeet and trap shooting, turkey shoots, and other gun sporting events also add to a collection nicely. They are colorful and a symbol of someone's skill in firearm shooting. Again, they also can often be found in a miscellaneous "smalls" section of an antiques booth or store for a small investment of $5 to $10 and they are almost always well worth it.

Illinois successful turkey hunting pin from 1995, **$10+.**

Archery could easily sustain a chapter of its own or even better, an entire book, but time and space only allows a brief introduction to this specialized area of collecting. At one time I owned a significant collection of bows and related items but like many things they were sold to make room for more fishing lures. The most collectible archery items are recurve bows made by Fred Bear, Ben Pearson or other early archer/manufacturers. Early cedar arrows are also popular items, as are some of the early glass bows by Shakespeare and others. Brand name is as important in archery collectibles as it is in any other sporting collectible and items by Bear usually garner the highest prices.

In addition to the above items and items mentioned in the previous chapter, collectors are interested in posters, calendars, die cuts, catalogs, pamphlets, brochures, envelopes, artwork, fobs, medals, awards, pinbacks, stickpins and numerous other categories impossible to include in this book. The book mentioned on Page 230 by Hal Boggess, *Classic Hunting Collectibles*, has separate chapters on many of these items and should be consulted for more details, photographic examples and current pricing values.

This chapter in no way can even attempt to cover in great detail all of the ancillary fields of collecting related to hunting. Separate chapters, or books, could be written on most of these topics. However, it is important to give the beginning to intermediate collector a taste of items that eventually will adorn his/her walls and shelves if collecting takes its normal path. With this in mind, I have selected only some of the most obvious items that I find interesting and that I think collectors will be able to find in the field.

I love Donna Tonelli's, *Top of the Line Hunting Collectibles*, Coykendall's books on sporting collectibles, and others, but unlike Tonelli, my audience is the beginning to intermediate collector who will likely have to settle for "average" hunting collectibles for the most part. My wife Wendy and I have a fairly decent personal collection, in my opinion, but it makes me feel a little underprivileged every time I view Tonelli's book, as she only shows the cream of the crop. It is important to realize that we will all find a few "top of the line" items but for the most part, most of us will have to be content with more common finds and ones we can also afford! The truth is that when you visit a

sporting collectibles' show or a flea market, the most common items are from the post-war period up through the 1960s. Thus, I think this chapter will assist collectors in recognizing collectible items from more recent time periods.

Again, most of the items being collected today are from distinctly different time periods with the big break being prior to 1940 and post-1940. This break in history is so important due to the many technological changes brought about after World War II in the manufacturing of decoys and related items. There is also the legal break of an antique being considered 100 years old or more and thus some concentrate only on items from the 1800s or very early 1900s.

The year 1940 was definitely the end of the golden age of hunting in America in terms of vintage decoys, vintage guns, vintage boats, vintage shot shell boxes, and the list goes on and on. Not that interesting things were not made after 1940, but that date signifies the gearing up for war for most factories in the country and we were not really able to get back into full production of items for consumer consumption until 1947. As a matter of fact, many, if not most, sporting goods companies did not even produce catalogs from 1941-1946. Then, at the end of the war, we had new synthetic materials developed for gun stocks, Tenite 1 and Tenite 2, many other types of Nylon,

Decoy collectors who hunt ducks and geese frequently get interested in other hunting collectibles. An early Nitro Club Remington/UMC two-piece 20-gauge box with Mallard drake, full, shows a little edge wear, but all the shells are perfect and the graphics are in great shape, **$400** or more. *Lewis Collection*

Durlon, Styrofoam, use of pulp by-products (paper mâché), etc., that were being used for the production of decoys and other items.

Items were now cheaper to produce, more small companies had a hand at it for a while, and many familiar items took on new forms. However, the period of 1947-1960 also gives us some very collectible items produced in mass quantities but not kept by collectors but used, thus making the items somewhat scarce today. So, whether you are a purist collecting only "vintage" items from pre-WWII, or if you are a baby boomer content to find items with which you are familiar from your tender years of youth dating from the 1950s, I am certain there are many items in this chapter to pique your curiosity.

Shot shell boxes

The most popular hunting collectibles outside of decoys and calls are without a doubt shot shell and other ammunition boxes. Old shot shell boxes display some of the finest in graphics ever seen in advertising and the artwork alone is worthy of display. Add to this the fact that certain gauges or loads are fairly rare and it is a collector's dream world. Most collectors are not content with just one Hi-Power Flying Mallard box; they want one of each gauge and load, including difficult to find 28-gauge shells. The same is true of other ammunition boxes. Many like to concentrate just on .22 shells, small, colorful, common and a weapon owned by most of us at least once in our lifetime. Or maybe the 30-30 is your favorite and you hope to find 30-30 shells made by all manufacturers. Or maybe you are a Winchester fan and you cannot be content until you have one example of every Winchester box made! A lifetime of collecting to say the least.

The shot shell box itself has an evolutionary history usually broken in time by the earlier two-piece box and the later one-piece box. The two-piece box had a bottom over which was placed a top that contained the graphics and the shot particulars. These boxes are more desirable by most collectors but are getting fairly hard to find as they mainly pre-date 1940, or earlier (most were not in production after 1932). Some of the two-piece boxes are also some of the finest examples of graphic design showing dogs in action, ducks in flight, etc. However, many of the one-piece boxes are equally pleasing on the eyes and also getting harder to find. The Hi Power duck boxes are about as beautiful as they come with their turquoise color schemes and the beautiful flying mallard on each size of the shot boxes.

Some collectors insist on having shells in the box and some prefer the boxes empty. To preserve the boxes, I recommend removing the shells or gravity will eventually win out and place small tears in the cardboard from pressure exerted on the box sides by the shells. Some collectors cut a piece of Styrofoam to place inside the box to preserve the shape. Others also cover the box with clear plastic wrap to protect the cardboard from dust and elements. Personally, I do not like to cover my display pieces but it would indeed protect them from deterioration.

In addition to shell boxes, the shells themselves make interesting displays and would add a nice bit of color secured in a shadow box. According the Remington Arms/UMC Web site, modern shotgun shells have a shelf life of 10 years as to use. So, once your collectible shells are found, most of them should not be used for hunting anymore anyway. A search of the Internet on shell collecting will turn up a wealth of sites for you to explore indicating the vast interest in this field of collecting.

Most boxes are affordable, with the two-piece boxes usually beginning at $50, with many bringing hundreds of dollars each; many of the more common one-piece boxes from the 1950s can be purchased for as little as $5, if empty. However, many of the finer examples of one-piece boxes will garner upwards of $50 if full or if they have nice graphics of flying ducks or rare photo images. Most of the shell boxes I have sold recently bring between $15 and $25 for empty early one-piece boxes by either Remington or Winchester-Western. The more expensive boxes tend to be unusual or rare gauges such as 10-gauge or 28-gauge boxes. The boxes in this price range are without special graphics, just standard earlier one-piece boxes. The addition of a dog/duck/goose would at least double this range for even the more recent boxes.

One more word needs to be said about shot shell box collecting. Be very careful if you become involved in shipping any boxes with shells, even with just primers, as it is likely a violation of federal law. It is perfectly legal to ship empty boxes through the mail but not full ones. UPS, DHL and FedEx will ship boxes but only under special provisions. Most on-line auctions no longer allow the sale of boxes with shot shells. I have experienced some buyers asking if I could mail them the shells, too. Of course, I would not comply with this illegal request and advise all of you to be especially alert of the legal ramifications of buying and selling ammunition.

The following photos show just some of the many collectible shot shell boxes found in the field. Any of the boxes showing game, dogs and field shots tend to bring a premium over standard design boxes.

A grouping of collectible Federal Hi-Power and Monarch boxes, **$35-$60** each.

A Hunters Red Dog 12-gauge box was made in Colgate, WI, **$50.**
Lewis Collection

A Western Super X 12 gauge, #5 shot, is pre-warning label, **$10-$15.**

Remington Kleanbore boxes were made in the mid-1930s. One is green shell without red trim, the other two are red shell with red/green/cream boxes, **$25** each empty.

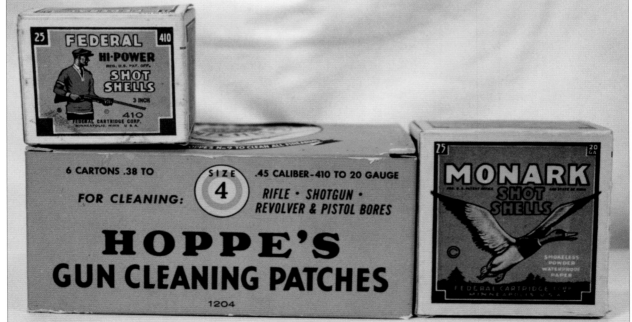

A Hoppe's Dealer display includes a Federal .410 box and Monark 20 gauge Mallard box, **$25-$50** each.

A Peters High Velocity Mallard drake box, **$50-$100,** depending on condition and if full or empty; value is more for odd gauges. *Lewis Collection*

A Mallard scene decorates this Peters Power Piston plastic shell box, full, with post-warning label, **$50** full. *Lewis Collection*

The Peters High Velocity 16 gauge, drake Mallard box, full, is a very highly desirable box, especially gauges other than 12s, **$100.** *Lewis Collection*

A very rare Peters High Velocity .410 drake Mallard box, full, **$150.** *Lewis Collection*

Full boxes of Nitro Express 2-3/4" shells and Shur Shot 2-5/8" shells are shown, **$100** each full. Note the color difference on "Wetproof," indicating shell colors. *Lewis Collection*

A Winchester Ranger Super Trap Load, pre-warning label, full, 12 gauge, 2-3/4" shells, **$50+** (paid $20 in 1995).

Western Xpert and Peters Victor 12 gauge boxes are shown with my favorite miniature mallard decoys. Both boxes are full and have 2-5/8" shells; the Victor box is harder to find, **$50-$100** each.

A Federal Monark 16 gauge Target Load, post-warning, shell details to show a colorful post-warning 1960s box, **$25.** *Lewis Collection*

Western Xpert and Remington Shur Shot 16 gauge boxes are grouped with my favorite Mallards again. Both of these early boxes are for 2-9/16" shells, **$40-$60** each.

Avon brand Good Shot after shave in the form of a Winchester shot shell, **$10+.**

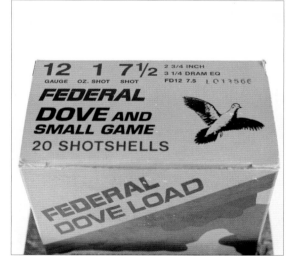

A newer Western Auto 16 gauge box and Winchester 12 gauge box show recent "animal" boxes and children's warnings, **$10** each. Even these inexpensive additions add color to a decoy collection. *Lewis Collection*

Federal Dove Load, **$10+.**

Other ammunition boxes

In addition to shot shell boxes, collectors are also interested in rifle, handgun and small caliber shell boxes. There is also an interest for powder cans, primer boxes, wooden shipping crates and other items related to shell manufacturing and use. Many of the old and colorful powder cans command over $100 each, and often much more. You should examine carefully the book *Classic Hunting Collectibles* by Hal Boggess, 2005, Krause Publications, for more details and pricing information. I wrote the introduction to this book and the introductory material for each chapter and refer the reader to those sections for more information. Hal shows some very rare shells, shell box inserts and one of the most complete sections to date on shell box wooden crates. Again, space is not available to reprint all of this data here but it is easily available by purchasing his book, with 1,100 color photos of all sorts of hunting collectibles.

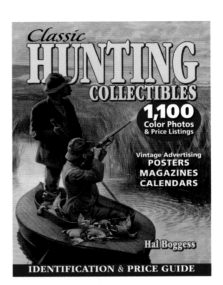

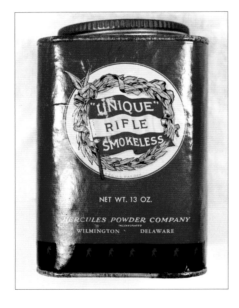

Hercules Powder "Unique" smokeless rifle powder can, **$25+.**

Dupont brand blasting caps tin, **$10-$15.**

Herter's brand .308 round nose jacketed bullets, **$20+.**

Western 38 Special, pre-zip in rough shape, **$5.**

Nicer Western sleeve packet for 35 Remingtons, **$20+.**

Western Super X .22 box from the 1950s, **$5-$10** full.

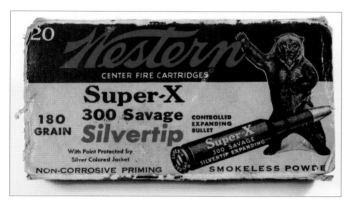

Great older Western box but rough shape for 300 Savages, **$10+.**

Older Savage box for .35 Remington, edge wear, **$20+.**

Winchester-Western box for 303 British, corner damage, **$10+.**

Federal "Rifled" slugs, really shot shell box, faded, **$10+.**

Peters .300 Savage sleeve box, edge wear, tape, **$10+.**

U.M.C. two-piece box for Remington and Mausers, **$25+.**

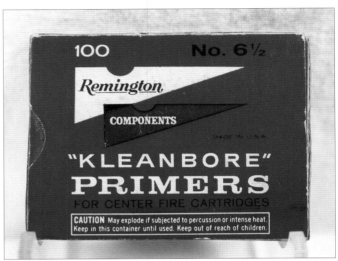

No. 6-1/2 Remington primers box with 100 primers, **$10+.**

Older Remington Hi-Skor .22 short cartridges box/full, **$25+.**

Remington Kleanbore 30-30 Winchester box with warning label, **$20+.**

Older Remington Kleanbore version without warning label for 30-06, **$15-$25.**

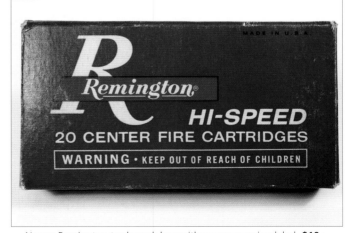

Newer Remington trademark box with newer warning label, **$10+.**

Shot shell crates

In addition to the shell boxes discussed, the wooden crates that shell boxes were shipped in up until the last 40 years have become very collectible in their own right. These are actually collectibles desired by three different groups: the household decorator, the sporting collectibles groups, and the gun collector. I recently sold about 30 of the crates and they ranged from unusual to common and the condition was excellent to poor and they averaged at about $25 each at an outdoor farm auction I had on Oct. 26, 2002. Some of the more unusual Remington and Winchester crates likely had a retail value of $50 to $75 each with some nice early Nitro cases and unusual sizes included. The boxes did quite well with one box reaching $45. A number of collectible and rare crates are illustrated in Boggess' *Classic Hunting Collectibles*.

Decoy weights, anchors, cages, etc.

Although I do not have many in my own collection, there have been a variety of decoy weights, anchors and cages that would make great additions to any collection. Some of the early anchors and any marked ones are becoming collectible at this time. The cages and leg holds were used to keep live birds in the field when live decoys were still legal.

The weights and anchors are often found on the decoys themselves but are sometimes found in antiques shops when dealers place a price on them not knowing what they are. Some of the weights were merely functional and some were fairly ornate themselves. Examples are shown in Chapter 1.

Reloading equipment and practice equipment

This is an area with many colorful and unusual additions to a collection. Many hunters reload their own shot shells due to the costs involved in buying factory-produced loads. This reloading effort resulted in a whole industry dedicated to the re-loader. Many tools are available that have beautiful wooden handles, many special shot shell boxes are available for the sale of wads and primers only, and many tools such as primer ejectors are available for collecting. This could itself be a full collection but just a few nice reloading tools complement any collection nicely.

Also related to this area is all of the practice shooting equipment available for collecting. One easy item to acquire is the hand trap thrower made by any number of major gun companies and some ammunition companies. Of course, there are also shot shell boxes marked "Trap" and "Skeet" which were meant for practice in duck and game bird hunting.

One of the most colorful items related to practice shooting is the "practice ball," or glass target ball, the predecessor of the clay pigeon. These are getting rare and difficult to find but are beautiful examples of hand blown and molded balls meant for a short life until shot! Also, many antique dealers do not know what they are and thus cannot price them accordingly. I have a nice array of target balls in amber, blue, cobalt, red, yellow, etc., all of which I picked up for a reasonable price in a shop because the owner did not know what they were. So keep your eyes open for such items in the future.

A glass target ball for early trap and skeet shooting, **$100+.**

Reloading shotgun shells was common in earlier times and these reloading tools are quite collectible. The old reloading tool shown should bring at least **$100.** *Lewis Collection*

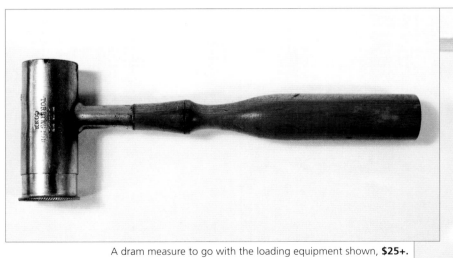

A dram measure to go with the loading equipment shown, **$25+.**

Duck stamps and artwork

Books have been written on the subject of duck stamps and I cannot do it justice here other than to mention the importance of duck and other related stamps to our sport. Federal duck stamps are required for all waterfowl hunting regardless of the state and many also added their own duck or waterfowl stamp. Iowa and some other states also added pheasant or grouse stamps. These game bird stamps are gorgeous and in some cases quite valuable. Some of the most valuable stamps are the artist proofs that are were available only from the artist of the stamp mounted in a limited edition of the original painting or print from which the stamp was initially made. Sad to say, many states such as my own state of Michigan, have gone to computer issuance of stamps and no longer require the beautiful state stamps (but still charge the fee!) that once adorned our state licenses, in addition to the Federal Migratory stamps.

In addition to the specialized resources on these stamps, general stamp collectors have a warehouse of knowledge related to these specialty stamps as well and dealers have long recognized a niche for these stamps. Unfortunately, the interest in stamp collecting is waning with an older population and I can only hope that new collectors of sporting collectibles keep an interest in these two beautiful art forms a live for some time to come.

Stamp values vary greatly depending on condition and whether the stamp was signed, with signed stamps normally decreasing the value greatly (unless it is signed by some famous individual, e.g. a president or great sports figure). Many of us began buying duck and trout stamps in duplicate years ago to save one unsigned for posterity and for that reason they are still available today. I began the practice in the late 1960s due to the beauty of the stamps coupled with the fact money from stamp sales assisted conservation efforts. Many of us interested in assisting wetland recovery and stream improvement made the same choices and for that reason we have "mint" stamps, unsigned, to collect.

Artwork related to ducks, waterfowl, bird hunting, deer hunting and other hunting, and decoys has indeed filled many texts. However, again you can add much color to a collection by some nice original paintings, limited edition prints, or mass-produced prints of hunting scenes. This area also includes the field of advertising art and many pieces of advertising art combine shot shell boxes and waterfowl hunting scenes or hunters and waterfowl. These make great additions to any collection and you should always be on the look out for an addition in this genre.

The following photos were taken from a non-copyrighted 2004 Duck Stamp Calendar printed by Norwood Litho. All stamp design is the property of the U.S. Department of the Interior. For current values of the actual stamps, refer to the texts cited above due to variations in values for used, new, on license, etc.

The first Federal Duck Stamp issued 1934-35.

The 1955 Federal Duck Stamp showing landing Ring-Necks.

Beautiful geese from the 1965 Federal Duck Stamp.

Everyone's favorite decoy is the Canvasback it seems, 1994.

Rare as a decoy find is this Pintail as seen on the 2002 stamp.

Hunting licenses

The collecting of hunting and fishing licenses has increased with an interest in sporting collectibles the past 20 years. Of course, one often collected licenses as part of a duck stamp or trout stamp collection as the items were most often affixed to licenses. However, now there is a market for licenses in general covering all areas of hunting and fishing, not just duck and trout stamps.

Some of the earliest licenses in some jurisdictions, such as Michigan, were in the form of a pinback, a round tin/celluloid license with a little tin pocket in the back of the license for the actual state issued permit to hunt or fish. Michigan only used this form of license for four years until the costs for production during the Depression forced a change to paper licenses. Some of the early pinbacks with the correct paper license in the insert have sold for hundreds of dollars with an average of about $100 being common. The most expensive ones are the non-resident licenses as they are the least common for most jurisdictions. Michigan issued pinbacks for deer hunting, small game hunting and fishing.

Along with the licenses themselves, collectors are also interested in the regulations booklets issued by each jurisdiction detailing the hunting and fishing regulations as to species, limits, sizes, transportation regulations, etc. Many jurisdictions also made hunters and anglers use transportation licenses for the fish and game and these too are collectible. In addition, many jurisdictions provided "tags" for deer, elk and moose; and even sturgeon. These metal tags are now collectible and more valued if never used.

In addition to the state issued licenses, regulations and other related items, collectors are now looking for badges of conservation officers, training materials for conservation officers and related items. These items are much rarer than licenses and can command a hefty price for early examples.

In general, the older the license the more valuable. Paper licenses from the 1960s and newer have little value, maybe $5 to $10 each at most. Of course, licenses handed down within a family make a great personal collection and a value is harder to place on such items. Since the advent of the Internet and the personal computer, most jurisdictions have ruined the beautiful old license by providing a computer-generated piece of paper with license details. Such a license has zero artistic value and near zero collector value or appeal. For instance, the beautiful trout stamp we used to have to add to our fishing license here in Michigan has now be replaced with a little paper license that says "all species." I am sure this will end the interest in modern licenses, other than as historical examples only. For my money, give me a pinback small game with a photo of a rabbit or pheasant or an early paper fishing license with a trout stamp attached and signed.

Collectors are especially after the following: the rare buttons issued for limited years (here in Michigan in the late 1920s to early 1930s); initial issuance stamps of state duck, waterfowl, grouse, pheasant, trout, or other species; the first and last year of issuance of a certain license type; game transfer tags that were often issued along with a license; particularly colorful licenses; early licenses in general; game laws of early years; licenses issued during one's birth year; and so on.

Four Michigan Small Game pinback licenses and a Resident Trout Fishing License pin. The small game pins were only produced for the four years illustrated and command at least **$50** each in excellent shape; **$75** if paper license is included with prices easily reaching **$100+** each. The trout pin from 1930 commands **$100+**.

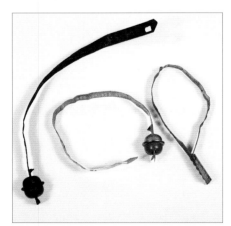

Deer kill tags used in Michigan until fairly recent times. Used ones are of little collector appeal and value but unused ones are being collected, **$5-$25** each for most.

DISPLAY IN MIDDLE OF BACK

S 216542

**1969 MICHIGAN RESIDENT
SMALL GAME LICENSE BACK TAG**

DISPLAY IN MIDDLE OF BACK

R 273560

R 1969

273560

**1969 MICHIGAN RESIDENT
DEER LICENSE BACK TAG**

Two 1969 back tags, Michigan, **$5-$10** each.

DISPLAY IN MIDDLE OF BACK

F 48327

MICHIGAN RESIDENT HUNTING LICENSE 1958

DISPLAY IN MIDDLE OF BACK

G 89333

MICHIGAN RESIDENT HUNTING LICENSE 1960

DISPLAY IN MIDDLE OF BACK

S 246252

1967 MICHIGAN RESIDENT HUNTING LICENSE BACK TAG

DISPLAY IN MIDDLE OF BACK

J 18123

MICHIGAN RESIDENT HUNTING LICENSE 1954

Some Michigan Resident general hunting licenses from 1954, 1958, 1960 and 1967: **$10** each for 1960s, **$20** each for 1950s. As a general rule, license prices double every 10 years going back in time, e.g. 1940s would bring **$40** each, etc. with the exception of the rare and in demand pinbacks from 1928-1932.

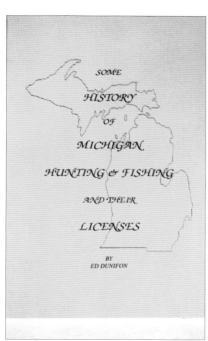

The book, *Some History of Michigan Hunting & Fishing and Their Licenses*, by Ed Dunifon, 1993, is a "must have" for collectors of licenses in Michigan giving the complete history of licenses and hunting and fishing history for many years as well. Each state needs to be researched as to values for licenses and you must be careful as there are no general rules to determine values from state to state. For example, Michigan pinbacks are rare with only 25 types issued from 1928-1932 but Pennsylvania used them for many years making them quite common; **$20+.**

Assortment of more common and more recent Michigan licenses and kill tags. Some include notes made by hunters regarding not seeing deer, numbers seen, etc. This information makes the licenses even more interesting to me giving them a little personal history. Also note the very non-descript smaller licenses generated by a computer, no thanks, I would like to see the old styles back with duck and trout stamps again affixed; **$5-$10** each at most for these recent ones.

Adult Resident Pennsylvania hunting license and tags, **$10.**

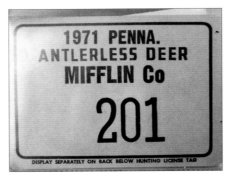

A 1971 Antlerless Deer for Mifflin Co, #201, **$10+.**

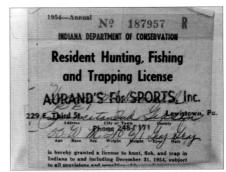

A 1954 hunting/fishing/trapping license for Indiana, **$20.**

Gunslick cleaning patches tin covered with paper, **$10-$15.**

Oilers, oil cans and cleaning tools

You cannot hunt for long in either a wet, nasty environment or a dry, sandy environment without running into the need to oil and clean your gun. Oil cans make for great collectibles due to their inherently interesting graphics and use of color. Most of the oil cans are worth from $15 to $25 but some of the rare and early ones are worth up to $500. One thing to note is whether the can has a lead screw top cap or a nylon cap. Once the nylon or plastic caps show up (early 1950s for the most part) the value goes down. In addition to the oil tins, small oilers, wrenches, and cleaning tools add interest to a collection. These are valued from $25 to well over $100.

Guns

I would love to add a section on guns here; however, it is not feasible for a number of reasons, the main one being it would be redundant. There are many fine gun-collecting books on the market and I would advise consulting any or all of them for more details.

My own personal favorite is the Marlin Model 90, over and under, introduced in the later 1930s. This is a wonderful duck gun in the 12 gauge and the 20 gauge is also a wonderful upland bird gun. According to one article I found on waterfowl hunting, the 20 gauge Marlin 90 is perfectly adept at decoy shooting as well. However, this article was written well before the mandatory use of steel shot and I think a 12 gauge superior in using the less

effective steel shot. Maybe as we perfect other non-toxic shot my 20 gauge Model 90 could once again go from the uplands to the duck blind but for now I will use the 12 gauge version.

If you would like to know what was available in 1953, a neat little book titled *Guns*, published in paperback by Maco Magazine Corporation, 480 Lexington Ave., New York, NY, is excellent. Written by Larry Koller and Pete Kuhlhoff, it has a section dedicated to guns for decoy shooting and guns designed for pass shooting. This little booklet is a great addition to a decoy collection showing the guns intended to be used with the silent ducks.

Miscellaneous items

This area has been added because many of these odd little items just do not neatly fit into any other category. Of course, this topic is virtually endless given its title; however, I have tried to show a few items that indeed have been associated with hunting over the years.

Keen Kutter sign, **$75+.**

Crow, duck, goose, turkey and other game calls are popular collectibles. The Lynch turkey call shown is **$75+.** See Chapter 2 for similar calls.

Higgins Gun Manual, **$10-$20.**

Two signs related to hunting, one for a sanctuary and the other a State Game Area sign from Michigan shown some disrespect by a hunter, **$20+** each.

A couple of the many Michigan Wild Turkey patches available from the 1990s. Similar to the successful deer hunting patches, these are becoming quite collectible, **$10+** each.

Rare Remington knife counter display unit. A former owner displayed pinbacks on it instead and thus the circles on the felt, **$200+.**

Framed Seagram's Canadian Hunter Whiskey sign, circa 1960s, **$50+.**

A pinback for the Lansing Oldsmobile Division of GM outdoor club, **$10+.**

A unique six-pack holder from Orro Products called DrinKaddy, **$20+.**

A beautiful cast Spaniel on the point, **$25+.**

Two unique bottle openers in cast metal from Scott Products, **$40+** each.

A hunting award patch with two sponsors, Williams Gunsight company and the Michigan television show dedicated to outdoor sports hosted by Fred Trost. Patch is from 1990 and shows a pretty buck, **$10+.**

This is the bottom of the bird bottle openers shown above.

Chapter 7

Traps and Related Items

In this day of PETA and other such organizations advertising on television nationally to end trapping, it may seem politically incorrect to many to cover this method of securing game. Be that as it may, trapping was, and still is, an important source of income in rural America and is of course a major part of our great American history. Without the major fur trapping economy developed in the 1700s-1800s, many would have stayed in their comfortable homes in the East and never ventured Westward or Northward as did my old colleague's Great Uncle Bill Sublette and many thousands of others.

I come from a family of trappers. Two uncles trapped well into their "senior years" and one owned and operated a trapping supply house. Many of my cousins earned their first dollar by trapping and selling furs. Many of my neighboring friends earned enough money trapping to buy their first .22 rifle or fishing pole. At one time in the late 1970s my farm hands were making a significant amount on weekends and evenings trapping raccoons, so much so they were wondering if "working" was worth it. Trapping has been an important part of our society for better than 300 years and it certainly should not be left out of a book on sporting collectibles because some may not like the concept.

Traps are similar to other sporting collectibles, with price being driven by condition of the trap, maker and age/rarity. Brand names are also important in this area with some of the better known traps being Newhouse and Victor. Size is also important, with prices reaching nearly $1,000 for excellent condition Newhouse Bear traps and $300-plus for good Wolf traps. The more common smaller traps made by Victor often sell for only $5 to $10 each. In addition to traps, there are books, trapping regulations, and small tags that marked the trap's owners that have also become collectible. This area of sporting collectibles is growing rapidly and our knowledge and pricing information is still sketchy compared to other areas in this book. I would estimate that our information on the collecting of antique traps is at about the same stage of lure collecting or decoy collecting about 20 years ago.

Keep in mind that trap collecting includes all kinds of traps, not just ones for fur-bearing animals. There are gopher traps, mole traps, rat traps, mouse traps, ant traps, and you could even add the area of fish traps, seines and minnow traps to this growing field of interest. I recently purchased a fairly complete trap collection of more than 200 traps and it included many early examples of each type of these traps. Shown here are just some examples of collectible traps and books on traps and trapping.

Artificial bait used in traps, **$40-$50+.**

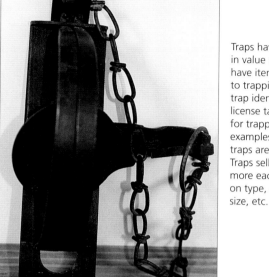

Traps have increased in value recently, as have items related to trapping, such as trap identification and license tags, and scents for trapping. Three examples of collectible traps are shown here. Traps sell for **$5-$500** or more each, depending on type, age, brand, size, etc.

At my April 7, 2007 auction, a number of traps sold for **$25-$300** each, with a cast-iron rat trap bringing **$165** and bear traps exceeding **$300** each.

Two unique trapping-related collectibles: a S. Silberman & Sons fur buyers watch fob and a neat little give away trap tie clasp, company unknown. Watch fob, **$75+**; tie clasp, **$25+**.

Andersch Bros. Hide & Fur House, Minneapolis, Minn., early 1900s *Hunters & Trappers Guide* illustrating fur bearing animals in North America. Andersch Bros. was a competitor of S. Silberman & Sons shown on Page 243 on the watch fob. This book is great for data and illustrations but the spine is loose making it of little value to collectors, **$20+.**

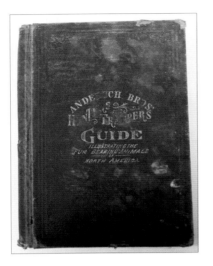

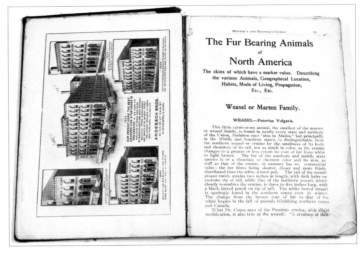

A hard-cover copy of *Mink Trapping* by A. R. Harding (there's also a soft cover), being held open by a trolley sinker, **$30+.**

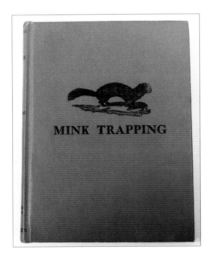

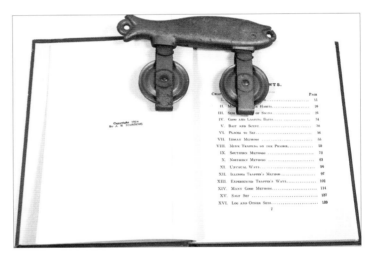

A more recent supply house catalog is this Bauer's 1975-76 catalog and the Fur Price List also by Bauer from 1975, **$5-$20** each.

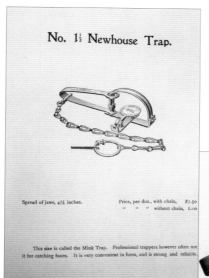

An early 1900s Oneida Community price list and catalog No. 28-A for animal traps. Oneida was of course the same Oneida that began as a communal society in the 1800s and produced many collectible trap brand names including Newhouse, Hawley & Norton, Victor and Jump. The Newhouse bear traps weighing in at 42 pounds bring collector prices of **$1,000** quite often and the wolf traps sell for up to **$300** if in great condition. Common smaller Victor traps are only worth about **$5-$10** each unless absolutely mint.

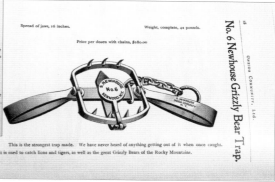

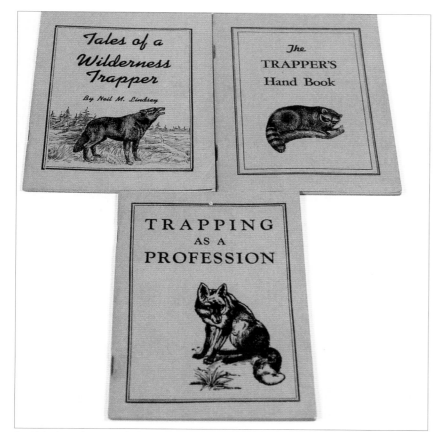

Fur-Fish-Game became the leading trapping magazine in America and was also known as Harding's Magazine to many. A. R. Harding was a leading educator related to trapping and wrote many books as shown above, **$10-$30** each.

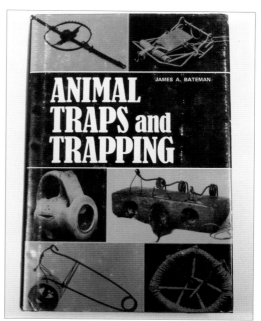

Animal Traps and Trapping, copyright 1971, 1973 by James A. Bateman, Stackpole Books, Harrisburg, Pa., **$20+**. This is a book about trapping in history and in all places, it includes insect traps, fish traps, bird traps, mammal traps, baits and chapters on ethics and legislation as well. The first edition was printed in Great Britain and would be worth the most. My copy was in its 12th printing in 1980 so there has been a lot printed to date. It is great for information on the history of trapping and the use of traps by both early and modern humans.

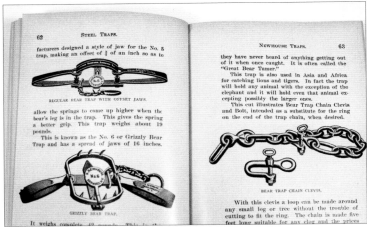

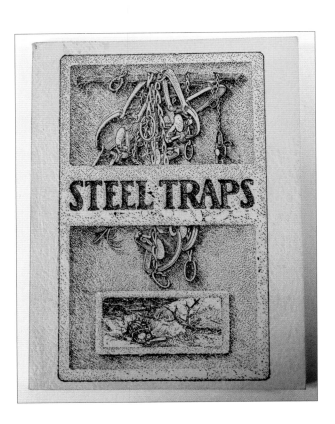

Steel Traps by A. R. Harding and published by A. R. Harding Publishing Co., Columbus, Ohio, no copyright data printed, **$25+**. This great little book shows the history of many American traps describing many and also discusses their use. The book shows a great selection of Newhouse traps and also has an interesting section on poorly designed traps that should not be used. This may make these traps even more collectible of course as they would not of sold as many models.

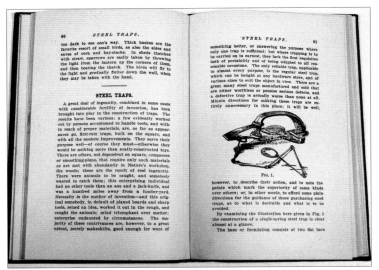

The Amateur Trapper and Trap-Maker's Guide by Stanley Harding, no publisher or copyright data, **$30+.** This great little book, circa early 1900s, shows a number of traps and historical trapping techniques.

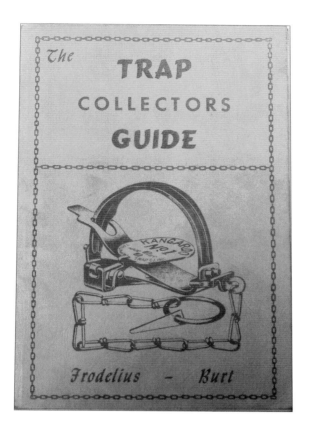

The Trap Collectors Guide copyright 1975 by R. B. Frodelius and R. E. Burt, published by Burts Printing Service, Dalton, N.Y., **$50+.** This is the first edition of one of the very few books discussing the collecting of traps and is thus a "must-have" for the trap collector. It shows a wide variety of makes and models and gives pricing information for them all. The biggest problem is that pricing is 32 years old as I write this and from my calculations such items as a Blake & Lamb bear trap or a Newhouse bear trap are priced at less than 1/3 of what they would bring today, but it is a great book with nice illustrations and great attention to the smallest details.

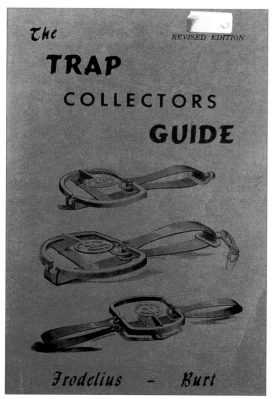

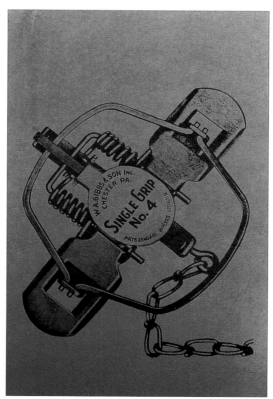

The Trap Collector's Guide, revised edition, copyright 1977 by R. B. Frodelius and R. E. Burt, published by Burts Printing Service. Again, a great book but it also dated being from 1977 and the pricing is 30 years old, but any trap collector should find one for reference, **$50+.**

Chapter 8

Sporting Books and Catalogs

As with many of the previous categories, there are already specialty books available covering collecting books and catalogs and other paper items. However, at least a brief mention needs to be made of the high demand that exists for certain sporting books and catalogs. Limited edition books, rare books, signed and autographed books, and nearly any catalog from the 1950s or earlier are collectible.

What do you look for in selecting paper items to collect? Actually, this depends if you are considering investment potential or personal interest. Let us cover investment potential first. The most important attribute of paper items is "condition, condition, condition" as we dealers like to say., but with paper items it is doubly true! A soiled paper item is of little value; a mildewed item, a torn item, a musty item—none of these are wanted in a collection. Not that a super rare piece will not be purchased, it is just that its value is no more than 10 percent of the value of a piece in fine shape, maybe only 1 percent. I have turned down paper items for free because they were so musty or dirty that I was afraid of ultimate damage to other items caused by them. Also, beware that paper items with must and mildew can also cause severe allergic reactions as I learned by experience with one "find" I made of old sporting magazines that ultimately had to be thrown out.

So, whether for value or reference, only select clean items in fine shape. Now, a tear or bent corner is not going to make an item worthless. These flaws are far easier to deal with than the areas of mildew and dirt. Some dirt will clean off with wallpaper cleaner and other cleaning items on the market, but again this should be done only in an item is needed for research or to fill in a gap in your collection.

With paper items, the most important attribute is "brand recognition" followed by general attractiveness of the layout of the item. In other words, a Heddon item is almost always going to garner more attention than even an older item by a small manufacturer such as Marathon or Worth. The Marathon or Worth item may be rare but that is not as important as the fact that far more collectors want to collect items related to Heddon, Creek Chub, Winchester, Remington, Bear, Ben Pearson, etc. So, you will find paper items related to the major brand names almost always coming at a premium price, especially rare advertising items such as store displays and counter display pieces.

As a former college president of an art and design school, I can attest to the layout of a graphic item as also being important for "attention getting" ability in paper collectibles. The area of layout includes the color of the brochure or other item, the quality of illustrations used, and the general design of the item and its use of illustrations. Look for nice strong colors, deep yellows and reds, a pleasing orange, an easily recognized green and yellow combination, etc. Then add nice line drawings and the use of good illustrations or photography. Finally, make sure the print is pleasing and easy to read. If an item has all of these qualities and brand recognition and is in pristine condition, it will command a premium price.

One final item of value is demand caused by other factors, including generation demand, crossover collector demand, and general attraction demand.

Generation demand is demand caused by one generation with a greater interest in an item, a brand, or an era. I have documented this type of demand well in my fishing collectibles books and it means that those of us "baby boomers" are far more interested in the items of the 1950s (and 1930s and 1940s) than we are of the first items on the scene. This is because we recognize them, remember them, hunted and/or fished with them, watched our fathers or mothers or brothers or sisters use them, in other words we saw them daily.

Crossover collector demand includes competition from collectors of related fields. Any Winchester item is a great example as it will be in demand by at least three groups: sporting collectors seeking the Winchester name, general antiques dealers knowing the value in the name Winchester and Winchester collectors wanting to add a brand name item to their own collection regardless of what it is. This tends to drive the price of an item up if it is of interest to two or more bodies of collectors.

General attraction demand is best illustrated by something I first noticed in fishing lure collectibles, called the "cute factor." If an item is just plain attractive, pretty, cute, and colorful, its value will increase accordingly because collectors from other fields will also be after it. In fishing lures, there is a lure known as a Heddon Punkinseed that is very "cute" and looks like a little bluegill or sunfish. These lures have gone far beyond their "normal value" as they now attract a large cadre of followers that just like their appearance, even if they are not that interested in lure collecting. Other areas of sporting collectibles will fall into this category for such items as duck decoys, some game calls, advertising items, etc.

All of the above covers collecting paper items for the sake of value; however, you cannot discount the intrinsic value of an item, either. For example, if you have a fine collection of Heddon Punkinseed lures, you are far more likely to spend money on paper items related to Punkinseeds than another collector would. Or, even if you simply had once owned a Heddon Punkinseed, you would then spend more on Punkinseed-related items. If we need something for our own research or to make ourselves feel good about a memory, we tend to buy it, regardless of price. I have developed a mathematical formula as follows: **item + quality of memory = price**. In other words, the greater the quality of a memory related to a particular item the greater will be its price. Only the buyer can determine this intrinsic value and it often will not be recovered in reselling an item unless one finds another buyer with similar feelings.

So, what is collectible in terms of paper items? Just about anything that meets the qualifications set forth above. But here is a guide:

Company catalogs and advertising items
Rod and reel manuals and advertising items
Gun manuals and advertising items
Brochures and advertising items for any sporting collectible
Advertising for hunting and fishing destinations
Trade catalogs from sporting goods shows
Introductory papers for any lure, rod, reel or gun
Introductory boxes for many items
Early (pre-1950) sporting magazines
Any other paper item related to sporting collectibles
Limited edition books on hunting and fishing
Early books on collecting sporting items, especially those rare and difficult to find
Specialty books on various items such as deer, muskies, etc.

Books on types of fishing, e.g. fly fishing, deep sea, etc.

Where do you find these items? Paper collectors are fortunate in the sense that there are many dealers specializing in paper items. Some of these folks sell online and many offer "lists" or catalogs for their specialty goods. It is my opinion that the online auction is the easiest source for finding a specific item to fill in a collection. However, you also find these items at many auctions in America, sometimes only a piece or two, sometimes an entire box full of items.

As with all items, the best way to find them is to also ask. Ask your friends, relatives, co-workers, at every garage sale attended, local auctioneers, hardware stores, sporting goods dealerships, former jobbers and salesmen, the local antiques stores, the library discarding books, just ask anyone you can think of about these items. I have found items in the most unusual places by never being too shy to ask.

To give a range of values is both necessary and difficult for this category, as it encompasses such a broad area. However, most paper items start at about $2 retail and can easily go up to $100 for rarer items. Rare catalogs from dates earlier than 1940 can bring upwards of $200 easily, with a Heddon catalog from pre-1920 fetching closer to a $1,000 or more depending on condition. I have purchased many 1930s-1960s catalogs for $50 to $150 each the past few years depending on brand recognition and condition. Simple eight- to 12-page advertising brochures will often bring $5 to $20 depending on the brand, item and condition of paper.

As a general rule, most paper items are not worth a significant amount if post-1950; however, certain manuals and catalogs would still command quite a bit up until about 1970. As you go back in time, there is nearly a doubling effect every 10 years. But then again, you must factor in the generation demand for any particular item as well. In my opinion, I should think the most valuable sporting collectible paper items in the near future will be from about 1930 until 1955 due to the interest of all of the "baby boomer" generation now collecting sporting collectibles.

This is a difficult area to give a price for particular items unless they have recently sold due to market fluctuation and demand differences. This is illustrated by a recent request made to a major paper dealer online when I asked him to send me $200 worth of paper items to scan for this book. He replied that he would rather not as he could not properly price it! This is a dealer in paper items declining to sell a certain amount because he was afraid he would price it wrong. He told me he would rather just sell it on an online auction and then he would know the value. He was very polite and understanding; he just did not want to sell an item for $15 that he later would see selling for $25. This is not uncommon among dealers of course; however, it does demonstrate the sensitive area of pricing and estimating prices for these types of items.

Antique and collectible books seem to be even more volatile in terms of pricing than paper advertising items. There are numerous value guides available regarding antique and collectible books and one or more of these should be consulted by the serious collector for more information on book valuation. However, I have found that books do not seem to have any easily determined formula in determining value in the field of sporting collectibles. Of course, limited edition books such as those by the Derrydale Press command high dollars and keep going up in value it seems; however, many of the books you would expect to command high dollars just do not always do so. It seems as a general rule the interest, and value, is greatest for books on fly fishing, white tail deer hunting, books that tell a good "tale" of sports, books once owned by famous sports figures or politicians, and, of course, any rare book. I have included some examples of what I would consider collectible books due to their contents or their rarity in previous chapters of this book. Any serious collector of rare books is directed to specialty dealers and references on rare books for more detailed information in this area.

One area of sporting collectibles-related paper items most fail to consider is the neat area of crate end labels used to ship fruits and vegetables in prior decades. Some of my most colorful paper items related to sporting come from this source. Crate label ends for the cedar fruit and vegetable shipping crates and similar tobacco paper labels usually begin at about $4 each and some can bring up to nearly $200 if rare and/or exceptionally interesting graphics are present. A superb site on the Internet dedicated to paper label collecting is located at http://www.paperstuff.com. This site has hundreds of labels for sale and gives a nice little history of these labels used primarily between 1920 and 1950 in America. Tobacco labels, pins and cigar box labels are similar in use, history and value. The little metal tobacco pins were used to mark tobacco as to the farm sending it to market and these are nice little advertising pins to collect.

The interesting thing about the crate end labels is that you can develop a collection within a collection by concentrating only on labels depicting farms and farming, or hunting, fishing, wildlife, or just fish, game birds, etc. Of course, some of the crossover labels such as fishing and wildlife tend to bring more due to competition among collecting fields. But there is likely not a more colorful area of sporting-related collectibles covering 70 of our past 100-year history of sporting collectibles.

A collectible crate-end label showing a trout fishing scene, **$5-$15.**

Little Joker Tobacco paper label, **$5.**

Magazines, catalogs, etc.

To me, this is the most exciting area of collecting as it provides knowledge for collecting, but the paper items themselves are collectible. An original Mason Decoy Factory catalog from 1920 is a wonderful item itself and has the added bonus of providing information on Mason decoys. The same is true of many early hunting magazines. Artwork by individuals such as Lynn Bogue Hunt adorn the cover of many magazines and the graphics inside of most ones from the 1930s and 1940s are worth the purchase price alone. But the advertisements inside the magazines are the invaluable sources of information on dating companies, introductions of new items and new techniques of manufacturing items, addresses of companies no longer in business, reviews of new items, and popularity of certain items. I would suggest that the uninitiated spend a good deal of time reading sporting magazines from 1930 through about 1955. This will give you a sense of the historical changes that took place in sporting goods manufacturing in American society during that time period of changing from vintage to classic, as I like to call the changes.

A commonly overlooked source of information on hunting collectibles, fishing collectibles and decoys is the wholesale catalog. These catalogs were produced by wholesale houses and jobbers throughout the country and made certain items of major companies available at reduced prices to retail outlets. For instance, many post-1940 decoys were offered in limited models and colors only, or primarily, through these outlets. Such names as Gateway, Belmont Hardware, Point Sporting Goods, etc. all put out catalogs that are veritable histories of sporting goods available at certain periods. The really nice aspect is that these wholesale catalogs are usually only a few dollars each compared with a catalog from a company per se.

Obviously, we would all like a catalog from Mason Duck Decoys, Herter's from the '30s, '40s, '50s, etc., an old Pratt and Stevens, a Dodge or two, an Evans brochure, and more. However, many of these are not available at any price or if available, are the cost of a good duck decoy or two. So, look at wholesale catalogs as an option, study magazines, buy a catalog if you can find one, and use reproductions when available. This is an area that you cannot go wrong on because the knowledge alone is usually worth the investment. Also, most paper investments have traditionally gone up in value consistently due to the fact that the supply is very limited and also very fragile.

The front and back covers of a 1933 Marble Arms catalog, **$150-$250.**

Know Your Fish booklet by Sports Afield, **$10+.**

A Duck's Unlimited's *Wing Watcher's Guide* and *Know Your Ducks and Geese* by Sports Afield, **$10-$20** each.

Sportsman's Guide to Wild Ducks written and copyrighted 1946 by the Wildlife Management Institute, Washington, D.C., and printed for the Michigan Department of Conservation, **$25+.** This is a beautiful full-color guide to duck identification, handy for decoy collectors and a must for hunters of waterfowl.

Examples of *The Decoy Hunter* magazine and details of the 1993 record-breaking Shang Wheeler Blackduck decoy shown on the cover of Issue 76, Nov.-Dec. 1993. This is a must have publication and back issues are great resources for decoy identification and valuation. These are **$5-$20** each, depending on content and age.

A variety of license regulations, conservation brochures, stamps, and other wildlife, fishing, hunting and trapping items, **$2-$5** each for most items. These are mainly from the last 20 years, but shown to give an idea of the historical variety to be found as well.

Recommended books for decoy, shell box collectors and general sporting collectibles

To purchase all the books listed would represent quite a sizable cash outlay, but each of them is a valuable tool in learning more about the collectibles area you're interested in, and some of the books are collectible in their own right. If you collect from all the various schools of duck decoy makers, for example, you will have to make an effort to obtain them all over time. Each book on this subject has indispensable data for collectors. If you specialize in one or two areas you are a bit more fortunate, but even study of areas in which you do not collect can be very helpful. The study of the entire area of decoy collecting is a fascinating and enjoyable task. You may get lucky if you make a trip to your local library.

There are, incidentally, some really good books about hunting and American folk art that have good sections on old decoys so do not overlook them in the card catalog or on the shelves of local used book stores. I spent about $150 once and walked away with over a half dozen books on waterfowl and decoys from a local used bookstore, one an out of print book on decoys alone being worth at least that much.

The list following contains many books that are out-of-print and no longer available from the publishers. There are, however, many booksellers who specialize in locating and obtaining out-of-print books. One Web site to begin your search is http://huntingrigbooks.com/Decoy_Books.htm.

The Art of Taxidermy by John Rowley, copyright 1898, D. Appleton and Company, New York and London. This is a 1915 edition of a great book written by the Chief of Taxidermy at the American Museum of Natural History in New York and the book contains 20 plates and 55 line drawings of interest; **$25+**; much more for the first edition in mint condition.

American Bird Decoys from the collection of William J. Mackey Jr. A catalog of a 1967 exhibit in St. Paul, Minnesota, and Oshkosh, Wisconsin. Out of print.

American Bird Decoys by William J. Mackey Jr. Copyright 1965 by William J. Mackey Jr. Originally published by E.P. Dutton and reissued by Schiffer Publishing Ltd. Various editions by Schiffer to 1985. Now out-of-print.

American Factory Decoys by Henry A. Fleckenstein Jr. Copyright 1981 by Henry A. Fleckenstein Jr. Schiffer Publishing Ltd., Box E, Exton, Pennsylvania 19431. Now out of print and very needed by factory bird collectors. It usually brings up to **$200** if you can find one.

American Decoys From 1865 to 1920 by Quintana Colio, copyright 1972. Science Press. Out of print.

American Sporting Collectors Handbook, edited by Allen J. Liu. Copyright 1976 by the Winchester Press. Out of print.

American Sporting Collectors Handbook, revised edition, edited by Allen J. Liu. Copyright 1982. Winchester Press. Out of print.

American Wildfowl Decoys by Jeff Waingrow. Copyright 1985, E.P. Dutton. Reissued by Weathervane Books, 1989. Both editions out-of-print.

The Art of the Decoy: American Bird Carvings by Adele Earnest.

Originally published in 1965 by Crown Publishers, New York, and Clarkson N. Potter, New York. Reissued in several editions and printing by various publishers. Present edition published 1981 by Schiffer Publishing Ltd., Box E. Exton, Pennsylvania 19341.

Auction Catalog of the Dr. George Starr Collection. Issued 1986 by the Richard A. Bourne Company. Hard cover edition, out of print.

Auction Catalogs, The William J. Mackey Collection-1973, 1974. A set of five catalogs issued by the Richard A. Bourne Company, out of print. Any of the Bourne Catalogs are a good investment and sell frequently on-line for **$5-$35** each.

Barnegat Bay Decoys and Gunning Clubs by Patricia H. Burke. Copyright 1985. Ocean County Historical Society. Limited edition of 1,000 soft cover copies. Now out-of-print.

Benj. J. Schmidt-A Michigan Decoy Carver, 1884-1968, by Lowell Jackson, C. 1970. Out of print.

The Bird Decoy, An American Art Form by Paul A. Johnsgard. Copyright 1976, University of Nebraska Press.

Canadian Wilds by Martin Hunter, reprinted articles from *Forest & Stream and Fur-Fish-Game* magazines telling of his trapping adventures, the Hudson's Bay Company, trapping with and by Indians and much more. Published by A. R. Harding Pub., copyright 1935, **$35+**.

Canvas Decoys of North America, Johnson, copyright 1994, soft cover.

Chesapeake Bay Decoys by R.H. Richardson. Copyright 1973, Crowhaven Publishers. Out of print.

Chincoteague Carvers and Their Decoys by Barry and Velma Berkey. Copyright 1977, Tidewater Publishers, P.O. Box 109, Cambridge, Maryland 21613.

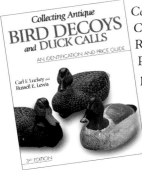

Collecting Antique Bird Decoys and Duck Calls, 3rd edition, by Carl F. Luckey and Russell E. Lewis. Copyright 2003. Krause Publications, Iola, Wisconsin. This 496-page book, with a 64-page color section, is the most complete book to date on both individual carvers and modern decoys, in addition to sections on calls, hunting collectibles and a review of advertising from 1927 through 1971.

The Collector's Guide to Decoys by Bob and Sharon Huxford. Copyright 1990, Schroeder Publishing Company. Collector Books, P.O. Box 3009, Paducah, Kentucky 42001. A compilation of major auction results for the four-year period 1985-1989. This is an excellent compendium of actual prices realized for decoy sales for this time period.

The Collector's Guide to Decoys by Gene and Linda Kangas, 1992, out of print.

Connecticut Decoys, Carvers and Gunners by Henry C. Chitwood, copyright 1987, Schiffer Publishing Ltd., Box E, Exton, Pennsylvania 19341.

Connecticut Working Decoys by Marshall Chitwood and Doug Knight.

Coykendall's Sporting Collectibles Price Guide by Ralf Coykendall Jr., copyright 1991, published by Lyons and Burford Publishers. He has additional volumes dating from as late as 1996 from the same publisher.

The Crow Shooter's Handbook by Nicholas Karas, copyright 1963 by Wightman Electronics Company, Inc., Easton, Maryland, **$20+**. A nice little booklet on crow hunting, conservation, decoys and calling.

Decoying St. Clair to St. Lawrence by Bernard W. Crandall.

Decoy Collecting by Ralf Coykendall, copyright 1985. An edition limited to 750 soft-cover copies. Out of print.

Decoy Collecting Primer by Paul W. Casson, copyright 1978. Out of print.

Decoy Collectors Guide by Harold D. Sorenson. Magazine reprints from 1963 through 1977. Volumes 1-3, 1963-65 in one, hard-cover volume is out-of-print. Volume 4, 1966-67, Volume 5, 1968 and Volume 6, 1977. Now out of print.

Decoy Ducks by Bob Ridges, copyright 1988, Gallery Books.

The Decoy as Art by James A. Warner and Margaret J. White, copyright 1985, Mid-Atlantic Press.

The Decoy as Folk Sculpture by Swanson and Hall, Cranbrook

Academy Art Museum, copyright 1987. A catalog of a 1987 exhibit of bird and fish decoys, 1,000 copies printed. Out of print but excellent source.

Decoys, 1991 by Gene and Linda Kangas, out of print.

Decoys-A North American Survey by Gene and Linda Kangas, copyright 1983, Hillcrest Publications, Inc., Spanish Fork, Utah 84660. Out of print.

Decoys and Decoy Carvers of Illinois by Paul W. Parmalee and Forrest D. Loomis, copyright 1969. Northern Illinois University Press. Original edition was issued in hard cover and is out-of-print. Reissued in soft cover in 1979 and 1983.

Decoys at the Shelburne Museum by William Kehoe and David Webster, copyright 1961, 1871. Hobby House. Out of print.

Decoys Celebration of Contemporary Decoys, c. 1994 by Aziz.

Decoys of Lake Champlain by Loy S. Harrell Jr., 1986, in print.

Decoys: North America's One Hundred Greatest, 2000, Krause Publications, Iola, Wisconsin, in print.

Decoys of Maritime Canada by Dale and Gary Guyette, copyright 1983, Schiffer Publishing Ltd.

Decoys of the Mississippi Flyway by Alan G. Haid, copyright 1981, Schiffer Publishing Ltd., Box E, Exton, Pennsylvania 19341.

Decoys of the Mid-Atlantic Region by Henry A. Fleckenstein Jr., copyright 1979, Schiffer Publishing Ltd., Box E, Exton, Pennsylvania 19341. Hard-cover edition is out-of-print with the exception of a deluxe, leather-bound limited edition. Soft-cover edition now available.

Decoys: St. Clair to the St. Lawrence by Bernard Crandall, copyright 1988, Boston Mills Press.

Decoys of the Susquehanna Flats and Their Makers by J. Evans McKinney, copyright 1978, Holly Press, out of print. New revised and expanded edition, copyright 1990, published by Joe Enders, *Decoy* magazine.

Decoys of the Thousand Islands by Jim Stewart and Larry Lunman, copyright 1991, Boston Mills Press.

Decoys of the Winnebago Lakes by Ronald M. Koch, copyright 1988, Rivermoor Publications.

Downriver and Thumb Area Michigan Waterfowling. The Folk Arts of Nate Quillen and Otto Misch by Kurt Dewhurst and Marsha Macdowell, copyright 1981, Michigan State University Press.

The Encyclopedia of Shotshell Boxes, c. 2000 by Bacyk, in hardcover and softcover.

Factory Decoys of Mason, Stevens, Dodge and Peterson by John and Shirley Delph, copyright 1980, Schiffer Publishing Ltd., Box E, Exton, Pennsylvania 19341.

Floaters and Stick Ups by George Reiger, published by George Reiger, copyright 1986, out of print.

George Boyd, The Shorebird Decoy—An American Folk Art by Winthrop L. Carter, copyright 1978, Tenant House Press, 200 copies printed, now out-of-print.

The Great Book of Wildfowl Decoys by Joe Engers, copyright 1990, Abbeyville Press.

Gun Powder Cans and Kegs, c. 1998 by Bacyk.

Gunners Paradise, Wildfowling and Decoys on Long Island by E. Jane Townsend, copyright 1979, Museums at Stony Brook.

Gunning the Chesapeake by Roy Walsh, copyright 1961, Tidewater Publishers, P.O. Box 109, Cambridge, MD 21613.

Joel Barber's America by Ralf Coykendall Jr., copyright 1983, limited edition of 200 copies, soft cover.

The Judas Birds by Hugh H. Turnbull, copyright 1983. This is essentially a catalog of an exhibit of rare Canadian and American decoys at Musee Marsil, Museum St. Lambert, Quebec, Canada.

R.A. Knuth—Wisconsin/Michigan Decoy Carver, 1892-1980 by Michael Holmer, copyright 1980.

Lake Champlain Decoys by Loy S. Harrel, copyright 1986, Schiffer Publishing Ltd., Box E, Exton, Pennsylvania 19341.

Louisiana Duck Decoys by Charles W. Frank Jr., copyright 1975, Pelican Publishing Company.

L.T. Ward & Bro., Wildfowl Counterfeiters by Byron Cheever, Hillcrest Publications, P.O. Box 246, Spanish Fork, Utah 84660.

Martha's Vineyard Decoys by Stanley Murphy, copyright 1978, David R. Godine, Publisher, Boston, out of print.

Mason Decoys by Byron Cheever, copyright 1974, Hillcrest Publications, P.O. Box 246, Spanish Fork, Utah 84660.

Modern Decoys By Joel Barber. Collected and edited by Ralf Coykendall Jr., copyright 1985.

New England Decoys by John and Shirley Delph, Schiffer Publishing Ltd., Box E, Exton, Pennsylvania 19341.

New Jersey Decoys by Henry A. Fleckenstein Jr., copyright 1983, Schiffer Publishing Ltd., Box E, Exton, Pennsylvania 19341.

Northern Lakes Decoy Exhibit by Jim and Mark Richards, copyright 1982, Lake Publishing; an exhibit catalog of 11 pages, 250 copies were printed.

Shang: A Biography of Charles E. Wheeler by Dixon Mac D. Merkt, copyright 1984, Hillcrest Publications, P.O. Box 246, Spanish Fork, Utah 84660.

Shorebird Decoys by Henry A. Fleckenstein Jr., copyright 1980, Schiffer Publishing Ltd., Box E, Exton, Pennsylvania 19341.

Southern Decoys of Virginia and the Carolinas by Henry A. Fleckenstein Jr., copyright 1983, Schiffer Publishing LTD., Box E, Exton, Pennsylvania 19341.

Traditions in Wood (A History of Wildfowl Decoys in Canada) by Patricia Fleming and Thomas Carpenter, copyright 1987, Camden House Publishing, Ontario, Canada.

Undercover Wildlife Agent, copyright 1981 by James H. Phillips, Winchester Press, Tulsa, OK, **$30+**. This interesting book deals with the journals and records kept by a federal conservation officer by the name of Robert O. Halstead and follows his career from the 1940s into the 1970s.

The Ward Brothers Decoys—A Collector's Guide by Ronald J. Card and Brian J. McGrath, copyright 1989, Thomas B. Reel Co., 2005 Tree House, Plano, Texas 75023.

Warman's Duck Decoys by Russell E. Lewis, copyright 2006, Krause Publications, Iola, WI. This 256-page 100-percent color paperback is the most recent book on decoys and shows superb photos of individual carvers, factory birds, some hunting collectibles and has pricing data current through sales held in 2006, including sales from Guyette & Schmidt and Decoys Unlimited, Ltd. which featured some of the Pitt Collection.

Waterfowl Heritage—North Carolina Decoys and Gunning Lore by William Neal Conoley Jr., copyright 1983 by William Neal Conoley Jr.

Wildfowl Decoys by Joel D. Barber. This classic for collectors was first published by Windward House in 1934. This is a collectors' edition worth much money. Subsequently, Dover Publications, New York, issued it in 1954 in a soft-cover edition, with several printings over the years, and is still available today although sometimes hard to locate. The Derrydale press Deluxe Edition of only 50 copies is bringing mid-level four-figure prices. There is also a later (1989) Derrydale Deluxe limited edition of 2,500 on the market.

Wildfowl Decoys of the Pacific Coast by Michael R. Miller and Frederick W. Hanson, copyright 1991, MBF Publishing, P.O. Box 6097, Portland, Oregon 97228-6097.

Wildlife Art—World's Championship Carvers, c. 1996, by Aziz.

Working Decoys of the Jersey Coast and Delaware Valley by Kenneth L. Gosner, copyright 1985, Art Alliance Press, out of print.

Sporting Collectibles Facts You Can Rely On

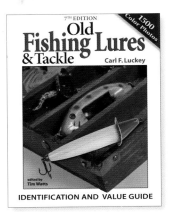

Old Fishing Lures & Tackle Identification and Value Guide

7th Edition
by Carl F. Luckey,
Contributing Editor Tim Watts

With 2,500 color photos, 5,000+ listings and updated prices the "lure bible" is better than ever! You'll find collecting data from leading lure companies, as well as small groups.

Softcover • 8¼ x 10⅞ • 768 pages
2,500+ color photos
Item# OFL7 • $34.99

Fishing Collectibles Identification and Price Guide

by Russell E. Lewis

From rods and reels to bait buckets, this must-have reference covers all your fishing treasures. Contains more than 2,000 color photos for easy identification, descriptions, values, and history.

Softcover • 8¼ x 10⅞ • 352 pages
2,000 color photos
Item# FISCL • $29.99

Warman's Fishing Lures Field Guide Values and Identification

2nd Edition
by Rob Pavey

Whether experienced fisher or novice collector, this handy guide offers easy access to lure knowledge, with 500+ color photos, details about size and color, and collector pricing.

Softcover • 4⁵⁄₁₆ x 5³⁄₁₆ • 512 pages
500+ color photos
Item# FLFG2 • $12.99

Classic Hunting Collectibles Identification & Price Guide

by Hal Boggess

1,100 color photos and pricing for hunting-related items from the late 1800s to early 1940s including posters, calendars, pin backs, catalogs, shot shell crates from Winchester, Peters Cartridge Co., Dupont, and others.

Softcover • 8¼ x 10⅞
256 pages
1,100 color photos
Item# CHNT • $24.99

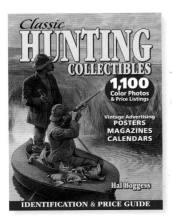

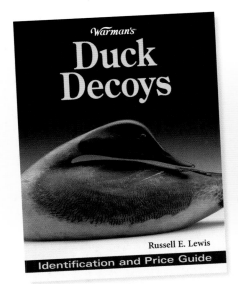

Warman's Duck Decoys

by Russell E. Lewis

Identify and assess wooden, modern and factory decoys with values, detailed descriptions and 1,000+ color photos included in this richly illustrated book.

Softcover • 8¼ x 10⅞ • 256 pages
1,000+ color photos
Item# Z0305 • $24.99

kp krause

An

700 East State Street • Iola, WI 54990-0001
715-445-2214 • 888-457-2873
www.krausebooks.com

Southborough Public Library
25 Main Street
Southborough, MA 01772

Order directly from the publisher by calling
800-258-0929 M-F 8 am - 5 pm
OR
Online at **www.krausebooks.com**
or from booksellers and antique shops nationwide.
Please reference offer **ACB7** with all direct-to-publisher orders.